HUMAN
RESOURCE
CHAMPIONS

HUMAN RESOURCE CHAMPIONS

THE NEXT AGENDA FOR ADDING VALUE AND DELIVERING RESULTS

Dave Ulrich

HARVARD BUSINESS SCHOOL PRESS
BOSTON, MASSACHUSETTS

Library of Congress Cataloging-in-Publication Data

Ulrich, David, 1953-
    Human resource champions: the next agenda for adding value and
delivering results / Dave Ulrich.
      p.   cm.
    Includes bibliographical references and index.
    ISBN 0-87584-719-6 (alk. paper)
    1. Personnel management.   2. Organizational change.
3.   I. Title.
    HF5549.U39   1996
    658.3--dc20   96-8754
                                                   CIP

CONTENTS

v

PREFACE

In the past few years, a number of articles, columns, and books have debated the question "Should we do away with HR?" This is a silly question and a senseless debate. Of course we should do away with HR—if it fails to add value and impedes performance. Of course we should keep HR—if it creates value or delivers results. A more useful question, the question addressed in this book, is "How can HR create value and deliver results?" Answering this question requires a fundamentally different way of thinking about HR.

Current HR thinking can be seen in any HR textbook. Titles and content may differ slightly, but nearly all the chapter headings focus on what HR people *do:* staffing, development, compensation, benefits, communication, organization design, high performing teams, and so on. These chapter headings reflect the paradigm that has dominated HR for the past forty years: making sure that HR is *done* in increasingly innovative, useful, and even elegant ways.

I want to turn this thinking on its side. I want to focus less on what HR professionals do and more on what they *deliver.* Delivery focuses on the outcomes, guarantees, and results of HR work. This book focuses on four generic outcomes: strategy execution, administrative efficiency, employee contribution, and capacity for change. Other possible innovative HR texts might define other outcomes by organizing material under such chapter headings as globalization, customer intimacy, operational excellence, learning culture, and so on, and then demonstrate how HR practices (what we do) make these deliverables happen. I hope that, partly as a result of this book, chapter headings in future HR texts will feature outcomes, or what happens because HR does good work.

Shifting the focus from doables to deliverables challenges traditional beliefs and assumptions about HR professionals, HR practices, and HR departments. HR professionals must become partners, players, and pioneers. They are more than people who pass through and happen to be assigned to work in HR; they are theory-based, competency-driven experts who draw on a body of knowledge to make informed business decisions. HR practices must be designed to create value and deliver results. HR practices are organizational processes that can enhance individual competencies and organizational capabilities (in other work Bob Eichinger, Michael Lombardo, and I have used the term *cultributes* to refer to this combination of organizational culture and attributes). When HR practices are aligned with the needs of internal and external customers, firms are more likely to succeed. HR departments must be held to a higher standard than they have been up until now. They must move their HR professionals beyond the roles of policy police and regulatory watchdogs to become partners, players, and pioneers in delivering value.

By prodding and pushing HR, I am predicting a more optimistic future than past. Some HR prophets tell HR professionals that they are doomed by their incompetence and headed for hell. I would rather tell them how to repent so that they can go to heaven. I am an optimist about HR, not just because I like HR professionals (which I do, for the most part), but because the issues with which HR professionals deal are at the heart of organizational success.

My colleague and friend C.K. Prahalad has taught me the importance of having a point of view—a clearly defined and articulated set of beliefs. I have a point of view for HR.

I believe that the next ten years will be the HR decade. The increased pace of change required by technology, globalization, profitable growth, and customer demands places work force competence and organizational capabilities at center stage. In recent years, many initiatives have become critical to firm success—for example, quality, reengineering, process improvement, core competence, learning, market discipline, principled leadership, and so on. Underlying these initiatives are the ways organizations get things done—their capabilities—and how they treat people—their competence. Understanding, leveraging, and crafting capabilities and competencies—HR issues—will lead to successful organizations and successful leaders.

I believe in patterns. Patterns represent accepted, familiar, and routine ways of getting things done. In many cases, however, HR professionals have developed bad patterns. They have come to their jobs with a set of skills based on outdated assumptions about work. These poor HR patterns have shaped client expectations to the extent that many clients have come to expect HR to focus only on administrative, transactional, and policy elements of HR work. HR work has become patterned in bureaucratic ways.

I also believe that patterns can be changed. New patterns emerge when ideas create new frameworks, new ways of doing work, and new expectations for the work held by both HR professionals and clients. In a recent seminar that I conducted, forty CEOs paired with their top HR professional talked about changing the patterns and expectations of HR. Together we discovered that when CEOs and HR professionals have new frameworks, ideas, and approaches to work, the bureaucratic pattern can be replaced with innovative, value-driven, and results-oriented work. This book is about changing HR patterns in ways that will impact both clients of HR (line managers and employees) and HR professionals.

I believe that HR should be judged by its future more than be bound by its past. The future of HR includes new initiatives, programs, and agendas. An HR professional from the 1940s would find it difficult to recognize the HR function of the year 2000, when the focus will be on global management, organizational capabilities, culture change, and intellectual capital. I also believe, however, that our past holds lessons for our future. HR issues of the past (for example, fair treatment of employees, shaping firms' values, sourcing talent) will continue to be central in the future.

I believe that questions are more important than answers. How does HR add value? Who does HR work with (line, staff, HR professionals, outside vendors)? What are the best metaphors for successful HR professionals (partners, players, pioneers, architects, designers, leaders)? Who is the client for HR initiatives (employees, customers, investors)? When should HR be proactive, reactive, or anticipatory? What are the criteria for successful HR practices (financial measures, employee morale, market share)? What are the new tools for HR? These, and other, questions will lead to answers, insights, and, of course, more questions not currently asked among HR professionals.

I believe in learning, but I also believe that it is easier to learn than to forget. For HR to master a new role, centered on deliverables with new patterns of behaviors, both learning and unlearning needs to occur. Learning means appreciating new alternatives; unlearning means letting go of the past. Both are necessary for HR's future to improve on its past.

I believe that when given the opportunity and direction, HR professionals act professionally. When they know theory, they set high standards; when they know how to add value, they do so; when they are given opportunity, they respond.

Now is the time.

Acknowledgments

This book integrates, borrows from, and leverages work from many colleagues. I have tried to cite this research in detail in the end notes. I realize that I may also inadvertently draw on work not formally cited, and I want to acknowledge and appreciate my colleagues.

My intellectual mentors in this work include J.B. Ritchie who teaches me how to think critically, Steve Kerr who teaches me how to think clearly, and Frank Doyle who teaches me how to think professionally.

My insights are drawn from colleagues in many walks of life. I have been privileged to work in an institution that values innovative thinking and teaching and to work with such colleagues as Ron Bendersky, Gordon Hewitt, Tom Kinnear, C.K. Prahalad, Ray Reilly, Dennis Severance, George Siedel, and Joe White.

I have collaborated with outstanding colleagues on projects where I have learned as much as or more than I have given, including work with Ron Ashkenas, Bob Eichinger, Jac Fitz-enz, Dale Lake, Michael Losey, Paul McKinnon, Norm Smallwood, Cal Wick, Warren Wilhelm, Arthur Yeung, and Jon Younger.

I have had the opportunity to practice my craft inside firms where executives were willing to learn with and teach me along the way, in particular, Wayne Anderson, Janet Brady, Ralph Christensen, Bill Conaty, Jim Donohue, Cliff Ehrlich, Bruce Ellig, Ellen Glanz, Pedro Granadillo, Hope Greenfield, Irv Hockaday, Howard Knicely, Frank LaFasto, Joe Miraglia, Mike Morley, Chuck Okosky, Pete Peterson, Judy Rosenblum, Tony Rucci, Janet Sansone, Rich Teerlink, Jacquie Vierling, and Mike Walters.

I have pursued a theory and research stream in which wonderful writers and researchers are constantly offering exciting new propositions, including work by Chris Argyris, Dick Beatty, Mike Beer, John Boudreau, Dave Bowen, Warner Burke, Jill Conner, Lee Dyer, Jay Galbraith, Gary Hamel, Mark Huselid, Bill Joyce, Ed Lawler, Jeff Pfeffer, C.K. Prahalad, Len Schlesinger, Craig Schneier, MaryAnn Von Glinow, and Jim Walker.

Many thanks to the editors at the Harvard Business School Press who put up with my aggressive desire to make sure my point of view came through in this work. They helped make this happen, in particular Marjorie Williams, Susan Boulanger, and Barbara Roth.

Special thanks to Ginger Bitter who is a superb manager of my sometimes chaotic and often confusing schedule. Special thanks also to Gerry Lake who edited this book and serves as managing editor of *Human Resource Management.*

Most special thanks to Wayne Brockbank who is my closest professional and personal friend. He is the best thinker I know in this business. He asks good questions, frames issues elegantly, and is fun to be around. He has taught me more than I could ever hope to repay.

Most of all, I find support from my family. My parents continue to listen and guide; my children, Carrie, Monika, and Michael, demonstrate continued patience; and my wife, Wendy, continually reminds me of what matters most.

Dave Ulrich
Ann Arbor, Michigan
August 1996

HUMAN RESOURCE CHAMPIONS

The Next Agenda for Competitiveness: Human Resources

I BEGIN MOST OF MY SEMINARS with the question, "To be competitive, what are the top five business challenges your executives must pay attention to?" Regardless of participants' level in their company's hierarchy or the company's industry or location, the responses are similar: The competitive landscape is changing, and new models of competitiveness are needed to deal with the challenges ahead. These responses reveal a new competitive reality demanding organization capabilities that will enable firms to better serve their customers and to differentiate themselves from their competitors.

This book is about creating organizations that add value to investors, customers, and employees.[1] In particular, it tells how line managers and HR professionals together can champion the competitive organization of the future. If organization capability has become a source of competitiveness,[2] and if line managers and HR professionals are to be the champions of organization capability, then a new agenda for both HR practices and HR professionals must emerge.[3] This book will help operating managers and HR professionals work together to achieve these goals.

This chapter lays out the next agenda of competitiveness by suggesting that HR holds the keys to success[4] in overcoming eight major challenges

1

facing executives. Each of these challenges defines why HR matters, requires partnerships between operating managers and HR professionals, raises questions about the agenda and role for HR practices and professionals, and requires new approaches to delivering HR. Collectively, these challenges require that HR practices add measurable value, that HR functions deliver business results, and that HR professionals develop the discipline of a profession, play new roles, and demonstrate new competencies. Fundamentally, the new competitive reality will require new ways of thinking about HR practices, functions, and professionals.

COMPETITIVE CHALLENGES AHEAD

Challenge One: Globalization

Globalization dominates the competitive horizon. The concept is not new, but the intensity of the challenge to get on with it is. Globalization entails new markets, new products, new mindsets, new competencies, and new ways of thinking about business. In the future, HR will need to create models and processes for attaining global agility, effectiveness, and competitiveness. As Joe Miraglia, former vice president of Motorola, has said, "What does it really mean when 75 percent of our profit is outside the U.S. and 60,000 people are outside the U.S.?"[5]

As the world becomes smaller through telecommunication, travel, information, ideologies, and partnerships, the global village is no longer on the horizon: It is here. Globalization can be characterized through comparison with an industry life cycle. When deregulation hit it, the U.S. airline industry rapidly consolidated from more than one hundred carriers to just eight (at least two of which are in financial difficulty), serving 80 percent of air travelers. While this consolidation was dramatic, the next phase of the industry's evolution—with global consolidation—may be more so, as USAir partners with British Air, Northwest with KLM, Continental with SAS, and so on. It seems safe to predict that in another ten years, a mere eight carriers *worldwide* may constitute 80 percent of the global air travel industry. Similar patterns exist or will soon emerge across almost every industry, including automotive, lodging, banking, securities, equipment, and education.

Effective global competition requires more than creating a product in a home market and shipping it as is to new markets. It requires a complex network of global centers of excellence that draw on technologies invented in one locale and shared worldwide; rapid movement of products, people, information, and ideas around the world to meet local needs; and management of the paradox of global economies of scale and local responsiveness. It requires a global mindset and a local commitment: Thinking globally but acting locally.

Another issue looming for global business is the uncertain politics of global markets. Those raised in Western cultures often take their democratic political processes as standard. Western rules do not necessarily apply, however, in countries where political and economic power can be influenced by religion, revolution, family, a single dominant political party, or even uprisings and revolutions. Learning to deal with volatile political realities constitutes a new global challenge for many Western firms. In the oil industry, for example, drilling for Siberia's vast oil reserves remains a risky venture because of the political uncertainties in the former Soviet Union.

Political volatility worldwide is likely to increase. In the early 1990s, for example, executives were falling all over each other to get into the growing, dynamic Mexican market. By the mid–1990s, when Mexico's politics had been turned upside down and its financial markets had collapsed, these same executives were desperately trying to extract themselves from the Mexican fiasco. More such dramatic shifts are likely to occur.

Businesses in technologically advanced countries amass enormous wealth very quickly when they become global players. As these businesses invest in weaker economies, the social and economic gap between those who have and those who have not widens, and the near future may bring as a response social unrest not only within but across countries. Unresolved, this inequity and unrest may fuel revolt and even revolution.

Despite such problems, U.S. companies do seek to establish themselves globally. For these organizations, the challenge is to create the capability to compete successfully at the global level. A recent American Electronics Association seminar, for example, examined the globalization challenges facing Quantum, a manufacturer of computer disk drives, a very competitive industry. In this industry, it is assumed that being a month late on a new product introduction costs about seven points (percent) in margin; if Quantum is three months late with a release, they may lose out on the new generation of products altogether. To compete in the face of this rapid development cycle time, Quantum is considering linking new development labs in San Jose, Asia, and Europe. The idea is that, when researchers in

Asia finish their day's work, they will then share it electronically with their San Jose counterparts who, in turn, will share their day's work with the European lab. By the time the researchers in Asia return to work, their ideas will have gone through two iterations of progress. We explored what, if any, particular organization capabilities would be required to make this plan work.

The answer is clear: To accomplish this ambitious agenda, Quantum will have to fundamentally redefine their organization as that of a global relay team. They will have to build global capabilities such as the ability to seamlessly move talent, ideas, and information around the world to create products and services faster and better than competitors. They will have to build a global shared mindset that supports the free exchange of ideas from any lab with all the other labs. They will have to build an employee infrastructure for hiring, training, and motivating employees that takes a global, not a national perspective.

Global capabilities also include considering the implications for the rest of the global business of decisions and economies taken in one country. Global capabilities require dealing with different forms of management thought and action. A business class for a group of Chinese senior executives, for example, included an entire day spent trying to understand why capitalism works and how a stock market can efficiently allocate ownership. What we in the West take for granted can be a major hurdle for people from other cultures.

In this new global world, the social and leadership contracts will also be changed. No one doubts any more that the old psychological contract of corporate security has been replaced with a new contract of self-security. In the future, security will come less from government and industry and more from an individual's talent and effort. Defining the elements of such self-security, however, especially in a global context, is more difficult and remains a work in progress.

Children of today's managers will need to be more globally agile and literate than their parents have been. Where economic literacy was once sufficient for success, global literacy will now be necessary. Beyond understanding exchange rates, businesspeople in the near future, among other skills, must comprehend the movement of technology across boundaries; possess political savvy in different countries; and be aware of global trade issues and underlying drivers for customers around the globe.

A company striving to create global organizational capability must begin with a basic assessment. What are the unique skills and perspectives necessary to be a successful global competitor? What percent of the existing management team has those global competencies? What percent are sensitive to the subtle differences in global markets and products? What percent could adequately represent the firm's interests to a broad global audience? What percent are comfortable with global issues? What percent could comfortably have a dinner conversation with key customers from other countries? What percent understand and could explain major cultural and religious differences around the world and how these impact the market for the firm's goods and services? How does the organization share information globally? What incentive systems will encourage employees to move around the world and to share ideas worldwide? How can employees gain global experience without the liabilities of expatriates? How can the company create a mindset that respects local conditions while leveraging global thinking?

Operating managers and HR professionals wrestling with these issues must create new ways of thinking about organizations. The global organization will be less concerned with geographic proximity (going to the same office every day) than with the virtual leveraging of global resources.

Challenge Two: Value Chain for Business Competitiveness and HR Services

A consistent theme for the competitive future is building and operating organizations that will be more customer responsive.[6] Responsiveness includes innovation, faster decision-making, leading an industry in price or value, and effectively linking with suppliers and vendors to build a value chain for customers. To support the value-chain argument, research indicates that employee attitude correlates highly with customer attitude.[7]

Refocusing HR practices more on the value chain (suppliers and customers) and less on activities within the firm has profound implications. For years, HR professionals and theorists have emphasized building HR practices within the firm. The shift to a customer focus redirects attention from the firm to the value chain in which it is embedded. HR practices within a firm should consequently be applied to suppliers and customers outside the firm. Training with a value-chain perspective weaves suppliers, employees, and customers into value-chain teams. Value-chain compensation programs focus on using suppliers and customers as evaluators and distributors of economic value within the firm. By shifting the focus from firm to value chain, all HR activities are rigorously redefined according to customer criteria.

On Motorola University's sixteen campuses worldwide, 50 percent of those trained are suppliers or customers. Motorola executives claim that their remarkable success in the Chinese market is due, in part, to their ability to train Chinese managers at Motorola University before they had product in the country. General Electric's Crotonville courses also have a strong supplier and customer bent. By removing boundaries between GE and those in its value chain, win/win relationships are forged, resulting in reduced costs, higher service, and better performance for both groups.

Relationships outside a firm go beyond its value chain to its value network. The complex of interrelationships among firms forms a value network. Motorola executives, for example, found that in one of their alliances with Intel, it was a supplier; in another, it was a competitor; and in a third, it was a customer. What are the HR implications of these complex networks of organization relationships? Which issues require collaboration and which competition? What types of organization reporting make sense in these relationships? What types of policies and practices on hiring, careers, training, rewards, and other HR practices?

One firm, for example, misunderstanding the complex value network in which it was embedded, and wanting to reduce its supplier costs, sent a formal, standardized memo to all suppliers, demanding a 7 percent reduction. It just so happened that one supplier (probably not the only one) was also a customer. It also happened that, as a customer, this firm bought three times what it supplied. The executives at this firm thought that reducing supply costs by 7 percent was a brilliant idea. They copied the letter and sent it to the original firm. HR in a value network would help ensure that policies within complex value networks are consistent and productive.

Managers and HR professionals must learn to create organizations that work along the value chain and across the value network.

Challenge Three: Profitability Through Cost *and* Growth

Profitability is a given. Firms that are not competitive as measured by profit, in the absence of a sustained monopolistic position, will fail. Profitability will continue to be a business issue in the future, but the accepted path to profitability will likely change. Increasingly, profitability must come from some combination of increased revenue and decreased costs.

During the last decade, most Western firms have been clearing debris. Downsizing, delayering, consolidation, productivity gains, reengineering, and focus on quality have redirected attention toward doing more with less, becoming more efficient, improving processes, and cutting costs as means to becoming more profitable. One company engaged in renewal compiled a list of the initiatives they had tried since the mid–1980s; it included the following:

Business-process reengineering

Business-unit restructuring

Continuous improvement

Consolidation

Corporate-centers study

Cost analysis

Cycle time

Decentralization

Downsizing

Economic value-added (EVA)

Empowerment

Excellence

Goal-setting

Japanese management (Theory Z)

Leadership development

Mission, vision, values

Quality

Restructuring

Rewards and recognition

Six Sigma

Variable pay

Workout

Most of these initiatives focus on the cost element of the profitability equation; they are designed to reduce the costs of people, processes, or other business expenses. While such a focus is not bad, it is only part of the profitability equation.

Increasingly, executives are discovering (or rediscovering) the second half of the profit equation: revenue growth. The point is not to replace cost with growth but to find ways to experience profitable growth. Hamel and Prahalad make this argument strongly in a number of their writings,[8] positing that, without a growth focus, executives lack a compelling and engaging vision of the future. The growth imperative has been further documented in research by Gertz and Baptista, who interviewed 180 U.S.–based chief executives and found that 94 percent were dedicated to growth, by far the dominant agenda acknowledged by these CEOs.[9]

Each of the three main paths to growth have HR implications. First, *growth through leveraging customers* involves efforts by a firm to induce current customers to buy more of its products. Almost every financial service firm, for example, identifies a number of potential financial transactions with customers, including checking accounts, savings accounts, stock funds, pensions, mortgages, credit cards, insurance, mutual funds, CDs, and so on. Successful financial service firms work to gain an even larger percentage of these transactions, thus growing portfolio by portfolio. General Electric has formed Boundaryless Customer Productivity Teams (BCPTs), teams of individuals from diverse GE businesses who work together to cross-sell GE products.

Organizations seeking to leverage customers must create processes and train people to connect quickly and easily with those customers' needs. Employees must be dedicated to and intimate with key accounts.

The second major path to growth, *leveraging core competencies,* that is, creating new products, raises the fundamental challenge of turning research knowledge into customer products. The organizational actions required for product introduction often revolve around forming competence or product-introduction teams. Cross-functional product teams identify core competencies and then turn those competencies into new products. New products often mean new revenue.

The third main path to growth involves *mergers, acquisitions, or joint ventures.* Almost anyone who has been involved with the post-merger integration process has witnessed the extent of the organizational response required by this business challenge. Financial and strategic compatibility is more easily assessed than cultural compatibility. As a result, many mergers fail because the organizational attributes of the merged companies were vastly different; the new company may achieve remarkable financial and strategic fit, but cultural fit may be dismal.

No matter which route is selected, profitable growth will require rethinking organization and HR tools so that growth aspirations can be realized through organizational actions. The implications of profitability through growth raise new questions for HR practices, including the following:

- How can executives create a commitment to rapid growth and the culture that supports it while simultaneously controlling costs?

- How can executives be sure that they hire people who can grow the business while reducing overall labor costs?

- How can executives create an organizational structure that provides both the autonomy needed for growth and the discipline needed to control costs?

- What are the HR implications of entering new businesses, of leveraging core technologies that lead into unfamiliar businesses, and of building the intimate customer relationships that bring an ever-increasing percentage of a customer's purchases into the same provider?

The challenge of achieving growth while reducing costs will push HR professionals to deal with their firms' inherent paradoxes. But even as these paradoxes are investigated, the firm will be taking on new challenges.

Deborah Engle, vice president of human resources for 3Com, has pushed the firm to reinvent itself even in the midst of its most rapid growth ever. Arguing that most firms wait until they have crested on the growth curve to get into restructuring and cost cutting, Engle has convinced 3Com executives to begin the transformation work while still climbing the growth curve. By examining the firm's culture, how its work gets done, its lines of communication, and the way employees are hired, trained, motivated, and organized, 3Com is managing both growth and costs simultaneously for sustained profitability.

Managers and HR professionals seeking profitable growth must find new ways to design and deliver organizational practices.

Challenge Four: Capability Focus

As strategic promises turn into daily actions, organization capabilities need to be redefined to sustain and integrate individual competencies. Organization capabilities are the DNA of competitiveness. They are the things an organization always does better than its competitors do. These capabilities may be hard, such as technology (for example, the ability to create new marketable technologies or the financial flexibility to respond aggressively in multiple markets simultaneously), or they may be soft, such as organizational capabilities (for example, the ability to move faster in the marketplace or to attract and retain effective global expatriates). Soft organizational capabilities are more difficult to create and replicate. We have seen this with firms trying to implement soft capabilities such as TQM or process reengineering. Most surveys show that efforts to implement these soft organizational capabilities have a 75 percent failure rate.[10] Less important than who builds the best product today is the question who has the organizational capability to build the best product over and over, adjusting to each global market.[11]

Recent research into soft organizational capabilities shows that organizations are working in four directions: building capabilities of confidence, in which individuals both inside and outside the organization believe that managers will do what they say and maintain their reputation;[12] becoming boundaryless, allowing information and ideas to move effortlessly across hierarchical, horizontal, and external boundaries;[13] achieving capacity for change, the flexibility and agility that allow constant innovation;[14] and learning, attaining change that builds on and maintains itself.[15] Company general managers have the obligation to identify and foster these and other capabilities to increase competitiveness.

HR professionals need to frame what they do in terms of the capabilities they must create. It is no longer sufficient to hire, train, or reward individuals; these activities must now be undertaken in the interest of creating a set of organizational capabilities. The San Francisco 49er football team illustrates how individual competence complements organizational capability. Athletes at each position are well trained and known as the best. The team and its system of play, however, is more important than any single individual. When Steve Young, the all-star quarterback, was injured and had to be replaced by the inexperienced Elvis Grbac, many fans felt the 49ers would be in trouble. Not so. Individual competence was less important than the teamwork capability shared among all the players. In successful organizations, whatever the industry or area, individual competencies are being turned into organizational capabilities.

Managers and HR professionals should constantly seek the capabilities necessary for success. They should routinely ask themselves and each other the following questions.

- What capabilities currently exist within the firm?
- What capabilities will be required for the future success of the firm?
- How can we align capabilities with business strategies?
- How can we design HR practices to create the needed capabilities?
- How can we measure the accomplishment of the needed capabilities?

Clear answers to these questions may not be readily forthcoming, but effective HR professionals will nonetheless continue to probe the underlying issues.

Challenge 5: Change, Change, and Change Some More

Although called by many names—among them, transformation, reengineering, culture change, reinvention, adaptation, flexibility, rapid learning, and agility—the competitiveness challenge is the same: Managers, employees, and organizations must learn to change faster and more comfortably. HR professionals need to help their organizations to change. They need to define an organizational model for change, to disseminate that model throughout the organization, and to sponsor its ongoing application. As cycle times get shorter and the pace of change increases, HR professionals will have to deal with many related questions, including the following:

- How do we unlearn what we have learned?
- How do we honor the past and adapt for the future?
- How do we encourage the risk-taking necessary for change without putting the firm in jeopardy?
- How do we determine which HR practices to change for transformation and which to leave the same for continuity?

- How do we engage the hearts and minds of everyone in the organization to change?

- How do we change and learn more rapidly?

Again, these questions do not have easy cookbook answers, but managers and HR professionals must address them.

A second issue with change entails a personal paradox. Most executives can give goose-bump speeches on the need for change and the dire consequences of failure to change. But, too often, the executives themselves don't change. They don't walk their talk. Because employees listen more to what executives do than to what they say, this inconsistency leads to the failure of many change efforts at both the personal and the organizational levels. HR professionals have the unique obligation to challenge powerful and successful executives to act according to their words. Learning how to insist without being insolent, to demand without being discourteous, and to persist without being pushy will be part of the HR professional's change challenge.

Managers and HR professionals who can create organizations that respond faster than their competitors to both predictable and unpredictable changes will be more likely to win.

Challenge Six: Technology

Technology innovations occur almost faster than we can keep up. The words designating new technologies—the Internet, video conferencing, global paging, networks, instant information and analysis—conjure entire new worlds of business action.

Technology has made our world smaller, closer, and faster. In an environment of burgeoning computer literacy, ideas and images spread quickly worldwide. Technology overcomes geographic distance as well as language and cultural difference. British television shows have a U.S. market, and U.S. shows have a global market. European fashions and design have cachet in the U.S. market, and U.S. popular culture has infiltrated even such cohesive cultures as Japan and France.

Personal use of technology has also changed the flow and use of information. Ideas are the currency of the next century, and intellectual capital can now be captured and communicated to others immediately. Staying ahead of the technology game requires constant investment in the competitive new services—Internet, CompuServe, Prodigy, America Online, Microsoft, and others as yet unknown.

Technology will dramatically affect how and where work is done, through teleconferencing, telecommuting, and shared data sources. Proximity was critical when a firm's boundaries were geographical. With the new technology, employees may work at home, in remote locations, or dispersed in customer offices and still remain connected to the business. Much of this book, for example, was written on a laptop while flying, then shared through modems with copy editors. Technology has redefined work time.

Managers and HR professionals responsible for redefining work at their firms need to figure out how to make technology a viable and productive part of the work setting. They need to be ahead of the information curve and learn to leverage information for business results.

Challenge Seven: Attracting, Retaining, and Measuring Competence and Intellectual Capital

In this ever changing, global, technologically demanding business environment, sourcing and retaining talent becomes the competitive battleground. Just as sports teams recruit aggressively for the best athletes, business organizations in the future will compete aggressively for the best talent. The skills required of agile, global, expatriate general managers become ever more stringent. Few people qualify. Successful firms will be those most adept at attracting, developing, and retaining individuals with the skills, perspective, and experience sufficient to drive a global business. The most sought after managers will possess the intellectual capital needed to create and distribute the products and services to global businesses.

Securing intellectual capital means upgrading the leadership bench. Leadership in the future will be team-focused and shared, rather than driven by a single person. It will become an on-going process of pioneering and risk-taking rather than a series of fiats derived from formal problem-solving. To cope with these trends, many of the business leaders of the future will have to be *GloPats,* managers comfortable in many global contexts, who appreciate and can leverage diverse cultures while balancing global economies of scale with local responsiveness. Filling a leadership bench with new leadership talents will require new leadership models. Leaders possessing the skills of the future may not be in place today, but they can be created or discovered.

Securing intellectual capital also involves learning to share ideas and information throughout a company more quickly. Some of the large professional service firms are experimenting with knowledge networks that use technology (for example, the Internet and electronic bulletin boards) to enable individual consultants to source and share information quickly. In studying learning organizations, we discovered that learning occurs where ideas are both generated (for example, discovery of a novel approach to work) and generalized through wide dissemination within the company. Securing intellectual capital means that new ideas must be generated and generalized. Managers and HR professionals must create the policies and practices that will encourage such learning.

Securing intellectual capital goes beyond learning to *rapid* learning. An organization capable of rapid learning spreads ideas and innovation quickly across boundaries through improved information-flow processes. Research by Cal Wick and I revealed that rapid learning follows when managers turn opportunities into vision, transform vision into action, and align action with customers.[16] Effective management of these processes creates an organization in which the half-life of intellectual capital becomes increasingly shorter. (In terms of knowledge, *half-life* means the time after which 50 percent of what is known has ceased to be current.) Creating organizations in which intellectual capital is constantly updated will be a significant aspect of HR work in the future.

The task of securing intellectual capital changes a firm's measurement processes. Traditional measures of success, focused on economic capital (for example, profitability or financial performance), must now be coupled with measures of intellectual capital. Seeking, finding, and using such measures will be among the primary challenges facing the HR professionals of the future.

Challenge Eight: Turnaround Is Not Transformation

In the last fifteen years, many companies have initiated turnaround efforts. Through downsizing, consolidations, and restructurings, these organizations have reduced costs and shed unprofitable businesses, while quality and reengineering efforts removed inefficient steps in work processes. All these efforts helped turn around businesses, making them sleeker, swifter, and more streamlined.

Turnaround, however, is not transformation. Transformation changes the fundamental image of the business, as seen by customers and employees. Transformation focuses on creating mindshare more than market share. Transformation results when customers and employees move from fundamentally different images of a firm to similar issues. When Harley-Davidson emerged from the control of AMF in 1982, it faced bankruptcy, not only economically, but in terms of mindset. Customers continued to see Harley as offering great technology—the sound and the feel—but they had a poorer image of Harley's quality.

Through aggressive leadership, Harley has transformed its image. It has become an icon of quality, an image of freedom, and a lifestyle symbol for old and new customers. The transformation at Harley-Davidson derived partly from product and product-related advertising but mostly from transforming employee mindset. As employees became re-committed to Harley-Davidson's values and business process, they began to build better quality bikes, to communicate their pride in their product to customers, and to transform their own mindset.

Transformation is occurring in a number of industries. Continental Airlines was seeking an identity throughout the 1980s and into the early 1990s, a period during which it had the reputation of offering low cost but with a correspondingly low level of service. In the 1990s, Continental executives worked to transform the company's image in the eyes of its customers. They began to listen to customers: They started an 800-line number, conducted customer surveys, articulated value in terms dictated by customers (for example, on-time arrivals), engaged employees in a customer-service focus, and worked backward, becoming the industry leader in customer service. Such transformations are not easy, but if achieved, they are more important than a new product launch or market expansion. The impact of a new identity for employees and customers outlasts any single product and extends beyond any market.

Managers and HR professionals who focus on transformation create fundamental and enduring change.

IMPLICATIONS OF BUSINESS CHALLENGES

Implications of Business Challenges on the Nature of Competition

The eight challenges outlined above redefine competition. When competition is defined as adding value to customers in unique ways,[17] companies must find new and unique ways to serve their customers. Parity suggests that competitors have learned to copy cost, technology, distribution, manufacturing, and product features. Organization remains unique. Traditional forms of competitiveness become table stakes.[18] Like ante in poker, firms will lose if these traditional forms of competitiveness are not attained; even where they are attained, however, they guarantee only that the firm will be "in play," not that it will be competitive.

New models of competition must go beyond the table stakes of cost, technology, distribution, and product features to identify other capabilities valued by customers. Response to the eight competitive challenges should focus on organizational capabilities such as speed, responsiveness, relationships, agility, learning, and employee competence. In brief, the new competitive reality first assumes product and cost parity and then argues that competitive advantage results from the creation of organizations that can continually produce better than their competitors can.

Implications of Business Challenges for the Leaders of the Future

Leaders at any level of a company must cherish and commit to winning. But wanting to win is not enough: Leaders must set a path that makes it happen. A firm's path to winning must increasingly go beyond mastering balance sheets, creating new manufacturing processes, and forming customer relationships; it must build organizations that change, learn, move, and act faster than those of its competitors. To make the best use of these organizational capabilities, executives must see their human resource practices as sources of competitive advantage.

The successful leaders of the future must be able to create organizational capabilities.[19] They must be able to identify the capabilities critical to business success and to design and deliver the human resource management practices that can create those capabilities. To create value and deliver results, the leaders of the future must become human resource champions.

Implications of Business Challenges for HR as a Profession

So what do these competitive challenges mean for the continuing evolution of HR? On the one hand, HR refers to the organizational systems and processes within a firm (for example, staffing, hiring, communication, and compensation) that govern how work is done. These processes must be judged by the extent to which they enhance competitiveness.

On the other hand, HR refers to the HR function or department. The new competitive realities outlined in this chapter suggest a new agenda for HR, an agenda focused on championing competitiveness. As champions of competitiveness, HR professionals must focus more on the *deliverables* of their work than on doing their work better. They must articulate their role in terms of value created. They must create mechanisms to deliver HR so that business results quickly follow. They must learn to measure results in terms of business competitiveness rather than employee comfort and to lead cultural transformation rather than to consolidate, reengineer, or downsize when a company needs to turn around.[20]

To achieve these goals, HR must recognize and correct its past. The human resource function traditionally has spent more time professing than being professional. The HR function has been plagued by myths that keep it from being professional (see Table 1-1). Regardless of whether these myths originate with HR people or with line managers, it is time they were overcome. It is time to talk less and do more; time to add value, not write value statements; time to build competitive, not comfortable, organizations; time to be proactive, not reactive. It is time to perform, not preach.

For too long the phrase *HR professional* has been an oxymoron. If HR practices are to be leveraged by the HR function, HR professionals must begin to act professionally. Professionals in other functional areas— physicians, attorneys, engineers, psychologists, controllers, and so on—share the following characteristics:

- Focus on defined outcomes (for example, physicians commit themselves to the Hippocratic oath and to healing).

Table 1-1 **Myths That Keep HR from Being a Profession**

Old Myths	New Realities
People go into HR because they like people.	HR departments are not designed to provide corporate therapy or as social or health-and-happiness retreats. HR professionals must create the practices that make employees more competitive, not more comfortable.
Anyone can do HR.	HR activities are based on theory and research. HR professionals must master both theory and practice.
HR deals with the soft side of a business and is therefore not accountable.	The impact of HR practices on business results can and must be measured. HR professionals must learn how to translate their work into financial performance.
HR focuses on costs, which must be controlled.	HR practices must create value by increasing the intellectual capital within the firm. HR professionals must add value, not reduce costs.
HR's job is to be the policy police and the health-and-happiness patrol.	The HR function does not own compliance—managers do. HR practices do not exist to make employees happy but to help them become committed. HR professionals must help managers commit employees and administer policies.
HR is full of fads.	HR practices have evolved over time. HR professionals must see their current work as part of an evolutionary chain and explain their work with less jargon and more authority.
HR is staffed by nice people.	At times, HR practices should force vigorous debates. HR professionals should be confrontative and challenging as well as supportive.
HR is HR's job.	HR work is as important to line managers as are finance, strategy, and other business domains. HR professionals should join with managers in championing HR issues.

- A shared body of knowledge (for example, attorneys learn the canon of law).
- Essential competencies (for example, engineers have the skills to build bridges, design machinery, or create computers).
- Ethical standards maintained by collegial jurisdiction (for example, licensed psychologists must adhere to an established set of ethical standards).
- Clear roles (for example, controllers help monitor the economic performance of their firms).

Outcome definition, knowledge, competencies, standards, and role criteria enable these occupations to be recognized and accepted as professions. The competitive challenges laid out in this chapter, when cast in these terms, will provide those who work in HR the opportunity to establish themselves as professionals.

PURPOSE AND OUTLINE OF THIS BOOK

This book is about building competitive organizations and what that means in terms of the next agenda for line managers and HR professionals. It is designed to help any manager create more competitive organizational processes, and, in particular, to help HR professionals to articulate new agendas for their roles in the competitive organizations of the future.

Most books on HR are organized around HR practices. Chapter headings might be, for example, staffing, training, appraisal, rewards, organization design, communication, and so on. In other words, traditional HR books focus on HR *means*. This book is organized differently. It is organized around the outcomes or deliverables of HR and the activities required to accomplish these outcomes.

Chapter 2 lays out a framework that defines four generic deliverables of effective use of HR: strategy execution, administrative efficiency, employee contribution, and capacity for change. These deliverables represent capabilities of competitive companies and must be championed by both line managers and HR professionals. These four deliverables also identify the roles that HR professionals play when creating value. The roles derived from these key deliverables are described in detail in Chapters 3 through 6.

Chapter 3 describes how HR can help make strategy happen. It reviews the role of HR as a strategic partner joined with line management in turning business strategy into action. The chapter provides a process for doing an organizational diagnosis through which line managers and HR professionals can leverage HR practices to deliver results.

Chapter 4 describes how HR can help build administrative efficiency. It reviews the role of HR as an administrative expert and highlights the ways in which work can be organized so that costs are reduced while quality of service is maintained. It recommends and describes the potential for reengineering HR and links that process to organizational design choices that include outsourcing, shared services, and the learning organization.

Chapter 5 describes how HR can ensure employee contribution. It reviews the role of HR as employee champion and highlights the management of intellectual capital to create value. The chapter discusses specific ways that managers and HR professionals can increase employee commitment and competence, despite post-reengineering trauma and burned-out employees, and keep employees committed in an era of increasing competitiveness.

Chapter 6 describes how HR can help make corporate change happen. It reviews the role of HR as a change agent and describes how to build capacity for change. Among the topics covered are processes for improving the capacity for change (for example, doing initiatives faster) and for creating fundamental transformation or culture change.

To accomplish these four deliverables, the HR function must be refocused at a fundamental level, and Chapter 7 introduces ways to rethink and redefine it. Applying organizational diagnostic tools to the HR function, the chapter shows how to do strategic HR, create HR strategies, and establish an HR organization. This chapter includes many examples of companies that have successfully transformed their HR functions, and it lays out the steps that led to these transformations.

Chapter 8 raises the question "What's next for HR practices, functions, and professionals and line managers?" Not a prediction, but a possible scenario, the chapter highlights the importance of continued examination of HR theory, tools, capabilities, leadership, and values.

Each chapter ends with a section outlining the implications for line managers and HR professionals of the concepts explored. These sections highlight ways line managers and HR professionals can co-champion HR issues to build competitive organizations.

SUMMARY

This chapter reviews eight competitive challenges facing firms today. To respond to these challenges, firms must create new organizational capabilities that derive from redefinition and redeployment of HR practices, functions, and professionals. Line managers and HR professionals must create these capabilities jointly. Line managers must strive for the following goals.

- Understand organizational capability as an essential source of competitiveness.

- Participate in the process of designing competitive organizations.
- See the organizational implications of competitive challenges.
- Dedicate time and energy to organizational capability.

HR professionals must achieve the following:

- See HR issues as part of a competitive business equation.
- Articulate why HR matters in business terms, starting with business value.
- Talk comfortably about how competitive challenges dictate HR activities.

As line managers and HR professionals jointly champion HR, the distinction blurs between HR staff and line managers as operators. The tools in this book are as relevant for managers who run businesses, operate plants, or direct staff functions as they are for HR professionals.

The Changing Nature of Human Resources: A Model for Multiple Roles

IF THE NEXT AGENDA for creating value is to come from Human Resources, the new roles for HR professionals will have to be defined. In the past few years, roles for HR professionals were often viewed in terms of transition from[1]

- Operational to strategic

- Qualitative to quantitative

- Policing to partnering

- Short-term to long-term

- Administrative to consultative

- Functionally oriented to business oriented

- Internally focused to externally and customer-focused

- Reactive to proactive

- Activity-focused to solutions-focused

More recently, these *from . . . to . . .* transitions have been seen as too simplistic: The roles undertaken by HR professionals are, in reality, multiple, not single. HR professionals must fulfill both operational and strategic roles; they must be both police and partners; and they must take responsibility for both qualitative and quantitative goals over the short and long term. For HR professionals to add value to their increasingly complex businesses, they must perform increasingly complex and, at times, even paradoxical roles.

A Multiple-role Model for Human Resources Management

To create value and deliver results, HR professionals must begin not by focusing on the activities or work of HR but by defining the deliverables of that work. Deliverables guarantee outcomes of HR work. With deliverables defined, the roles and activities of business partners may be stipulated.

The framework in Figure 2-1 describes—in terms of deliverables—four key roles that HR professionals must fulfill to make their business partnership a reality. I devised this framework over the course of my work with dozens of companies and hundreds of HR professionals; many companies have since used it as a way to describe the deliverables of their HR work.[2] The two axes represent the HR professional's *focus* and *activities. Focus*

Figure 2-1 **HR Roles in Building a Competitive Organization**

FUTURE/STRATEGIC
FOCUS

	Management of Strategic Human Resources	Management of Transformation and Change	
PROCESSES			PEOPLE
	Management of Firm Infrastructure	Management of Employee Contribution	

DAY-TO-DAY/OPERATIONAL
FOCUS

ranges from long-term/strategic to short-term/operational. HR professionals must learn to be *both* strategic and operational, focusing on the long *and* short term. *Activities* range from managing *processes* (HR tools and systems) to managing *people*.[3] These two axes delineate four principal HR roles: (1) management of strategic human resources; (2) management of firm infrastructure; (3) management of the employee contribution; and (4) management of transformation and change. To understand each of these roles more fully, we must consider these three issues: the *deliverables* that constitute the outcome of the role, the characteristic *metaphor* or visual image that accompanies the role, and the *activities* the HR professional must perform to fulfill the role. Table 2-1 summarizes these issues for each of the roles identified in Figure 2-1.

Management of Strategic Human Resources

The strategic HR role focuses on aligning HR strategies and practices with business strategy. In playing this role, the HR professional works to be a

Table 2-1 **Definition of HR Roles**

Role/Cell	Deliverable/ Outcome	Metaphor	Activity
Management of Strategic Human Resources	Executing strategy	Strategic Partner	Aligning HR and business strategy: "Organizational diagnosis"
Management of Firm Infrastructure	Building an efficient infrastructure	Administrative Expert	Reengineering Organization Processes: "Shared services"
Management of Employee Contribution	Increasing employee commitment and capability	Employee Champion	Listening and responding to Employees: "Providing resources to employees"
Management of Transformation and Change	Creating a renewed organization	Change Agent	Managing transformation and change: "Ensuring capacity for change"

strategic partner, helping to ensure the success of business strategies. By fulfilling this role, HR professionals increase the capacity of a business to execute its strategies. Translating business strategies into HR practices helps a business in three ways. First, the business can adapt to change because the time from the conception to the execution of a strategy is shortened. Second, the business can better meet customer demands because its customer service strategies have been translated into specific policies and practices. Third, the business can achieve financial performance through its more effective execution of strategy.

When Marriott, for example, made the strategic decision to enter the Hong Kong market, executives knew that successful HR practices would increase their probability of success. Since quality of service is a primary differentiator of Marriott hotels from their competition, and since the quality of employees correlates with the perception of service, Marriott executives knew they had to attract and retain the most qualified employees in the area. To do so, the HR and line executives examined the company's HR practices, seeking ways to distinguish them in the marketplace. In this case, the customer was the pool of highly talented potential employees who might at the time be working for a competitor and who must be enticed into working for Marriott. After considering many options, the company offered potential employees at the Hong Kong Marriott a five-day workweek rather than the six-day workweek traditionally required by competing hotels. While this may seem a simple policy, it was very important to the potential employees. The five-day workweek became a cornerstone of Marriott's strategy for achieving high-quality service, enabling the company to advertise, solicit, and secure the talented employees who would provide that service in the Hong Kong market.

The deliverable from the management of strategic human resources is strategy execution. HR practices help accomplish business objectives. There are many examples. As Sears worked to reduce costs, HR managers implemented compensation, job rotation, and downsizing practices that reduced labor cost per store. As Whirlpool sought to gain more global market share in appliances, HR strategies modified hiring practices and career paths to ensure multinational competence. When Colgate-Palmolive wanted to increase its global revenue, the compensation system was changed to reward sales growth. When Motorola wanted to gain access to Russian markets, it offered training and development opportunities to Soviet customers. Each of these HR practices helped execute business strategy. The HR executives who designed these new practices were strategic partners: They mastered the skill of organizational diagnosis and aligned HR practices with business strategies.

The metaphor for this role is the "strategic partner." HR professionals become strategic partners when they participate in the process of defining business strategy, when they ask questions that move strategy to action, and when they design HR practices that align with business strategy.

The primary actions of the strategic human resource manager translate business strategies into HR priorities. In any business setting, whether corporate, functional, business unit, or product line, a strategy exists either explicitly, in a formal process or document, or implicitly, through a shared agenda on priorities. As strategic partners, HR professionals should be able to identify the HR practices that make the strategy happen. The process of identifying these HR priorities is called *organizational diagnosis,* a process through which an organization is audited to determine its strengths and weaknesses.

In the past decade, increasing attention has been paid to the importance of moving HR professionals into the strategic role. But in answering the call to become "more strategic" and "more involved in the business," many HR professionals have inappropriately identified this as the only HR role.[4] The implications of this are discussed below under "Paradoxes Inherent in Multiple HR Roles."

Management of Firm Infrastructure

Creating an organizational infrastructure has been a traditional HR role. It requires that HR professionals design and deliver efficient HR processes for staffing, training, appraising, rewarding, promoting, and otherwise managing the flow of employees through the organization. As a caretaker of the corporate infrastructure, HR professionals ensure that these organizational processes are designed and delivered efficiently. While this role has been down-played and even disclaimed with the shift to a strategic focus, its successful accomplishment continues to add value to a business.

HR professionals create infrastructure by constantly examining and improving the HR processes. Marriott, for example, works diligently to improve its staffing, development, and assessment processes. When opening a new facility, Marriott temporarily relocates employees into that facility to implement the best practices used at other facilities. Marriott works to share its facilities' best practices by holding workshops for HR professionals from the various divisions and sites. The company encourages experimentation within a site to foster development of new HR practices and to find economies of scale for some HR activities (for example, by creating an employee benefit service center), while decentralizing and increasing site ownership of other activities (for example, creating high performing work teams at a facility).

The deliverable from the infrastructure role is administrative efficiency. HR professionals accomplish administrative efficiency in two ways. First, they ensure efficiency in HR processes. For example, through reengineering HR processes, one firm recently found twenty-four separate registration systems for training; new efficiency and cost savings were achieved by streamlining and automating them into a single system. Another firm, finding that it required an average of six months to staff key positions, improved the process and cut the time needed to one month. A second way in which HR executives can improve overall business efficiency is by hiring, training, and rewarding managers who increase productivity and reduce waste.

By delivering administrative efficiency, HR managers highlight their role as administrative experts, mastering and leading reengineering efforts that foster HR and business processes. At a simplistic level, most HR functions today (like most other business functions) are being asked to do more with less—and accomplishing this feat should be the outcome of undertaking this role.

The metaphor for work on a firm's infrastructure is the "administrative expert." As implied above, HR professionals acting as administrative experts ferret out unnecessary costs, improve efficiency, and constantly find new ways to do things better.

To be effective as administrative experts, HR professionals need to undertake activities leading to continual reengineering of the work processes they administer. In many firms, this reengineering of HR processes has led to a new HR organizational form called *shared services,* through which HR administrative services are shared across company divisions while maintaining service quality for their users (line managers, employees, and executives). (See Chapter 4 for a review of shared services.)

Management of Employee Contribution

The employee contribution[5] role for HR professionals encompasses their involvement in the day-to-day problems, concerns, and needs of employees. In companies in which intellectual capital becomes a critical source of the firm's value, HR professionals should be active and aggressive in developing this capital. HR professionals thus become the employees' champions by linking employee contributions to the organization's success. With active employee champions who understand employees' needs and ensure that those needs are met, overall employee contribution goes up.

The deliverables from management of employee contribution are increased employee commitment and competence. HR practices should help employees to contribute through both their competence to do good work and their commitment to work diligently. In an era when downsizing has eroded the employer-employee psychological contract, HR executives can be business partners by continuing to be employee champions who pay attention to employee needs. Again, there are many examples of appropriate, successful response in this area. Microsoft holds all-employee meetings during which employee views are voiced and heard. Apple has created an employee services center, which employees can call using an 800 number, staffed by people who can answer questions about company policy and administration. Marriott has organized employees into high performance work teams that provide emotional support to employees within the work teams. Regular employee surveys at Hewlett-Packard monitor employee concerns and stimulate appropriate responses. In each case, HR professionals working as employee champions strive to understand and fulfill employees' needs.

The metaphor for this HR role, as implied above, is "employee champion." These champions personally spend time with employees and train and encourage managers in other departments to do the same. With employee champions who understand the needs of employees and ensure that those needs are met, overall employee contribution goes up. Employee contribution is essential to any business, not only for its own sake (the social desirability of committed employees), but also because it affects a business's ability to change, meet customer expectations, and increase financial performance. When employees are competent and committed, employee intellectual capital becomes a significant appreciable asset that is reflected in a firm's financial results.

The main activities for the management of employee contribution are listening, responding, and finding ways to provide employees with resources that meet their changing demands. As higher and higher demands are placed on employees, HR professionals and line managers who serve as employee champions creatively seek and implement the means for employees to voice opinions and feel ownership in the business; they help to maintain the psychological contract between the employee and the firm; and they give employees new tools with which to meet ever higher expectations. At Marriott, for example, the ideal for HR managers, fulfilled by the best at any given facility, is sensitivity to employees. The best HR managers know the employees by name and spend time walking around the property listening to them. They help employees to feel part of a team dedicated to customer service. These managers are responsible for encouraging employee suggestions both from individuals and at forums; for ensuring fair hearings for employees who have difficulties with management; and for maintaining overall employee contribution.

Management of Transformation and Change

A fourth key role through which HR professionals can add value to a firm is to manage transformation and change. *Transformation* entails fundamental cultural change within the firm; HR professionals managing transformation become both cultural guardians and cultural catalysts. *Change* refers to the ability of an organization to improve the design and implementation of initiatives and to reduce cycle time in all organizational activities; HR professionals help to identify and implement processes for change.

The deliverable from management of transformation and change is capacity for change. As firms undergo transformation, HR executives serve as business partners by helping employees let go of old and adapt to a new culture. As change agents, HR executives help organizations identify a process for managing change.

As implied, the metaphor for work in this role is "change agent." As change agents, HR professionals face the paradox inherent in any organizational change. Often, change must be grounded in the past.[6] For the HR professional serving as change agent, honoring the past means appreciating and respecting the tradition and history of a business while acting for the future. HR professionals may need to force or facilitate a dialogue about values as they identify new behaviors that will help to keep a firm competitive over time. Being change agents is clearly part of the value-added role of HR professionals as business partners.

The actions of change agents include identifying and framing problems, building relationships of trust, solving problems, and creating—and fulfilling— action plans. In research on the competencies of HR professionals, my colleagues and I have found that the domain of competencies related to managing change was the most important for success as an HR professional.[7] HR professionals who are change agents help make change happen; they understand critical processes for change, build commitment to those processes, and ensure that change occurs as intended.

Case Study: Application of the Multiple-Role Model at Hewlett-Packard

Hewlett-Packard (HP) has a legacy of commitment to human resource issues, although not until 1990 did a professional HR executive, Pete Peterson, become a corporate vice president. In his years as a vice president of human resources, Peterson made dramatic changes. The ratio of HR people to employees went from 1:53 to 1:80, while maintaining the same high quality of services. These improvements derived from reengineering all HR processes, redefining HR roles, and reassigning accountability for managing people to the line managers.

In 1990, Peterson challenged his worldwide personnel team to "create the environment" by increasing value for the company, providing higher quality services for employees, and utilizing human resources more effectively. Team members were to focus on becoming business partners who helped their organizations become more competitive. To translate this vision into action, HP's human resources professionals were assigned four specific goals.

First, the HP human resources team was to facilitate, measure, and improve the quality of management and teamwork. Second, HR was to contribute to business strategy, identify human resource implications, and facilitate change consistent with HP's basic values. Third, HR was asked to accelerate individual and organizational learning across HP. And fourth, HR was to manage people-related processes, that is, functions within the HR department.

The HP human resources function has been very successful in fulfilling these goals. So successful, in fact, that Hewlett-Packard won the *Personnel Journal* Optimas Award for General Excellence. The journal cited HP's human resources organization in terms of its seven categories.[8]

Competitive advantage: HP's worldwide employee survey provides employee feedback on managers' and directors' business goals.

Financial impact: HP's human resources department saves HP $35 million per year through a reduced HR-to-employee ratio.

Global outlook: HP's "Practices Hotline" links company HR professionals worldwide.

Innovation: A women's conference on technology helps to advance the careers of HP's women scientists and engineers.

Managing change: HP is committed to improving diversity among its work force.

Quality of life: HP consistently rates as one of the best U.S. companies to work for because of its commitment to its work force.

Service: HR has created several technical systems that continue to improve HR processes.

The HP human resources team continued to move the function forward by establishing a development course called Personnel as a Competitive Advantage. Discussions during this course concerned the continually changing roles of HP's human resources department. The team applied the framework from Figure 2–1 to Hewlett-Packard's situation as a way of defining its changing HR roles. While the HP example uses somewhat different terms than does Figure 2-1, it does demonstrate application of the figure's basic concepts to the HR function at Hewlett-Packard. These applications are described in Figure 2-2, which defines personnel goals in terms of apportionment of responsibility, and in Figure 2-3, which defines the characteristic activities of each role.

At Hewlett-Packard, the HR role begins with customer need. *Customer* may be variously defined as the entire organization, its employees,

Figure 2-2 Hewlett-Packard's Application of HR Professional Roles

STRATEGIC LONG-TERM

Customer Need: effective business and HR strategies Ownership: 85% line; 15% HR HR Function: alignment PM Role: strategic HR management PM Competencies: • business knowledge • HR strategy formulation • influencing skills	Customer Need: organizational effectiveness Ownership: 51% line; 49% HR HR Function: change management PM Role: change agent PM Competencies: • change management skills • consulting/facilitation/coaching • systems analysis skills
Customer Need: administrative processes efficiency Ownership: 5% line; 95% HR HR Function: services delivery PM Role: function manager PM Competencies: • content knowledge • process improvement • information technology • customer relations • service needs assessment	Customer Need: employee commitment Ownership: 98% line; 2% HR HR Function: management support PM Role: employee champion PM Competencies: • work environment assessment • management/employee development • performance management

 PROCESS   PEOPLE

OPERATIONAL/DAY-TO-DAY

Source: Hewlett-Packard. Reprinted with permission.

and/or its managers. The HR role statement, as illustrated in Figure 2-2, indicates who has ownership, or primary responsibility and accountability, for fulfilling the duties corresponding to each role in the model. Hewlett-Packard gives line managers primary ownership of strategic HRM (top left cell) and of the management of employee contribution (bottom right cell). It accords joint ownership to management of transformation and change (top right cell); and it allows the HR team primary ownership of firm infrastructure (bottom left cell). The primary role of HR and the competencies required to fulfill that role are further identified. Figure 2-2 lays out a vision of the Hewlett-Packard HR function

Figure 2-3 Sample Activities Related to HR Roles at Hewlett-Packard

STRATEGIC/LONG-TERM

Strategic HR Management	Change Management
HR is a major contributor to business strategy.	*HR partners with line managers to lead and facilitate change.*
• Design HR strategies to align with business objectives • Consultation in the development of the organization's values, mission, business planning • Member of management team contributing to business decisions • Participation in hoshin process; leads efforts on CEO people hoshin • Participates in business task forces (e.g., ISO 9000) • Program management of workforce planning, skills assessment, succession planning, diversity, retrainng • Foster systems thinking/quality focus	• Change management facilitation • Consulting for increased organization effectiveness (assessment/diagnosis, contracting, action planning, evaluation, follow-up) • Organization design • System/process redesign • Reconstructing / re-engineering • Competency analysis • Long-range team and management development

PROCESS ⟷ PEOPLE

HR Services Delivery	Employee Commitment
HR provides more service, better quality, and greater accessibility resulting in lower cost and increased customer satisfaction.	*HR facilitates, measures, and improves the quality of management and teamwork.*
• Wage review • Requisition tracking • Applicant sourcing/interview • Benefits program/delivery • Reclassification/promotions • Data base maintenance and transaction processing • New program introductions • Data reporting and analysis • Classroom training delivery • Interviewing logistics	• Champion HP Way • Facilitate employee surveys • Promote inclusive environment • Promote work/life balance • Management coaching • Communication with employees • Investigation of open door issues • Performance evaluation review • Corrective actions with employees and managers

OPERATIONAL/DAY-TO-DAY

Source: Hewlett-Packard. Reprinted with permission.

focused on meeting customer needs, assuring deliverables to the business, assigning accountability, and defining the HR competencies needed to enact the vision. For each role, leaders of the HR function have identified activities to be fulfilled by the personnel professionals occupying these roles; the activities are identified and described in Figure 2-3. These represent the set of day-to-day activities required to fulfill the vision of a multi-role HR contribution.

The firm's definitions of HR roles (as outlined in Figure 2-2) and of the activities related to those roles (as outlined in Figure 2-3) give HP's human resources professionals a clear sense of purpose and a clear definition of what and how they add value to the firm. By focusing on all four roles, HP practice legitimizes all HR professionals, not just those working on the upper-cell strategic activities. The accountabilities assigned for each role focus attention on the responsibility of line managers to become actively engaged in people-related work.

The framework and concepts illustrated in Figures 2-2 and 2-3 help HP human resources employees to know their expected outcomes, their responsibilities, their duties, and the images they should project within the organization. The sum of these efforts constitutes a professional role statement for the HR function at Hewlett-Packard.

Case Study: Application of the Multiple-Role Model at Clorox

Clorox senior line executives have been working at weaving their people strategy into their business strategy. Each of the three proposed strategies for Clorox's corporate success—customer interface, work simplification, and people strategy—serve different consituents—customers, investors, and employees, respectively—and have critical success factors that relate directly to HR issues. As the vice president of human resources, Janet Brady worked to identify the roles that would allow Clorox HR professionals to help accomplish business goals. Using the multiple-role model illustrated in Figure 2-1, Brady articulated specific actions for Clorox HR professionals in each of the four roles.

HR professionals at Clorox succeed as *strategic partners* when they fulfill the following criteria.

- Act as an integral part of the business team.
- Speak for Clorox's needs when part of any team revising existing or developing new HR programs.

- Engage a business team in systematic organizational audits that result in establishing clear priorities.

- Provide HR resources to the business.

- Possess a complete up-to-date understanding of Clorox's business and the implications for HR stemming from prevailing business conditions.

Clorox HR professionals succeed as *administrative experts* by fulfilling the following criteria.

- Develop and manage guidelines, plans, and policies for effectively managing human resources.

- Act as consultants in a field of expertise, supporting other HR professionals as well as HR clients.

- Take responsibility for continuous improvements in programs and operations in a field of expertise.

- Keep up to date on issues and concerns in a discipline, thus maintaining status as a recognized expert in that area.

Clorox HR professionals who are *employee champions* succeed by fulfilling the following criteria.

- Speak for employee needs and management's concerns about employee relations.

- Know employees and anticipate their concerns, needs, and issues.

- Be available to and approachable by employees.

- Become and remain experts in the tools and techniques for assisting employees with work-related concerns.

- Provide employees with the resources they need to commit themselves to meeting company objectives.

And, finally, Clorox HR professionals acting as *change agents* succeed by fulfilling the following criteria.

- Influence and drive organizational-change strategies in support of business strategies.

- Manage the "pilot's checklist" to help ensure successful change efforts.

- Take continuously the organization's pulse regarding both internal and external matters and perspectives.

- Remain up to date about the tools, techniques, and practices of change in order to effectively and efficiently manage change and respond to the organization's requirements.

- Educate the organization about HR trends that affect the business.

By turning the four HR roles into specific behaviors and actions, Brady created a world-class HR organization. She set high expectations for what the function will deliver and defined the behaviors necessary for the company's HR professionals to accomplish those deliverables.

Hewlett-Packard and Clorox are examples of companies that have applied the multiple-role model illustrated in Figure 2-1 to their particular settings. While using language and terms tailored to their own businesses, they have defined HR roles in terms of deliverables, identified multiple rather than single HR roles, specified the HR practices and professional attributes necessary to fulfill the four roles, and used the ideas to discuss how HR creates value in their respective enterprises.

BUSINESS PARTNERS PLAY MULTIPLE ROLES

The experiences of Hewlett-Packard, Clorox, and other companies suggest that it is time for the human resources function in general to become more professional. A number of companies' experiences also provide some insights into the multiple roles that HR professionals must play.

Today's HR professionals are often labeled *business partners.* Too often, however, the term *business partner* is narrowly defined as an HR professional working with general managers to implement strategy, that is, working as a *strategic partner.* Even in the original conception of the multiple-role framework (illustrated in Figure 2-1), the role governing management of long-term processes was construed as that of a *business,* not *strategic,* partner, as if the terms were indistinguishable.[9] Based on discussions with HR executives such as Pete Peterson of Hewlett-Packard, the original "business partner" concept has changed.[10] Today, a more dynamic, encompassing equation replaces the simple concept of *business partner.*

Business Partner = Strategic Partner + Administrative Expert + Employee Champion + Change Agent

Business partners exist in *all four roles* defined in the multiple-role model (see Figure 2-1), not just in the strategic role.

Strategic partners (top left cell) are business partners because they align HR systems with business strategy and set HR priorities for a business entity. Administrative experts (bottom left cell) are business partners because they save their businesses money through more efficient design and delivery of HR systems. Employee champions (bottom right cell) are business partners because they ensure that employee contributions to the business remain high, in terms of both employee commitment and competence. Change agents (top right cell) are business partners because they help businesses through transformations and to adapt to changing business conditions. Being a business partner requires competence in diagnosing organizations, reengineering processes, listening and responding to employees, and managing cultural transformation. The HR business partner adds value to a firm through strategy execution, administrative efficiency, employee commitment, and cultural change.

HR professionals who work primarily in any one role should have no lack of respect for those working in the others. In a play, the entire ensemble contributes to success. If one actor or actress becomes arrogant and disrespectful of the others, the entire production suffers. So, too, in human resources. Each of the four roles is essential to the overall partnership role. Too often, businesses today esteem the HR strategic partner and/or change agent roles while discounting the administrative expert and employee champion roles as traditional and dated. This thinking drives wedges among HR professionals and weakens the overall effectiveness of the HR function.

IMPLICATIONS OF MULTIPLE ROLES FOR HR PROFESSIONALS

As discussed above and illustrated in Figure 2-1, HR professionals may add value to a business in four ways: They can help execute strategy, build infrastructure, ensure employee contribution, and manage transformation and change.

Assessing the Current Quality of the HR Function

The multiple-role model can help in assessing the overall quality of HR services. The HR role-assessment survey in the appendix to this chapter offers one effective and flexible means for undertaking this task. The survey operationalizes specific descriptors of HR concepts, activities, and practices for each role, and tabulating the results yields a profile of HR quality for each. This assessment, which can be done at the corporate business unit, or plant level, will define the roles as currently played within a business.

The scoring sheet, included with the survey, provides two kinds of information. First, the total score for all four roles (ranging from 50 to 200) constitutes a general assessment of the overall quality of HR services within a business. Total scores above 160 may be considered high, indicating a perception of high quality in delivery of HR services. Total scores below 90 indicate HR services perceived as being of low quality overall.

Second, the allocation of the points among the four roles indicates the current perception of the quality of HR services for each, providing a picture of the HR function that allows a business to evaluate it more effectively. Most companies that have collected these data scored higher in the operational quadrants and lower in the strategic quadrants, a result consistent with traditional HR roles. The largest range of scores is found for employee contribution, with some firms shown to be heavily invested in enhancing employee commitment while others appear to have relegated employee concerns to the back burner. In general, the management transformation and change role receives the lowest scores.

Reviewing the Evolution of the HR Function

The HR role-assessment survey in the appendix provides not only a view of current overall quality of HR services but also an assessment of the evolution of a business's HR services. This can be done either by changing the questions to request perceptions of "past versus present or future" quality for each role or by repeating the survey over time.

Had a business collected this data several times over the past twenty years, for example, the evolution of its HR roles would have been evident, showing, most likely, movement from a focus on operational roles to a focus on strategic roles. Focus on employee contribution has also decreased at most businesses over the past two decades. In recent years, most firms have undertaken productivity initiatives, such as reengineering, downsizing, and consolidation, which demand that HR professionals focus on infrastructure and their roles as administrative experts. Over the same period, an emphasis on strategic intent initiatives, such as globalization, customer service, and multi-generational product design, have encouraged HR focus on strategy execution and fulfillment of the strategic partner role. Finally, culture change initiatives, such as process improvements, culture change, and empowerment, have meant that the HR professional must increasingly manage such culture change in the capacity of change agent. This shift in emphasis has meant that HR professionals have done less and less in their role as employee champion to manage employee contribution.

By using the HR role-assessment survey, businesses can identify areas in which the HR function is growing stronger or weaker in each role.

Comparing HR and Line Manager Views of the HR Function

Another use for the HR role-assessment survey in the appendix is to solicit responses from line managers as well as HR professionals and to compare the results. Asking both HR professionals and line managers to rate the current state of HR performance in each of the four roles yields an audit of the extent to which the two perspectives align. Examination of the results can contribute to improved understanding of the HR function and company expectations in a number of ways.

Matched expectations

Matched expectations mean that HR professionals and line managers see the HR function in the same way. Alignment of HR and line expectations may be good news since it indicates agreement on the roles and delivery of HR services. Alignment may, however, be bad news. In one firm, for example, the HR and line managers agreed that current delivery of HR services was in the 15 to 20 point range (out of 50) for each of the four roles. But while this alignment implied that HR was meeting line managers' expectations, these expectations were uniformly low. Meeting low expectations implies that neither HR professionals nor line managers had a stretch vision for HR. The multiple-role framework offered here presents a way to define stretch goals, to raise expectations, and to specify value-added targets for HR professionals.

Mismatched expectations

Mismatched expectations occur when the perceptions of line managers and of HR professionals differ. The most common mismatch seen on surveys collected thus far shows HR professionals rating themselves higher than do their line managers. In these cases, HR professionals perceived their work to be better than did the clients of that work. Such positive self-rating, isolated from correction by client perceptions, may lead to self-deception and denial, where HR professionals believe that their services are appropriate and add value to a firm but the clients do not.

In a number of firms, client surveys include assessments of HR not only by line managers but also by employees. In one case, such client surveys found the HR function to be the lowest-rated function in the firm. The firm's HR professionals felt they were designing and delivering excellent services, but these services were either misunderstood by employees or failed to meet their needs. The HR professionals had been judging their services by their own good intentions, while their clients were judging them by the impact and results of the services received.

The HR role-assessment survey thus constitutes a diagnostic tool for identifying the expectations of line managers and other HR clients. The data generated by comparing ratings made by HR professionals, line managers, and others can lead to productive discussions in which expectations are set and shared, and roles are clarified and communicated.

HR Function versus Individual HR Professionals

A business may find, in doing the above audits of HR roles, that individual HR professionals do not have competence in all four roles, but at the same time, it should find that the function—as an aggregate of individuals—does share a unified vision and competency. In one company, for example, it was found that the individuals fulfilling the components of the HR function were committed and competent; the field HR professionals were strategic partners with business leaders; HR functional leaders were administrative experts in their domains; employee relations experts worked effectively to understand and meet employee needs; and organizational effectiveness experts appropriately managed change. As a team, however, this group of talented individuals was woeful. In one-on-one interviews, these HR professionals acknowledged that they did not respect or even like one another.

A team of HR experts needs to forge individual talent into leveraged competencies. At the above firm, the individual HR experts began to share their concerns, openly discuss differences, and focus on common goals and objectives. With focus, time, and commitment, tensions and distrust were overcome; resources and lessons were shared. They began to speak with one voice about the purposes and value of the HR function. They began to call on each other and leverage each other's strengths. In brief, they began to work as a team.

Use of the survey as a diagnostic instrument may thus indicate that although individuals in a business have unique talents in one of the four roles, the overall HR function needs to unify these individual talents to gain strength and efficacy.

Clarifying Responsibility for Each Role

Each time a business reviews the multiple roles of HR, this question arises: What is the line managers' responsibility in each cell? This is a crucial question and has a two-part answer.

First, HR professionals in a business have unique responsibility and accountability for ensuring that the deliverables from each role are fulfilled. If, for example, a rating of 10 represents the complete accomplishment of the deliverables for each role, it is HR professionals who own the achievement of a 10 rating.

Second, accomplishing the goals and designing the processes for achieving the goals are *different issues*. While HR professionals own the accomplishment of each of the four roles, they may not have to do all the work of the four roles. That is, HR professionals must guarantee that a 10 be achieved for each role, but they don't have to do all the work to make that 10 happen. Depending on the process established for reaching the goal, the work may be shared by line managers, outside consultants, employees, technology, or other delivery mechanisms for doing HR work.

In many cases, responsibility for delivering the four roles is shared, as indicated by an allocation of points. Figure 2-4 indicates one prevailing pattern of allocation. The allocation of points clearly will vary by firm. The distinction, however, between commitment to the outcome (10/ 10) and delivery of the outcome (sharing responsibility or dividing the 10 points) remains a consistently important point for discussion. HR professionals need to guarantee the outcome and to help define the shared responsibility for delivering it. As are the roles themselves, delivery

Figure 2-4 **HR Role in Building a Competitive Organization: Shared Responsibility**

processes and allocations are subject to change and trends, some of which are discussed below.

Management of employee contribution

The employee contribution HR role has experienced the greatest change in the recent past. Traditionally, HR was allocated 8 out of every 10 points for delivery of employee commitment. Today, many firms are dividing delivery: 2 points for HR, 6 points for line managers, and 2 points for employees. In other words, in many firms, when employees have grievances or concerns, HR's job is not to fix the problem but to ensure that managers have the skills needed to respond effectively to employees and that employees themselves have the skills to overcome challenges. Over time, many firms hope the employees in high performing teams will have even more responsibility for their own development.

Management of firm infrastructure

For efficient delivery, many firms today put 5 of the 10 points for infrastructure HR services into corporate/shared service organizations. This shift is counterintuitive, but has its own logic. In a traditional setting, promotion to the corporate level usually means doing more strategic work. In many modern organizations, however, promotion to the corporate level means becoming part of a shared service organization that performs administrative work in order to remove the administrative burden from the field HR professionals. The remaining 5 points are divided between outsourcing administrative transactions (3 points) and information technology (2 points). Outsourcing HR activities has been an experiment at many firms that are trying to find ways to reduce HR costs while increasing the quality of services. Information technology uses computers to do much of the administrative work of HR; over time, that use will probably increase.

Strategic HRM

The responsibility for strategy execution in most firms today is shared between HR professionals and line managers (5 points each). As partners, each brings to the strategy discussion unique skills and talents. Together, they team up to accomplish business goals.

Management of transformation and change

In their responsibilities for culture change, HR professionals are asked to deliver approximately 3 of the 10 points, while line managers are allocated 4 points and outside consultants the remaining 3. The low allocation of 3 points to HR professionals indicates that many of them are not fully comfortable or competent in the role of change agent. Traditionally, HR professionals have been distant from the change process.[11] In fact, HR work was viewed as antithetical to change, with HR systems providing impediments to, not impetus for, change. The emerging responsibility for transformation currently rests with external consultants, with many firms delegating responsibility for driving change to external consulting firms.

External consultants offer disciplined, objective approaches to transformation, with the competence and confidence to make the change happen.

PARADOXES INHERENT IN MULTIPLE HR ROLES

Strategic Partner versus Employee Champion

Success in the multiple-role framework requires that HR professionals balance the tension inherent in being a strategic partner on the one hand and an employee champion on the other. As strategic partners with managers, HR professionals partner with managers and are seen as part of management. Taken to an extreme, this may alienate employees from both HR and management. Employees at one company that was moving its HR function into strategic partnership saw the HR professionals, whom they felt provided the only channel through which their concerns were voiced to management, participating in more management meetings, becoming active in strategic planning, and becoming synonymous with management. As a result, the employees felt betrayed and rated the HR function as not meeting their needs.

As employee champions in partnership with managers and employees, HR professionals ensure that the concerns and needs of employees are voiced to management. Taken to an extreme, this may alienate the HR function from management, who may not want to work with HR people whom they see as insensitive to business realities and advocates of employees.

Resolving this conflict requires that all parties—HR, management, and employees—recognize that HR professionals can both represent employee needs *and* implement management agendas, be the voice of the employee *and* the voice of management, act as partner to both employees *and* managers. A classic example of a successful response to this paradox is provided by Doug Fraiser, who joined the Chrysler board of directors in the late 1970s as part of a plan for employee investment in the firm. When union members challenged Fraiser's new "management" commitment, he retorted with something like, "How can I better meet your needs than by sitting with and influencing management?" To be a successful partner to both employees and management requires that both sides trust the HR professional to achieve a balance between the needs of these potentially competing stakeholders.

When HR professionals are not called on to represent employees' concerns to management, uninformed decisions may be made. It is not uncommon, for example, for merger and acquisition decisions to be made based solely on financial and product/strategic analyses that demonstrate the value of the venture; only after the decision is made is HR asked to weave the two companies together. Sadly, more ventures fail because of cultural and human differences than because of product and strategic differences. Where HR professionals are asked to represent employee and organizational concerns during pre-merger diagnosis, more informed decisions are made about *all* costs of merger activities, including the merger of cultures and people.

Change Agents versus Administrative Experts

HR professionals must also balance the need for change, innovation, and transformation with the need for continuity, discipline, and stability. This tension between their roles as change agents and as administrative experts yields a number of paradoxes that must be managed. Businesses must balance *stability* and *change*. A business must have stability to ensure continuity in products, services, and manufacturing. Businesses that change constantly lose identity and chase mythical successes that never materialize. On the other hand, businesses that fail to change in the end simply fail.

Businesses must balance the *past* and the *future*. A business must honor its past but also move beyond it. It must recognize that past successes ensure current survival but that only by letting go of the past will the future arrive. Old cultures should ground new cultures, not become impediments to change.

Businesses must balance the benefits of *free agency* and *control*. A business needs to encourage free agency and autonomy in making decisions, sharing information, and soliciting ideas. Conversely, a business requires discipline among employees to make the value of the whole greater than that of the parts, to forge individual efforts into team accomplishment, and to create boundaries for freedom.

Businesses must balance *efficiency* and *innovation*. New ideas and programs require risk capital, both economic and human. HR professionals need to encourage risk and innovation while maintaining efficiency. Thus, risks need to be bounded, not haphazard.

To resolve these and other paradoxes, HR professionals dealing with cultural change need to be both cultural guardians of the past and architects of the new cultures. In practice, this means that in discussions with those who want to move slowly, HR professionals need to drive for dramatic change. On the other hand, in discussions with those who want to demolish history and tradition, HR professionals need to be advocates of moderation and respect for earned wisdom. It means that when working to create new cultures, HR professionals should simultaneously consider the impact of the new culture on administrative processes (for example, how to hire, train, and reward employees in a manner consistent with the new culture) and recognize the hold that the old culture retains over both employees and company practices.

This balancing act requires that new cultures lead to new administrative practices and that administrative practices support culture change. Sometimes, advocates of dramatic culture change, not realizing the infrastructure required to support the change, may make bold statements that stretch credibility and exceed a business's capacity for implementation. Part of the role of the HR professional as change agent is to moderate such statements. The administrative infrastructure may be the last thing to change as companies forge ahead in new strategic directions.

SUMMARY

Being an effective HR professional does not mean simply moving from operational to strategic work. It means learning to master both operational and strategic processes and people. Success in these roles requires an understanding of the *deliverables, metaphors,* and *actions* specific to each.

Deliverables are the guaranteed outcomes of HR. They represent what HR does to add value to a firm. HR has four generic deliverables: strategy execution, administrative efficiency, employee commitment, and transformation and change. HR professionals articulate and guarantee these deliverables to their businesses. *Metaphors* are the images that characterize HR professionals in each of their roles. The four images that characterize the HR professional of the future include strategic partner, administrative expert, employee champion, and change agent. HR professionals as business partners operate in each of the four roles. *Actions* are the personal activities and organizational systems undertaken by HR professionals and line managers to fulfill these roles.

For line managers, these new HR roles—each encompassing its deliverable, metaphor, and action—require specific responses:

- Define the desired and feasible deliverables from HR activities.
- Operationalize, measure, and communicate the value created by HR.
- Define who has what responsibility and accountability for HR activities.

HR professionals, too, in order to meet the demands of their new roles, must learn to act in new ways and with new expectations. They must accomplish the following goals:

- Stop *talking* about being a business partner and *do* it.
- Define *business partner* in terms of value created for the business.
- Profile accurately—with the participation of their clients—the *current* and the *desired* quality of their deliverables.

For today's HR professionals to deliver value to a firm, they must fulfill multiple, not single, roles. They must specify deliverables to the firm from each of their roles, define images that characterize these roles, and act to accomplish the deliverables pertaining to their roles. They must also recognize the paradoxical position they occupy within a firm, accepting accountability for accomplishing results while building the shared commitment needed to achieve those results.

APPENDIX

Human Resource Role-Assessment Survey

Dave Ulrich and Jill Conner

The attached survey explores different *roles* that the HR function may play within your business. Considering the HR professionals in your business entity (for example, corporate HR if you are at corporate, business unit HR if you are in a business), please rate the current quality of each of the following HR activities, using a five-point scale (1 is low; 5 is high).

	Current Quality (1–5)
HR helps the organization . . .	
1. accomplish business goals	_____
2. improve operating efficiency	_____
3. take care of employees' personal needs	_____
4. adapt to change	_____
HR participates in . . .	
5. the process of defining business strategies	_____
6. delivering HR processes	_____
7. improving employee commitment	_____
8. shaping culture change for renewal and transformation	_____
HR makes sure that . . .	
9. HR strategies are aligned with business strategy	_____
10. HR processes are efficiently administered	_____
11. HR policies and programs respond to the personal needs of employees	_____
12. HR processes and programs increase the organization's ability to change	_____
HR effectiveness is measured by its ability to . . .	
13. help make strategy happen	_____
14. efficiently deliver HR processes	_____
15. help employees meet personal needs	_____
16. help an organization anticipate and adapt to future issues	_____
HR is seen as . . .	
17. a business partner	_____
18. an administrative expert	_____
19. a champion for employees	_____
20. a change agent	_____

	Current Quality (1–5)

HR spends time on . . .
21. strategic issues   ————
22. operational issues   ————
23. listening and responding to employees   ————
24. supporting new behaviors for keeping the firm competitive   ————

HR is an active participant in . . .
25. business planning   ————
26. designing and delivering HR processes   ————
27. listening and responding to employees   ————
28. organization renewal, change, or transformation   ————

HR works to . . .
29. align HR strategies and business strategy   ————
30. monitor administrative processes   ————
31. offer assistance to help employees meet family and personal needs   ————
32. reshape behavior for organizational change   ————

HR develops processes and programs to . . .
33. link HR strategies to accomplish business strategy   ————
34. efficiently process documents and transactions   ————
35. take care of employee personal needs   ————
36. help the organization transform itself   ————

HR's credibility comes from . . .
37. helping to fulfill strategic goals   ————
38. increasing productivity   ————
39. helping employees meet their personal needs   ————
40. making change happen   ————

Scoring Sheet for HR Role Survey

Using the assessments in the quality column of the survey, complete this worksheet. Put your score from the quality column next to the number for each question, then add the total for each of the four roles. See pages 38–45 for information on understanding and using the results of the survey.

Strategic Partner		Administrative Expert		Employee Champion		Change Agent	
Question	Score	Question	Score	Question	Score	Question	Score
1		2		3		4	
5		6		7		8	
9		10		11		12	
13		14		15		16	
17		18		19		20	
21		22		23		24	
25		26		27		28	
29		30		31		32	
33		34		35		36	
37		38		39		40	
TOTAL		TOTAL		TOTAL		TOTAL	

Becoming a Strategic Partner

PARTNER HAS BECOME the term of choice for HR professionals who help accomplish business goals. As discussed in Chapter 2, HR professionals acting as business partners play many roles, one of which is *strategic* partner, charged with turning strategy into action. Consider the following cases in which HR professionals were asked to create organizations to accomplish specific business strategies.

Case 1

In just two years in the mid-1980s, Engcon,* a global engineering construction firm, faced a major downturn, moving from more than $250 million in profit to more than $500 million in losses. This downturn led to the decision to place a new executive team at the head of the firm. The new CEO worked vigorously to restructure the company, to refocus its efforts, and to return it to profitability, and by 1990, the firm was again profitable. The board of directors at this point asked the CEO to assess the firm strategy; specifically, its global focus and mix

---

*Engcon is a fabricated name for a firm that faced a situation much like this vignette.

of products, services, and customers. During a year-long audit, the strategy was reassessed, after which adjustments were made. The board then asked the CEO to determine whether the firm had the right technology and systems in place to support and sustain its strategy. Following a technology audit, systems were upgraded and better aligned with strategy. The board members then asked the CEO for a third audit: They now wanted to know whether the firm had the right organization to implement and sustain its strategy. To accomplish this organizational audit, the executive committee turned to the senior vice president of human resources, who was asked to determine the strengths and weaknesses of the organization, to assess whether the organization in place was the right one to implement strategy, and to recommend improvements. The HR senior vice president led this effort by creating an advisory team of senior managers, which in turn created an assessment process using input from employees, customers, and suppliers. The resulting recommendations were given to the board, and organizational changes were made and implemented.

Case 2

Frontier Communications, formerly Rochester Telephone Corporation, found itself in the unenviable position of having a number of large competitors (for example, AT&T, MCI, and Sprint) enter its local telecommunications market. Without a cultural transformation, which would involve adjustments in its products, services, and management practices, Frontier would be unlikely to survive in the changing telecommunications marketplace. To advance this transformation, Ronald Bitner (chairman, president, and chief executive officer) proposed the following plan: become the "premier telecommunication company in the world" through high-quality products and customer focus. He has stated that "No vision can be achieved without an able and dedicated employee body. . . . We're undertaking a fresh, critical assessment of the skills and competencies each of our employees must have to move forward. Where we lack that expertise, we're committed to move it in from the outside."[1] To help facilitate the necessary cultural transformation, Bitner hired a senior HR executive, Janet Sansone, who was given the explicit task of championing the change effort. Sansone's responsibility was to make sure that culture change was part of the discussion, that models for culture change were created and implemented, and that executive attention to culture change remained high. Sansone was to create a process whereby the company's organization could be continually realigned with changing business requirements. In the local markets, for example, Frontier's organization had to become much more cost competitive. (In the long-distance markets, Frontier acquired other firms to become the fifth largest long-distance carrier in the United States.) To accomplish this goal, Sansone worked to construct cost-competitive local organizations within the context of evolving organizational processes necessitated by Frontier's acquisitions/mergers. As a member of the executive committee, Sansone developed a disciplined process for assessing and aligning organization practices with business strategy.

Case 3

Coopers & Lybrand (C&L), one of six world-wide professional service firms, is dedicated to client service. The company leaders believe that their advantage in the marketplace is their ability to anticipate and meet client needs more effectively than their competitors. At the same time, they know that their intellectual capital, represented by their employees' competence and commitment, is their major resource for serving clients. Under the direction of Judith Rosenblum, vice chairman of learning, education, and human resources,* the company developed a strategy called Nexus to integrate the employee commitment and client-service initiatives. C&L based Nexus on two premises:

1. Our people are *our customer's* most important asset.

2. We want to be the employer of choice of employees our customers would choose.

Rosenblum argued that a collaborative service firm meets professional requirements as a benchmark but does so collaboratively, so that both the engagement team (C&L employees dedicated to a particular client) and the client's team share common values. Her work has led to a series of cross-organization workshops in which the C&L engagement team and the client team meet to identify common values and define behaviors that each can and should develop to serve the other; they then operation-

---

*Rosenblum has since moved from Coopers & Lybrand to become chief learning officer at Coca-Cola.

alize a new team structure that focuses on creating unity across traditional boundaries. From these workshops, collaborative networks of resources have been created through which C&L employees become more committed to serving clients, and clients are better able to use C&L employees' talents.

In each of these cases, HR professionals acted as strategic partners. They were given the task of answering the question a strategic partner must answer: *How do we create an organization to accomplish business objectives?* Business objectives may be stated many ways—as financial targets, balanced scorecards, visions, intents, missions, aspirations, or goals. Regardless of the objective's form or content, an organization must be created to make it happen. When HR professionals work as strategic partners, they work with line managers to institute and manage a process that creates an organization to meet business requirements.

CHALLENGES OF BECOMING A STRATEGIC PARTNER

Becoming a strategic partner requires both fortitude and discipline. Some HR divisions have inserted phrases such as *strategic partner* in their mission statements, hoping that the words alone would make it happen. Unfortunately, hopes without understanding create more cynicism than change. To become a strategic partner requires overcoming five challenges:

1. Avoid Strategic Plans on Top Shelf (SPOTS).
2. Create a balance scorecard.
3. Align HR Plans to Business Plans.
4. Watch out for quick fixes.
5. Create a capability focus within the firm.

Challenge 1: Avoid *Strategic Plans on Top Shelf* (SPOTS)

More strategies are written than acted upon. More visions are created than realized. More missions are espoused than executed. More goals are stated than accomplished. Without creating a disciplined, rigorous, and thorough mechanism for translating aspirations into actions, strategies remain *Strate-gic Plans on Top Shelf* (SPOTS).[2] Bookshelf funerals for strategies occur all too often: Ever so much thought goes into the written document, which then ends up in a binder on a shelf. Strategy fails to impact practices.

All too often, the strategic planning scenario unfolds like this. The top management team goes to a "strategic offsite" and spends a week working on strategy. Team members review customer expectations, business trends, technological innovations, and core competencies; they debate alternative investments of resources; they draft statements about aspirations, visions, and missions. During this week and the weeks following, executives work long hours and participate in intensive and thoughtful debates about how to compete for the future. At the end of these forums, provocative and often profound statements are made about the future. Unfortunately, these statements—variously called missions, visions, aspirations, goals, or objec-tives—fail to acknowledge and, therefore, to involve all the organizational processes required for their accomplishment.

Becoming a strategic partner means turning strategic statements into a set of organizational actions. Overcoming the challenge of SPOTS requires that HR professionals force organizational issues into the strategic discussion *before* strategies are decided. At Engcon, the organizational diagnosis cham-pioned by the head of human resources helped the company turn its global strategy into effective HR practices. The diagnosis revealed that Engcon's culture was predominantly North American: Senior managers were North American, career paths to the top jobs were primarily within North America, and communication methods focused on North American assumptions (for example, using baseball and other North American sports metaphors). Because of this organizational diagnosis, the company knew it had to make major changes to accomplish its global strategy. By facilitating the organizational diagnosis, the HR senior vice president turned strategies into actions.

Challenge 2: Create a Balanced Scorecard

The concept of a balanced scorecard is not new,[3] but its application has become increasingly popular.[4] A balanced scorecard focuses on serving multiple stakeholders (investors, customers, and employees) and can be a total performance index assessing executive performance. AT&T executives, for example, are judged on the extent to which they add value for each stakeholder. The categories apply to any large or complex business.

- **Economic value-added (EVA):** Meeting the financial numbers expected of the executive.

- **Customer value-added (CVA):** Meeting customer-service goals.

- **People value-added (PVA):** Meeting employee expectations.

At AT&T, these three indicators form an overall, balanced scorecard measure for tracking executive performance.

If HR executives are to be strategic partners, they need to absorb and apply the concept of the balanced scorecard in two ways. First, they need to be equally accountable for all segments of the *balanced* scorecard, not just for the employee dimension. Perhaps based on previous HR models, HR executives may believe that their success should be judged only by the extent to which they meet employee needs. As the balanced scorecard indicates, employee commitment is only one criterion for effective HR performance, and HR professionals in strategic partnership will be held accountable for the same dimensions as are other managers. Rosenblum at Coopers & Lybrand recognized the linkage between the company goals of being "employer of choice" and having the "employees its customers would choose." By creating the Nexus initiative linking employee and customer values, Rosenblum enacted a balanced scorecard approach to management within Coopers. Hal Burlingame, AT&T's HR senior vice president, is evaluated by the same balanced scorecard as are the company's other executives: His performance is judged not just by the PVA score, but by all three scores. This approach requires that HR professionals master their business's financial and customer issues and recognize their contribution to attaining these goals.

Second, although accountable for all three dimensions of the balanced scorecard, HR professionals should provide intellectual leadership on the employee dimension. The easy trap in measuring the employee as stakeholder is to create a commitment or satisfaction index. The best HR professionals define the employee dimension of the balanced scorecard not only in terms of employee attitude, but also in terms of organizational processes. The processes represent those activities that *affect* employee attitude, such as leadership, teamwork, communication, empowerment, shared values, mechanisms for treating individuals with dignity, and so on. By measuring these processes as well as employee attitudes, HR professionals fully define the employee stakeholder dimension of the balanced scorecard.

Challenge 3: Align HR Plans to Business Plans

Almost all HR departments do planning, with approaches arrayed along a continuum ranging from an afterthought, or "add-on," to business strategy through integration with business strategy to an isolated planning process.[5] (See Table 3-1.) At the "add-on" end of the continuum, HR planning is little more than a postscript to the business planning process. In this approach, only after extensive business planning, during which business product, market, and technological directions are defined, are questions about HR practices raised. These questions deal with the structure, competencies, accountabilities, organization, and leadership required to make the business strategy work. At this end of the continuum, HR issues are an afterthought, subsidiary to business strategy; they receive relatively little attention and become an accessory to business planning. At this extreme, line managers consider HR questions as an appendage and appendix to

Table 3-1 Approaches to Merging Strategic and HR Planning

Afterthought/"Add-on"	Integration	Isolated
The focus is on business planning, with HR practices considered as an afterthought.	The focus is on a synthesis of business and HR planning.	The focus is on HR practices and how the HR function can add value to the business.
Line managers own the HR discussions, with tangential involvement of HR professionals.	Line managers and HR professionals work as partners to ensure that an integrated HR planning process occurs.	HR professionals work on the plan and present it to line managers.
The outcome is a summary of HR practices required to accomplish business plans.	The outcome is a plan that highlights HR practices that are priorities for accomplishing business results.	The outcome is an agenda for the HR function, including priority HR practices.

"real" planning efforts, which focus on how the business positions itself in its market.

At the "isolated" end of the continuum, HR planning is a distinct and separate planning process. The HR department not only initiates the effort but designs and administers the HR plan. In these cases, the HR plan becomes a process for shaping HR rather than business priorities. In extreme cases, HR plans are created with little or no notice by or input from managers outside the HR function. While the result may be an elegant document, these isolated HR plans add little value to the business because they remain separate from the business planning process.

The real challenge of HR planning is to occupy the continuum's middle ground, to integrate HR practices into the business strategy. In these initiatives, HR planning becomes an integral part of a business planning process. HR professionals work with line managers to identify HR practices that accomplish business strategy. The outcome of integrated business/HR plans is an architecture or framework for incorporating HR practices into business decisions to ensure results. At Frontier Communications, the work by Janet Sansone has resulted in the use of a set of HR questions to help create business plans. Her participation with the executive committee has helped ensure that each business decision pass the HR test. In a series of acquisitions, for example, HR issues were systematically considered *before* the acquisition. Management was prompted to ask key questions: Will the acquired firm's talent add value to Frontier? Will HR practices (for example, compensation, training, appraisal, and retirement) of the acquired firm be congruent with Frontier's, and, if not, what will be the cost of integration? Will the acquired firm's management style and corporate culture be consistent with those of Frontier? By asking these questions, Sansone becomes a strategic partner, integrating her work with the company's business plans.

Challenge 4: Watch Out for Quick Fixes

Everyone wishes there were a magic elixir to fix every problem. Reports about early success with a weight-loss drug used on obese mice brought thousands of calls to Amgen, the drug's producer. Diet books, marriage manuals, easy-learning books (foreign language tapes, for example) sell briskly with promises of quick fixes. The fact is, action/improvement in these areas is difficult and takes time and commitment. Successful weight loss diets, successful marriages, and acquisition of a foreign language require work. Likewise, HR professionals need to avoid the lure of the quick fix. Two traps encourage this temptation: *benchmarking* and *frou-frou*.

Benchmarking

Benchmarking, or learning about *best practices,* has become almost a religion in some companies. With great fervor, teams of employees identify and visit other companies recognized as world-class. These field visits provide businesses with information on how to gauge their work relative to the best in class.

Traditionally, benchmarking has been done on the harder, more objective, aspects of a business, for example, technologies, systems, financial ratios, or quality. Increasingly, firms also benchmark softer management practices. General Electric deployed a senior management team to examine management practices in some of the best managed firms in the world to identify key processes for improving productivity. This team derived a set of principles and processes to help GE businesses become even more productive. These concepts became institutionalized in a course entitled "Productivity/Best Practices" attended by over 1,000 GE managers.

Digital Equipment Corporation[6] benchmarked twelve companies and concluded that best practice in human resources should focus less on a particular practice than on a set of general principles. They identified the following five principles as central to firms with HR best practices.

- They have an integrated theme: "What the company is known for."
- They leverage a system of HR practices by focusing on two or three key strategic initiatives that promote the integrative theme.
- They use discipline and follow-through to achieve the integrative theme and its HR focus.
- Line managers are accountable for HR management as a key piece of total business management.
- The HR function has added value that is credible and understood by both line and HR management.

I describe HR benchmarking at GE and Digital to illustrate that it not only can be but has been done. Information derived from benchmarking organizational practices and principles can become a valuable tool for management. It can force broader thinking, show commitment to change, and help establish a baseline against which to measure progress. To build organizational competitiveness, benchmarking is a valuable precondition.

The benchmarking trap

The benchmarking trap occurs when managers who want to improve organizational capability select one organizational practice (training, for example), identify a handful of companies who have excellent reputations in the area, and visit those companies to examine that one practice. These best practice visits give managers in-depth insights and perspective on what other companies do *on the single practice* on which they are focused. The visits become traps, however, if the practice is assessed in isolation from other organizational issues. Someone wanting to learn about training, for example, may visit three or four corporate training centers but may not come to understand management's commitment to training or how training programs fit within the company's overall management philosophy.

In another form of the benchmark trap, benchmarks may be too narrowly derived by relying only on things that are "easy to count." Some firms measure revenue per employee because these numbers are in an annual report and can be tracked easily. The good news with these measures is that they are replicable; the bad news is that they may be inconsequential and even invalid, providing the wrong information. A firm may have a very high productivity measure (high revenue/employee ratio), for example, because it outsources many activities. The high productivity ratio thus may not reflect organizational capability as much as the firm's structure.

HR professionals who are strategic partners need to avoid benchmarking traps by making sure that HR benchmarks are not isolated in a single practice area but represent a confluence of HR practices. They also need to assure that the information collected from benchmarking research and analysis becomes part of a dialogue, not unthinkingly established as a standard. In fact, while many who benchmark use the information as a standard, it should in reality be used only as a baseline. The most successful companies benchmark to find out what others do, not so they can do it that way, but so they can do it better.

The frou-frou trap

In our study of state-of-the-art practices for *Human Resource Planning Journal*[7] Bob Eichinger and I coined the term *frou-frou* to describe some of the cute, popular, and faddish HR trends that really don't add long-term value. After completing this study, we devised a list of the attributes of HR practices that qualify as frou-frou.

1. It is simple and easy and claims to solve complex problems.

2. It claims to apply to and help everyone.

3. It is not anchored or related to any known and generally accepted theory.

4. Proponents hesitate to present it in academic settings or write about it in refereed journals.

5. Proponents cannot tell you exactly how it works.

6. It is a "track" topic at 75 percent of the conferences you attend.

7. Its proponents claim that it has changed their lives and that it can change yours, too.

8. Its greatest proponents are those with the least experience in the field.

9. Proponents claim that the only way to really understand it is to try it personally; it cannot be explained or demonstrated.

10. It is just too good to be true.

HR professionals as strategic partners need to avoid frou-frou. Just because an idea is popular does not make it right. HR professionals need to understand the theory, research, and application of ideas in order to apply them appropriately in their business.

Challenge 5: Create a Capability Focus Within the Firm

A number of authors have focused on the importance of building core competencies or capabilities within a firm.[8] Capabilities refer to what a firm is able to do or needs to do to accomplish its strategy. Eli Lilly and Company, for example, uses a three-pronged strategy. One prong focuses on product groups, the diagnostic categories in which the company will invest and produce products. The second prong focuses on the geographic areas around the world in which those products will be distributed. The third prong focuses on critical capabilities necessary to accomplish the company's product distribution strategies, including scientific innovation, disease prevention and management, cost competitiveness, biotechnical expertise, information technology, and preeminent organization effectiveness. These capabilities become the bridge between strategy and action.

At a number of companies, processes have been used as surrogates for capabilities. Processes represent the flow of information, decisions, materials, or resources to serve customers. An organization has numerous processes, which, taken collectively, represent its means for dedicating its internal resources to its customers. Defining processes begins with a customer focus: What are the flows that add value for customers? General Electric, for example, has identified six core processes, applicable to many business configurations.

1. **Order to Remittance (OTR):** The processes for conveying notice of specific customer requirements to the organization and for fulfilling those requirements.

2. **New Product Introduction (NPI):** The process for creating and distributing new products.

3. **Quick Market Intelligence (QMI):** The process for infusing customer needs into the organization.

4. **Globalization:** The process for transmitting and using the firm's services in countries throughout the world.

5. **Supplier Management:** The process for managing supplier relationships to reduce costs.

6. **Productivity:** The process for increasing efficiencies through higher or lower output.

Like groups at many other companies, the GE Corporate Business Development staff has created tools and techniques to improve each of these processes across the twelve major GE businesses. By so doing, the managers have engaged in a process, or capability, focus throughout the firm.

The focus on capabilities clarifies how strategies can be put into practice. To accomplish a strategy, a firm requires a series of capabilities.[9] (Common capabilities that may exist within a firm are listed in Table 3-2.) As firms generate these capabilities, two things happen. First, strategies such as customer intimacy, leveraged technology, operating efficiency, and so on, are translated into the specific capabilities necessary to accomplish them, which then in turn are translated into HR practices.[10] Second, as these

Table 3-2 Critical Capabilities

Capabilities are those processes and practices within a company that enable a company to add value for customers in unique ways. Possible capabilities include the following:

_____ Align performance measures to strategic priorities.

_____ Assess competitor capabilities.

_____ Attract and retain high-caliber people.

_____ Be the low-cost producer in the field.

_____ Be technology leader in the field.

_____ Be the quality leader.

_____ Be the customer service leader.

_____ Be creative.

_____ Be agile in work processes.

_____ Centralize decision-making.

_____ Collaborate with governments.

_____ Compete across the economic cycle.

_____ Create and share strategic vision for the future.

_____ Create a shared mindset.

_____ Create capacity for change.

_____ Demonstrate cultural flexibility.

_____ Demonstrate entrepreneurship.

_____ Develop clear accountabilities/ consequences.

_____ Display flexibility.

_____ Engage in a large-scale transformation.

_____ Ensure trust between leaders and workers.

_____ Ensure confidence.

_____ Form alliances with a variety of organizations.

_____ Have high productivity.

_____ Have a culturally diverse workforce.

_____ Have high-quality engineering.

_____ Have dominant distribution channels.

_____ Have committed employees.

_____ Have a global mindset from "top to bottom."

_____ Identify and develop the next generation of leaders.

_____ Improve productivity every year.

_____ Improve profitability every year.

_____ Improve speed.

_____ Increase cash flow.

_____ Innovate.

_____ Learn more quickly than competitors.

_____ Maintain long-term view.

_____ Maintain good investor relations.

_____ Manage financial-management systems.

_____ Move quickly into new markets.

_____ Organize around customer requirements.

_____ Possess cultural unity.

_____ Practice participative management.

_____ Provide continuous learning.

_____ Reduce product introduction time.

_____ Reduce order-to-remittance process.

_____ Reduce organizational layers.

_____ Reengineer work systems.

_____ Share information.

_____ Take risks.

_____ Think and act globally.

_____ Work in teams.

_____ Work in a boundaryless way.

capabilities, or core competencies, are created, they can be used to generate new business. As Honda, for example, created its core competence for making engines, it applied this know-how to multiple products, among them cars, lawn mowers, snow blowers, motorcycles, and so on.[11]

HR professionals work as strategic partners when they identify and improve capabilities, both to implement strategy and to leverage new products.

Overcoming Challenges

By overcoming these five challenges, HR professionals become strategic partners. At Hewlett-Packard, for example, strategic partners need to link business objectives with HR processes and programs. To do so, executives stress the following basic requirements.

- Participation in the *hoshin* (business planning) process.
- Understanding of business issues.
- Participation in business task forces (for example, outsourcing and ISO 9000).
- Fostering systems thinking (for example, learning).
- Ensuring program management of workforce planning, skills assessment, succession planning, retraining, and diversity.
- Providing support to group-wide or sector initiatives.
- Championing the company way and management practices.

As these activities are accomplished, partnership replaces challenges.

FRAMEWORK FOR ORGANIZATIONAL DIAGNOSIS

Translating strategy into action requires discipline. The concept for moving from strategy to action is *organizational diagnosis,* that is, the systematic assessment and alignment of organizational practices with business goals. In the three cases at the beginning of the chapter, HR professionals at Engcon, Frontier, and Coopers & Lybrand were asked to create organizations that accomplished strategies. To do so required that they create processes for organizational diagnosis that allowed them to audit their organizations' strengths and weaknesses and then to work to improve areas of weakness uncovered.

The concept of organizational diagnosis may be new to organizational process, but it is not new within organizations. When financial professionals examine a business's financial processes, they are doing a financial audit. The HR parallel to the financial audit is the organizational audit. In financial audits, experts systematically assess the management of financial issues (for example, receivables, payables, inventories, turnover, and so on); they then recommend ways to improve financial processes. In an organizational audit, organizational systems and processes are examined with the goal of improving them for the better achievement of strategic goals.

A complete organizational diagnosis requires four steps. HR professionals who are strategic partners ensure that these steps are accomplished by HR professionals working with their clients, the line managers.

1. Define an organizational *architecture.*

2. Create an *assessment* process.

3. Provide leadership for *improvement* of practices.

4. Set *priorities.*

Step 1: Define an Organizational Architecture

Organizational consultant David Nadler and his associates, with straightforward logic, use an architecture metaphor to describe the systems that exist within an organization.[12] Organizations, like buildings, have numerous systems. *Organizational architecture* specifies the systems that constitute organizations. The ability to design, integrate, and operate these systems is the essence of effective organizations.

Numerous frameworks or architectures have been used to describe how organizations operate. Jay Galbraith's *star* organization model defines five essential factors within organizations: strategy, structure, rewards, processes, and systems.[13] The 7-S organization framework used by McKinsey & Company uses seven elements: strategy, structure, systems, staff, style, skills, and superordinate goals (shared values).[14] The U.S. Department of Commerce uses an organizational architecture to define its Malcomb Baldrige award for quality.

To undertake an organizational diagnosis, HR professionals must begin with a clear architecture that defines their organization's systems and processes. In some ways, it matters less *what* architecture is used and more that *an* architecture is articulated. The architecture keeps HR professionals and their clients from taking a myopic view of the organization's systems. Without an architecture that defines the multiple systems within an organization, for example, management might assume that organization equals structure; but this formulation would fail to account for the other essential elements of an organizational infrastructure. When financial audits are done, they follow an architecture that defines the essential financial processes within a business. Organizational audits, likewise, must follow an architecture.

Table 3-3 shows an architecture based on the work of Nadler, Galbraith, and McKinsey. This architecture focuses on building the organization to accomplish strategy. The first row (strategic intent and organizational capabilities) describes the firm's direction. Below this row are the six factors that define how organizations operate and identify the systems that must change if the organizations are to accomplish strategy. These factors are listed and defined below.

- **Shared mindset:** *Shared mindset* represents the common identity and culture within a business.

- **Competence:** *Competencies* represent the knowledge, skills, and abilities that exist among and across employees and groups of employees.

- **Consequence:** *Consequences* represent the performance management standards, including measures, appraisal systems, and rewards.

- **Governance:** *Governance* represents the organization's reporting relationships, decision-making processes, policies, and communication processes.

- **Work process/capacity for change:** *Work processes* represent how organizations improve processes, manage change, and learn.

- **Leadership:** *Leadership* represents how firms shape, communicate, and commit to direction.

The architecture proposed in Table 3-3 implies that shared mindset and leadership integrate organizations. Shared mindset, or common culture, represents the glue that holds an organization together. Leadership represents the foundation on which organizations build practices. The pillars explore the breadth of HR tools necessary for sustaining strategic intent. Grounding the four pillars requires successful deployment of HR practices.

Each pillar represents an organizational requirement for making a business strategy effective. The competence pillar ensures that the organization achieves and maintains the knowledge, skills, and abilities to accomplish its business strategy; the consequence pillar ensures that the organization develops processes to allocate the consequences of meeting or missing business objectives; the governance pillar ensures that the organization establishes structures and communication routines to shape employee behavior; and the work-process/capacity-for-change pillar ensures that processes exist for adapting and transforming the organization. When an organization inculcates competence, consequence, governance, and work process/capacity for change, it will have the capability of translating business strategies into mindsets into actions. Following this architecture, business strategies do not become fodder; they become courses of commitment.

The four pillars provide a framework that defines the choices that must be made if strategy is to be translated into action. Identifying and executing choices in each of the four pillar areas assures a stable base on which to build an implementation strategy. At times, executives may misallocate all of their attention and resources to one pillar, to the exclusion of the other three, thus creating an unstable foundation for strategy execution. In one case, for example, executives established a global strategy and then worked diligently to create an organizational structure that would govern global business requirements. After installing the global organizational structure, they assumed that they had not only created the appropriate strategy but had also taken all necessary steps to accomplish the strategy. Yet, the global strategy did not succeed, and they were frustrated. Structure alone will not implement a global or other business strategy. The firm in this example needed to work on building competencies for global issues; it needed to design performance management systems that had consequences for a global position; and it needed to create a change process that would move the firm from being a domestic to being a global player. Working on only one pillar of the architecture led this firm to a false sense of security about its organizational infrastructure. The executives responsible had failed to realize that all four pillars required dedicated attention if strategy was to be moved into infrastructure. All companies must learn to acknowledge that choices

Table 3-3 **Architecture for Organizational Diagnosis**

Strategic Intent: What Are We Trying to Accomplish?

Strategy: Intent, plan, focus, drivers, etc.   Environmental Context: Regulation, economy.
Customers: Segmentation, value-added.   Core Competency: Technology.
Finance: Measures, return, value-created.

Organizational Capabilities: What are the organizational capabilities we require?

Shared Mindset: What we want to be known for by our customers.

Competence Pillar	Consequence Pillar	Governance Pillar	Work-Process/Capacity-for-Change Pillar
What are the competencies we require to accomplish our strategy?	What are the standards and consequences required to accomplish our strategy?	What is the organization we need to accomplish our strategy?	How able are we to manage the work processes and to change in order to accomplish our strategy?
Staffing Who is hired into the organization? Who is promoted through the organization?	**Appraisal** What are the performance standards for individuals, groups, and departments within the organization?	**Organization Design** What should be the shape of the organization (e.g., how many levels, what roles, what reporting relationships, what division of labor, etc.)?	**Work-Process Improvement** What types of initiatives should we offer to ensure that our management processes work well (e.g., quality, reengineering, etc.)?

Staffing (continued)	Appraisal (continued)	Organization Design (continued)	Change Processes
Who is outplaced from the organization?	What are the mechanisms for giving feedback to employees about their performance against standards?	How do we make appropriate decisions?	What are the critical processes for making change happen?
Development		**Policies**	**Leveraging Learning for Change**
Given our business environment and business strategy, what training should be offered?	What are the processes used to ensure accurate, meaningful, and effective appraisals?	What policies (e.g., safety, health, labor) do we have?	How can we share ideas and learning across organizational boundaries?
Given our business environment and business strategy, what alternatives to development should be offered?	**Rewards**	**Communication**	
	What are the financial and non-financial consequences of meeting standards?	What information should be shared with whom in the organization?	
	How will the reward system ensure that individuals are motivated in appropriate directions?	Who should share and receive information?	
		What mechanisms should be used for information sharing?	

Leadership: What is the quality of leadership given our strategy?

in one pillar will most likely affect choices in the others. Alignment across the pillars must be achieved.

When HR professionals use organizational architecture to guide their analyses, they define how their organization operates and set the stage for effective organizational diagnosis.

Step 2: Create an Assessment Process

An organizational diagnosis turns the architecture into an assessment tool. As such, the factors identified in the architecture become assessment or audit questions with which to probe the organization's strengths and weaknesses. Table 3-4 transforms the architecture in Table 3-3 into a diagnostic tool. At left are listed the six factors that constitute an organization; these are then stated as questions in the second column, posed to emphasize the extent to which the factor will help accomplish the firm's strategic intent. *Firm* in this case may refer to the entity being audited, whether the corporation overall, a business unit within the corporation, a plant or site, or a function. The *Rating* column employs a simple metric (1 = low, 10 = high) for use in evaluation; during the diagnostic process, companies find the numerical score less important than the discussion it evokes. The Best Practice column identifies practices for improvement, the third step of the diagnosis.

The assessment phase may be used formally or informally. But whatever the manner, HR professionals managing organizational audit processes are functioning as strategic partners, helping systematically to turn strategy into organizational action.

Used as an informal tool, the assessment structure in Table 3-4 can help HR professionals participating in any strategy discussion to engage a management team in focused discussions about building an organization that can meet business goals. When an electronics plant was shaping a cost-reduction strategy, for example, the HR professional forced the plant management team to discuss the organizational implications of the cost reductions. He asked the team the six questions in Table 3-4 to assess their organizational readiness to make cost reduction a reality. At the end of the discussion, the managers had created not only a cost strategy, but an organizational action plan to make it happen.

Table 3-4 Assessment: Organizational-Capability Architecture

Strategy: Given our business priorities and expected capabilities, how would we rate ourselves on each of the following management actions necessary to accomplish our strategy:

	Question	Rating (1–10)	Best Practice
Shared Mindset	To what extent does my firm have the right shared mindset (culture)?		
Competence	To what extent does my firm have the required competencies (knowledge, skills, and abilities) to reach future goals?		
Consequence	To what extent does my firm have the right performance management system (measures, rewards, and incentives) to reach future goals?		
Governance	To what extent does my firm have the right organizational structure, communication systems, and policies to reach future goals?		
Work Process/ Capacity for Change	To what extent does my firm have the ability to improve work processes, to change, and to learn in order to reach future goals?		
Leadership	To what extent does my firm have the leadership required to reach future goals?		

Used more formally, the structure in Table 3-4 can facilitate performance of organizational audits. Some companies have begun systematic organizational audits to complement financial audits. At General Electric, Bill Conaty, the vice president of human resources, has instituted a policy of having HR professionals accompany the corporate business audit team. These HR professionals weave into GE's traditional business audit HR/ organizational questions similar to those identified in Table 3-4. In retail chains, too, organizational audits are considered an essential complement to financial assessment. Once every quarter, a percent of employees within a store complete a short organizational assessment questionnaire similar to that in Table 3-4. The scores of these randomly selected employees become an organizational audit measure for the store.

HR professionals may further lead and structure the audit process by determining answers to the following series of questions about the source, nature, and use of organizational audit data.

Who will collect the organizational audit data?

Three different groups can collect the audit data, either independently or collectively. First, line managers may collect the data, acting as a task force responsible for organizational diagnosis. Second, HR professionals may collect data as part of their HR responsibility. Third, a third party, such as a consulting firm, may be contracted to perform the audit. In the Engcon case at the beginning of this chapter, for example, all three groups participated in the organizational audit. The senior vice president of HR led the task force for organizational diagnosis; the line managers on the task force actually conducted interviews; and a consultant was retained to help define the process and refine the questions.

Who will provide the data?

Organizational audits are often based on perceptual data, so multiple perceptions are important to the process. There are three sources of input for audit data. First, employees within the firm may assess organizational factors. If employees are making the diagnosis, it is critical that a cross section of employees be consulted, since the perceptions of top managers may differ significantly from those of employees at other levels of the organization. Second, suppliers and customers in the firm's value chain can be consulted about their perceptions of the organization's effectiveness. Involving suppliers and customers in the diagnostic process helps cement their commitment to the organization. Third, comparisons may be made between the firm's organizational practices and the best practices of industry competitors and of high-performing firms in other industries. The synthesis of input from these three data sources ensures a thorough organizational audit process.

What type of data will be collected?

Organizational audit data may be both perceptual and evidential. *Perceptual data* comprise the thoughts and feelings of those who interact with the organization. Both because perceptions often reflect reality and because people act on their perceptions, these data are valid and important. *Evidential data* come from ratios and other indicators of the status of organizational factors (for example, percent of budget spent on training, ratio of revenue per employee, ratio of salary grade of senior- to lower-level employees, ratio of supervisors to employees, and so on).[15]

Financial audits often collect specific information about practices, but then form overall indices to determine the financial health of a company. As organizational audits become more commonplace, an organizational capability index will probably emerge that will indicate the organization's overall ability to accomplish its business goals.

How will the data be turned into action?

Organizational analysis often overdoes data collection and underdoes analysis and action. Reams of data are collected, reports are generated, statistics are presented; but, because the data remains unfocused, little action follows. Data should be turned into action as the diagnosis process unfolds, that is, as common themes are identified, as managers with decision-making responsibility take ownership of the data, and as alternative actions are proposed.

Step 3: Provide Leadership in Improvement Practices

An organizational diagnosis must go beyond assessment to improvement. Improvement occurs when HR professionals generate alternative actions and practices for each of the six organizational factors, adding value by framing choices and identifying best practices through research at other firms. Several excellent texts summarize emerging and best HR practices.[16] Table 3-5 briefly highlights the key words, phrases, and concepts often used to describe HR practices for each of the six factors.

HR professionals should take the lead in proposing, creating, and debating best practices in culture change, competence (staffing and development), consequence (appraisal and rewards), governance (organization design, policies, and communications), work processes (learning and change), and leadership. Generating possible alternative HR practices in each of these areas becomes the responsibility of the HR professional, bringing to bear technical expertise and state-of-the-art knowledge.

Table 3-5 **Architecture for Organization Capability: Best Practices**

Strategic Intent: What Are We Trying to Accomplish? Organizational Capabilities: What are the capabilities we require?			
Mindset: What do we want to be known for by our customers?			
Competence Pillar	**Consequence Pillar**	**Governance Pillar**	**Work-Processes/ Capacity-for-Change Pillar**
What are the competencies we require to accomplish our strategy?	What are the standards and consequences required to accomplish our strategy?	What is the organization we need to accomplish our strategy?	How able are we to manage the work processes and to change in order to accomplish our strategy?

Competence Audit
Competence Enhancement
• Staffing (Buy)
  In:
  Up:
  Out:
• Development and Learning (Build)
  • Competence to results
  • Individual to team
  • Bounded to unbounded
  • Shelf to tailored
  • General management to process
	Building Performance Management System
	• What are we trying to accomplish?
	• How should we measure it?
	  • Behaviors + outcomes
	  • Individual and team
	• How can we tie rewards to measures?
	  • Financial
	  • Non-financial
		Organization Design
		• Focusing on process not hierarchy
		• Removing boundaries
		  • vertical
		  • horizontal
		  • external
		Communication
		• Aligning message with medium
		• Building a communication plan
		Engaging Employees
		Participation, involvement, empowerment
		Managing Policies (safety, health, labor)
			Reengineer Processes
			• Indentify processes
			• Select process champions
			• Streamline processes
			Manage Change
			• Profile capacity for change
			Increase Learning Capability
			• Generate ideas with impact
			• Generalize ideas with impact

Shared Leadership

• Personal credibility   • Real change leaders

• Organizational capability   • Middle managers as leaders

As HR professionals work through Step 3, providing leadership in improving practices, they generate a range of HR practices to be instituted. One firm working through this step derived a list of fifteen HR initiatives for the following year. Their plans to establish all fifteen went awry, however, when they found that this large number of initiatives dissipated their efforts.

Step 4: Set Priorities

Step 4 of organizational diagnosis is setting priorities, that is, focusing on the most important, of what may be many critical issues. Figure 3-1 demonstrates how to use two basic criteria to evaluate which HR practices should be given highest priority. The first criteria is *impact,* which combines the following qualities:

- **Alignment:** The extent to which the HR practices will accomplish strategy.

Figure 3-1 **Setting Priorities for HR Initiatives**

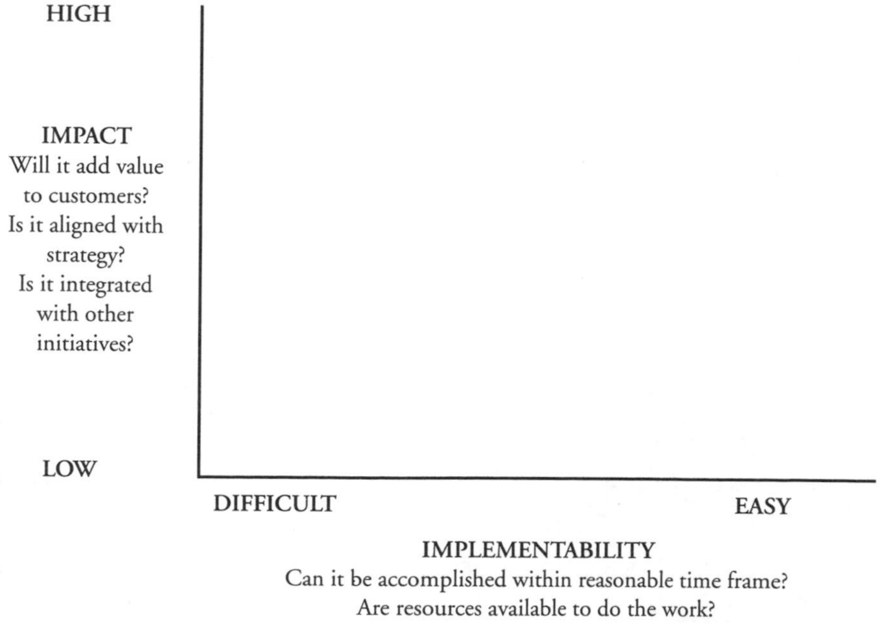

HIGH

IMPACT
Will it add value
to customers?
Is it aligned with
strategy?
Is it integrated
with other
initiatives?

LOW

DIFFICULT   EASY

IMPLEMENTABILITY
Can it be accomplished within reasonable time frame?
Are resources available to do the work?

- **Integration:** The extent to which the HR practices integrate and affect each other.

- **Customer focus:** The extent to which the HR practices influence external customers.

These three items taken together determine the placement along a continuum from low to high impact of each HR practice under consideration.

The second criteria is *implementability.* This criteria combines these qualities:

- **Resources:** The extent to which resources exist to accomplish an HR practice (for example, money and talent).

- **Time:** The extent to which management attention can be focused on the HR practice.

Resources and time determine whether implementation of a specific HR practice will be difficult or easy.

A firm using the impact and implementability criteria employed the following method to turn strategy into action. The firm's HR professionals generated several possible HR practices that could align with strategy. Since they knew that all of them could not be implemented in the near term, they held a meeting to discuss the impact and implementability of each HR practice under consideration and used the following matrix to establish priorities.

HR Practice	Impact	Implementability
Competence-based hiring		
Succession planning		
Career development		
Action-learning training programs		
Global leadership development		
Team-based incentives		
More pay at risk		
Flexible benefits		

HR professionals and line managers together assigned each cell a rating of low, medium, or high. Through this dialogue, they were able to prioritize the HR practices under consideration and to determine which they should invest in.

Ratings from this type of review can be transferred to a chart such as Figure 3-1 for a clear visual representation of the consensus, with each initiative assigned its precise location. By using the chart in Figure 3-1, HR professionals can prioritize the possible HR practices (actions) that come out of their organizational diagnosis. Implementation according to these priorities can then be planned and scheduled using the timing sequence illustrated in Figure 3-2. The thick line in this figure represents a time line (often one or two years); each step represents a priority to be accomplished within a set period. The higher the step, the more complex the change required. Given a time line of two years, most organizations can fulfill no more than four or five priority initiatives.

SUMMARY: BECOMING A STRATEGIC PARTNER

HR professionals play a strategic partner role when they have the ability to translate business strategy into action. This process begins by recognizing

Figure 3-2 **Organizational Capability Plan: Priorities and Support**

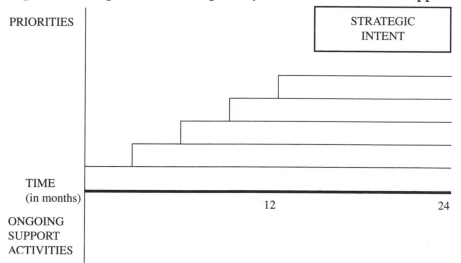

the challenges to becoming a strategic partner and then building the necessary organizational structures to overcome these challenges. To do so requires that HR professionals learn to perform disciplined organizational audits. This involves four steps: architecture, assessment, improvement, and prioritization.

Organizational diagnosis may be performed at any level. At the overall corporate level, HR professionals may lead an executive committee through an organizational assessment based on structured questions designed to determine whether and how the organization can accomplish its business objectives. Similar analyses can be done within a plant, business unit, or function (for example, R&D, engineering, marketing, or HR).[17]

As HR professionals lead managers through the diagnostic model outlined in this chapter, they become value-added partners. As partners, they should encourage line managers to share responsibility for organizational diagnosis. When line managers focus on turning strategy into action, they undertake the following tasks.

- They must ensure that every business plan has an organizational action plan for implementation.

- They must make sure that strategic promises to customers, employees, and investors are kept.

- They must question HR practices to evaluate priorities and focus.

HR professionals as strategic partners do not always agree or go along with the decisions of the executive team, but they should force serious discussion of how organizations should be created to accomplish strategy. As partners, HR professionals should not become servants of the team but advocates for creating a balanced scorecard within the organization. As partners, they earn respect and credibility by being outstanding at what they do—delivering organizational excellence through diagnosis. As partners, HR professionals challenge from a base of confidence. To function as strategic partners, HR professionals must fulfill the following tasks.

- They must establish an organizational architecture and be able to use it to translate strategy into action.

- They must learn to perform effective organizational diagnosis by asking good questions and generating creative and apt alternative practices.

- They must be able to set priorities for initiatives and then to follow through on them.

By jointly performing organizational diagnosis, line managers and HR professionals collaborate to turn strategies into actions.

Becoming an Administrative Expert

IN RECENT YEARS, line managers and HR professionals have had to discover more efficient ways to get work done. These efforts have been loosely labeled reengineering, and they include the reengineering of human resources itself.[1] As HR professionals reengineer their delivery of services, they become administrative experts creating efficient infrastructures, both for HR processes and for their businesses as a whole.

The following cases, examining Johnson & Johnson, Inc., and Lotus Company, illustrate the types and extent of HR reengineering. The HR professionals who led these reengineering efforts at J&J and Lotus were administrative experts; their work resulted in more flexible and dynamic HR organizations.

Case Study: Johnson & Johnson, Inc.

Johnson & Johnson (J&J),[2] operating in more than 150 countries, is the world's largest and most comprehensive manufacturer of health care products. The corporation encompasses 118 businesses clustered into three major sectors: pharmaceutical and diagnostic products, professional and consumer pharmaceuticals, and consumer and personal care products. The business units have independent philosophies and operating histories as well as unique customers, products, and cultures. J&J corporate executives, however, discovered that much of the sales, general, and administrative costs detailed in the businesses' financial statements could be traced to bureaucratic controls, duplication, and inefficient HR processes. This led J&J to look for ways to reduce both cost and bureaucracy and to increase HR efficiency, effectiveness, quality, and services of HR processes.

To accomplish the desired improvements in HR, J&J executives worked with Amherst Consulting.[3] Together they created and implemented the centers of expertise concept, in which the HR technical resources within a business unit were combined. J&J's centers of expertise included the following.

- Compensation/benefits;
- Affirmative action/diversity;
- "Live for life," a combination of medical, safety, wellness, and employee-assistance programs and risk-screening service;
- employee relations; and
- organizational effectiveness.

J&J leadership also worked to redefine the allocation of HR professionals' time. As indicated in Table 4-1, J&J HR professionals had formerly allocated their time to corporate or to business units, depending on their assignments. Under the new system, HR professionals allocate their time to service-center and contracted activities. HR reengineering success at J&J will be measured by improved indicators for both efficiency (reduced costs, improved productivity) and service (improving customer perception of HR services).

Lotus Company

Lotus Company[4] was founded in 1982 in Cambridge, Massachusetts, as a software firm producing consumer products, the most market-dominant being *Lotus 1-2-3* and *Lotus Notes*. One reason for the company's success was its culture, which was based on open communication (anyone could see the president at any time, for example) and an entitled workforce (well-trained, highly committed, knowledgeable workers).

Table 4-1 Johnson & Johnson's Estimated Allocation of HR Time

	Field HR/ Dedicated Service	Service Center	Center of Expertise	Contracted Service	Total Time
Past: In a centralized HR organization	20		70	10	100
Past: In a decentralized HR organization	80		10	10	100
Present: Where we are today	40	30	10	20	100
Future: Where we are headed	20	40	10	30	100

Employees were considered neither blue nor white collar, but gold collar because of their high competence.

In November 1991, the executive committee recognized that the firm was confronting a series of new business realities. These included the following needs.

- Productivity and value-added focus: Business plans were becoming too complex and too rigid, leading executives to search for new ways to keep people "connected to the rights of the organization," among them flexible work, policies, and HR processes. ("Rights of the organization" is Lotus language for the psychological contract between employees and the company.)

- Strengthened relationships between managers and employees.

- Decentralization of HR information to desktop databases that gave managers HR responsibility.

- Facilitated administrative processes, to eliminate redundancies such as the need for three signatures on a senior executive move.

- Organizational processes for examining the HR staffing needed to service a larger organization effectively.

- Redefined roles for HR professionals, moving the function from that of social worker to that of knowledge worker adding value to the firm. HR, known as a "corporate Switzerland" where managers could hide out, needed a new defining image.

For Lotus in general and the HR department in particular, these new business realities compelled the HR department to create a new vision. The vision statement they derived read "We view ourselves as a business dedicated to helping all our customers achieve maximum value from our products and services." The key concepts in this statement are *business,* showing that HR is accountable for business results; *customers,* including managers and all other employees; *achieve value,* meaning that customers must find utility in the HR services; and *products and services,* defining HR practices as products and services rather than as policy.

To achieve these goals, the Lotus HR function engaged in a reengineering effort to strengthen the relationship between managers and employees; to move information from within HR to the manager's desktop; to automate administrative procedures to provide faster, more direct service; to respond to new demands without exponentially increasing HR headcount; and to transact HR programs and initiatives with customer needs as a priority. These results would replace the many handoffs, the long cycle times, and the duplication of efforts that had occurred under the old Lotus HR function.

In the reengineered Lotus organization, corporate HR personnel (in compensation, OD/training, staffing, and diversity, for example) became less focused on policy creation and more focused on consulting. Technology brought information closer to managers and employees who could then use it to make quicker decisions. Employees with questions now went straight to a manager, each of whom had been given a compact disk containing answers to commonly asked HR questions and a link to the HR on-line information resource, Direct Connect, available at the HR Call Center. Managers with administrative questions can also take them to Direct Connect. HR strategic partners were assigned to the business management team of a specific business, and thus managers with questions about business issues with HR implications can turn to their HR strategic partners for answers.

Following are some of the key practices and lessons from the Lotus HR reengineering effort.

- Place all possible HR information on-line (at Lotus, was called Direct Connect). Twenty-three three-ring reformatted into Direct Connect, which is continuously updated with information on new policies and practices.

- Empower "responder" accountability among the Direct Connect staff to ensure quality service delivery. Direct Connect employees respond to eight to ten cases per person per day, with the responsibility for fixing each problem.

- Track all calls. Direct Connect incoming calls are tracked to ascertain possible company-wide problems, issues, and concerns. This information becomes an important HR database, sorted by location, manager, or other data classification.

- Work hard to deliver Direct Connect service. The Direct Connect responder answers 79 percent of all calls within three minutes; 21 percent of employee questions are referred from the responder to an HR staff person.

- Distribute data about Call Center use to line managers. It is useful for managers to know, for example, if most calls concern training, benefits, the company position on a specific issue, the correct handling of a required form, and so on.

- Do aggressive marketing. The benefits of using Direct Connect in lieu of talking with a live person must be marketed through demonstrations (for example, in the lunch room and at information kiosks), communication (such as letters to employees' homes), and focus groups.

As these practices were implemented, the image of Lotus's HR organization changed dramatically for the better.

ACTIONS NECESSARY TO BECOMING AN ADMINISTRATIVE EXPERT: THE TWO PHASES OF REENGINEERING

HR professionals work as administrative experts at two levels. On the one hand, they may help a firm go through the reengineering of *business processes.* As organizations identify and improve core processes, HR professionals may actively serve on the improvement teams working toward greater simplicity, efficiency, and effectiveness. Too often business reengineering has been driven by technologists working mechanistically and rationalistically, with little input from HR professionals sensitive to the human issues related to change. Perhaps the lack of HR involvement in business reengineering contributes to the failure of all but about 25 percent of such efforts.[5]

On the other hand, HR professionals must also apply their administrative expertise to *HR processes*. Even if not invited to participate in business reengineering, HR professionals should demonstrate their ability to deliver HR services efficiently by reengineering their own processes as needed. By so doing, they not only improve their firm's infrastructure but earn credibility for participation in subsequent business change efforts.

In reengineering either business or HR processes, HR professionals can add enormous value by recognizing and responding appropriately to the two phases common to any reengineering effort. Phase 1, improving processes, focuses on identifying ineffective processes and devising alternative methods of delivering services. This phase represents the most common type of reengineering and employs traditional reengineering tools (for example, process mapping, flow charting, and so on). Phase 2, rethinking value creation, goes beyond simplifying and improving processeses to rethinking the structures that enable work to get done. The following sections review ways in which HR professionals can add value at each phase. Creating value is described in greater detail, since this set of activities is less familiar.

Phase 1: Improving Processes

Phase 1 of HR reengineering applies business reengineering principles to improving HR processes. Arthur Yeung, a professor of business at the University of Michigan, has laid out the following steps in HR reengineering.[6]

1. Define the target processes.
2. Develop "as is" models.
3. Challenge underlying assumptions.
4. Develop "should be" models.
5. Implement, roll out, market.
6. Measure business impact.

For each of these six steps, Table 4-2 summarizes activities, tools, responsibility, and output. Underlying all these efforts is a relatively simple goal: stopping some HR activities and simplifying others, most often through investments in technology.

Yeung's summary of the practices at a number of companies that have applied these six steps appears in Table 4-3. The table illustrates the range of activities involved in HR process reengineering—among them streamlining, simplification, and redesign. HR professionals participating in these efforts apply principles of process reengineering common to both business and HR work. The tools in Table 4-3 become foundation skills for HR professionals working toward HR process reengineering.

Phase 2: Rethinking HR Value Creation

By the mid-1990s, the HR function at almost every American business had completed reengineering Phase 1 and improved its processes. While these improvements brought more efficient delivery of HR services, they often did not go far enough. Being an administrative expert requires more than cutting costs and simplifying work: Phase 2, rethinking HR value creation, is just as important. Value creation goes beyond reengineering HR processes to reframing and rethinking the conceptualizations and methods of accomplishing HR work. Administrative experts draw on three conceptual frameworks when rethinking HR value creation.

Framework 1: Avoid the centralization/decentralization quandary

The dominant paradigm for organizing HR (and other) work has traditionally been centralization versus decentralization, that is, respectively placing the design and coordination of HR activity at the corporate or field unit (business unit or function) level. Figure 4-1 frames this debate in terms of degree of integration (centralization) versus degree of differentiation (decentralization). The fundamental debate is around power and authority: Who has authority to design HR systems, to deliver HR practices, and to make decisions about how HR work is done? Power generally concentrates either at corporate or in the field unit.

The centralize/decentralize debate will never be satisfactorily resolved because it asks the wrong question. Centralize/decentralize questions focus on what goes on inside the function more than who uses the services of

Table 4-2 Road Map for Reengineering HR Processes

Step	Activity	Tools	Responsibility	Output
1 Define the Target Processes	• Define key HR activities as processes. • Prioritize key processes. • Break processes into manageable chunks. • Identify and document key process variations. • Involve subject matter experts.	Brainstorming, customer focus groups	Champion for HR reenginering + steering committee	Prioritize reenginering efforts
2 Develop "As Is" Models	• Conduct workflow analysis (who does what when, where, how) and identify hand-offs. • Audit existing constraints in systems (e.g., compatibility, integrity, and consistency of data) • Determine problems in current process from customer's and administrator's perspectives. • Identify key measurement related to process (e.g., cost, quality, time, rework, etc.).	Workflow analysis, activity analysis, systems audit, focus groups, interviews	Assessment team (HR and line managers)	Flow map of existing processes and their performance in terms of cost and quality
3 Challenge Underlying Assumptions	• Challenge each activity in the current process (why is it done, why is it done there, why is it done then, why does that person do it, why is it done this way, etc.). • Challenge current policies, practices, and philosophy. • Explore alternative delivery methods. • Cut across functional silos. • Incorporate and leverage information technology.	Visioning, scenario building, brainstorming, critical thinking	Process team + assessment team + technical team	Identify opportunities for radical improvement

4 Develop "Should Be" Models	• Solicit information from broad base about alternatives. • Benchmark other companies. • Integrate separate processes. • Finalize specification of new information systems. • Draft new process flow. • Assess potential impact of new process (cost/benefit, risk, etc.).	Benchmarking, conflict resolution, issues resolution, simulation, consensus building	Process team + technical team	Design new processes, select best information technology to support process, determine impact of new processes
5 Implement, Roll Out, Market	• Implement incremental approach. • Conduct pilot testing. • Implement systems integration. • Market the program, create curiosity, implement trial use. • Offer training to support users. • Manage resistance. • Anticipate and address morale problems.	Marketing, communication, training, coaching, experimentation	Transition team + technical team	Facilitate the smooth migration to the new systems and user's acceptance of the new processes
6 Measure Business Impact	• Capture business impact of HR processes before and after reengineering. • Measure business impact, not just budget and milestones in programs and activities. • Separate short- from long-term impact.	Activity analysis, cost analysis, customer service survey, focus groups	Full-time program staff	Monitor progress and impact

Source: Arthur Yeung's teaching materials, based on reenginering models from a variety of consulting firms, among them Wyatt, TPF&C, Index, and Hewitt. Reprinted with permission.

Table 4-3 **Examples of Reengineering HR Processes**

Company	Reengineered HR Processes	Reported Results
Sears	• Associates update records from personal computers at stores; the system enables them to route tax changes automatically to payroll for electronic processing. • Employees call a toll-free number to change profit-sharing and medical coverage. • Hiring managers no longer need to fill out data-entry sheets, which used to crawl across desks in HR as clerks manually computed tax rates, withholdings, and deductions. Now, the hiring manager inputs basic information on-line and the computer spits out an employee number and updates employee records. • Before reengineering, each of twenty-four HR centers was processing work differently. After reengineering, Sears charted processes and established a consistent set of rules.	• Reduced HR staff from 573 people to 125 in three years. • Consolidated HR centers from twenty-four to two. • Slashed HR costs by 75 percent.
CalFed Inc. (Los Angeles)	• Workflow automation eliminated twelve of fifty-five processes and significantly changed those remaining. • HR reengineering took seven months to map out. • Previously, a special check request could take days to process as the paperwork stalled on various desks waiting for approval. By creating an electronic form that could be sent directly to employee-services, cycle time was reduced to ten to fifteen minutes. • A time clock system rerouted information directly to payroll. The computer reads the time cards and calculates pay, withholdings, and deductions for 4,000 employees.	• Trimmed 50 percent of HR staff. • Cut cycle time on some activities by 90 percent. • Recouped technology investments in one year.

National Semiconductor	• Traditionally used a paper-based system to track more than 50,000 resumes per year. Now, with scanning and data storage software from Resumix, key word searches are done. The system also accepts electronic mail and fax. Once a document is on a screen, HR can E-mail or fax it to a hiring manager for review. • Uses E-mail as a gateway into COPS (Career Opportunity Programs System) which provides up-to-date job openings. The menu-driven system sorts jobs into 20 categories, provides detailed job descriptions, and offers data on training or education requirements. • COPS automatically updates itself by logging onto the HRIS computer every night. It can grab requisitions and make them available on-line.	• Reduced cycle time in hiring from 110 to 62 days. • Found better workers. • Did away with hundreds of pages of paper listings.
Florida Power and Light	• A sophisticated employee-records system now transfers information from scanned resumes and applications, pulls together several other types of employee documents, and stores everything on optical laser discs. • HR or managers can pull up records on a PC.	• HR department eliminated 65 percent of the paper and 50 percent of staff from 1991 to 1995.
J.M. Huber Corporation (Edison, NJ)	• HR began by documenting existing workflow, carefully studying it and creating detailed strategies for improving efficiency. Top management, line managers, and others participated in the discussions. The most crucial issue was to change from an old mainframe to a client-server system that could access data more freely. • The automated system allows employees to sign up and change benefits using an interactive voice-response system. • Authorized field managers will be able to pull up an employee's salary history, job description, and a host of other data to determine if an employee is qualified for a promotion or a salary increase. Once the request has been initiated and approved, the system will process it and the changes will be reflected on the appropriate paycheck.	• Process redesign reduced HR department's hand-offs by 42 percent, cut work steps by 26 percent, and eliminated approximately 20 percent of original work.

Table 4-3 Continued

Company	Reengineered HR Processes	Reported Results
Hewlett-Packard	• Uses an agent (Edify Corporation) to automate quarterly age reviews for 13,000 people. The PC-software dials into the personnel system and downloads a list of who works for each of 1,200 sales managers. • Using E-mail, each manager is sent a list for verification. Managers E-mail changes back to the system, which automatically updates files. • Finally, the agent repeats the process, this time sending proposed salary changes for review. The managers either approve the raises or make modifications by calling an interactive voice-response system to update records.	• HP has a computer handling the work formerly done by twenty administrators.
IBM	• Revamped its national benefits administration and pared thirty-six phone centers down to a single location in North Carolina. The firm equipped representatives with personal computers capable of conducting powerful hypertext searches on benefits policies. It then divided the representatives into two work groups. Tier 1, the largest group, composed of generalists, receives the most basic questions, which make up the majority of calls. Tougher questions go to a smaller number of Tier 2 specialists. • A new salary system routes pay increase requests to the proper person for approval. Once it is signed off, the confirmation returns to the manager initiating the request and is sent automatically to payroll for processing. • A 24-hour interactive voice-response system processes more than 170,000 benefits requests per year. Within twenty-four hours, it provides an employee with data on his or her retirement plan.	• Cut 40 percent of original staff in benefit administration and handles a record number of calls. • Between 1987 and 1994, IBM slashed HR workforce from 3,300 to 900.

Source: Arthur Yeung, teaching materials based on S. Greengaard, "New Technology Is HR's Route to Reengineering," *Personnel Journal,* July 1994.

Figure 4-1 **Centralization versus Decentralization Quandary**

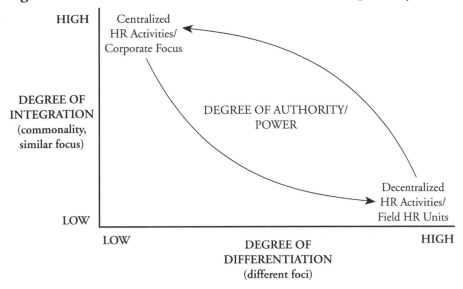

the function. Because the centralize/decentralize debate results in frequent changes in allocation of authority, employees become cynical about how the HR work is really done. The centralize/decentralize debate puts attention on power and authority rather than on service.

HR professionals as administrative experts need to avoid the centralize versus decentralize debate by rethinking and reframing the basis of their roles within a service entity.

Framework 2: Define a value-creation framework and delivery options

The debate about power, influence, and control should shift to a debate about value creation. Value creation begins not with what happens inside a group, but with what the group's user or customer receives from it. Value must be defined by the receiver, not by the giver of services. I like to send my wife flowers on her birthday, for example. I think this is a valuable gift, and the $50 expenditure means a lot to me. To her, however, it means that I express my affection by spending less than two minutes ordering flowers. She thus does not receive the value I intend. To give her a present of value, the value must have meaning to her, not me.

HR professionals as administrative experts must learn to create value, not as they perceive it, but as the managers and other clients perceive it. HR professionals must start with the question: What value can my work create for this business? Starting with this question shifts focus from what is done to what is delivered.

When power and authority are the criteria for HR work, two delivery mechanisms prevail: corporate and field. When value creation becomes the focus of HR work, four additional delivery mechanisms are possible: broker of services, service center, centers of expertise, and integrated solutions. See Figure 4-2 for an illustration and Table 4-4 for a description of these six delivery mechanisms.

Broker of Services.   One option for HR services is to broker HR work. A number of firms have done some targeted brokering or outsourcing, and a debate is emerging about the extent to which nearly all HR services should be outsourced.[7] The assumption underlying the brokering mechanism is that HR work contracted with outside agencies may be guaranteed in terms of fulfillment of cost and service commitments. The question that determines brokering of work is this: To what extent is industry average

Figure 4-2 **Delivery Mechanisms for Creating Value Through HR**

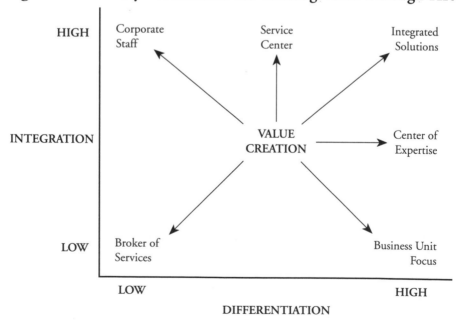

in cost and quality acceptable for this service? For some HR work, accepting industry average adds value. Some firms, for example, have accepted that processing benefits or payroll can be done at an industry-average cost, so these firms outsource this administrative processing work. These firms' HR administrative experts manage the elements of brokering services: negotiating contracts, bidding services, establishing agreements, and monitoring agreements.

IBM's Workforce Solutions (WFS) effort, begun in 1991, provides an example of brokering in practice. In this reorganization, IBM integrated a number of HR activities into a shared service organization called Workforce Solutions. According to George Krawiec, general manager of WFS, the HR headcount was reduced by more than 40 percent, from 2,200 in 1991 to 1,200 in 1993. HR costs were decreased by $100 million, a savings of more than 30 percent. WFS brokered services included the following.

- HR research and consulting

- Leadership development

- Compensation and benefits administration

- Occupational health services

- Work force diversity programs

- Equal opportunity compliance and records

- Recruiting and employment

- Resource programs and operations

- Information technology

- Executive programs

Each of these HR services was brokered both inside IBM to business units and outside IBM to the general market of potential users. By the mid-1990s, however, WFS had backed off from this aggressive brokering strategy. The company had found that some of the outsourced HR services were elements of IBM's distinctive competence and that buying and selling these services as commodities lessened IBM's uniqueness.

Service Center. A second delivery option for HR services is the creation of service centers for sharing HR-related work transactions. These service centers standardize routine transactions at a single location, allowing

Table 4-4. **Summary of the Alternatives for HR Delivery**

	Corporate Staff	Business Unit Staff	Broker of Services	Service Center	Center of Expertise	Integrated Solutions
Image	Strong corporate staff groups	Distinct business unit staff groups	Contracted services	Back-room operations	World-class technical experts, working with business	Integrated staff services working together
Key Success Factors	• Standardized policies • Efficient operation	• Alignment • Ownership	• Clear short- and long-term contracts • Relationships across boundaries	• Technology • Information • Standardized work	• Technical depth • Contracting with business • Business requests technical solution	• Integrated projects across staff groups • Contracting with business clients for projects
Primary Focus	• Corporate-wide policies • Long-term direction of the firm	Build staff systems to align with business needs	Contracting for services	Efficiently delivering staff services	Providing technical expertise for each staff area	Offering integrated and responsive consulting services to business

Strengths	• Consistency • Efficiency	• Dedicated resources • Adaptable programs	Clear price for services rendered	Efficiency	Technical excellence on each staff area	Offering integrated and responsive consulting services to businesses
Weaknesses	• Lack of flexibility • Ownership	• Duplication • Low quality of expertise • Isolation	• Small numbers bargaining • Incomplete contracting informations	Work not done alone; not all work is transactional	• Keeps boundaries between staff groups • Requires high degree of collaboration	Requires staff groups to collaborate
Operational Norms	Strong senior corporate experts	Locally dedicated staff services	Outsource services	Leverage technology; define administrative and transactional work	Technical experts in each staff group contract with businesses to meet needs	Integrated staff group where services are integrated within staff and with the business
Measures	Efficiency, firm-wide logic	Local ownership	Cost	Response time	Technical support	Integrated support

more efficiency throughout the corporation. Benefits processing, for example, similar across different business units, can be delivered more efficiently through standardized processes, with service centers handling common employee calls and concerns.

Transaction-based services deal with routine standardized administrative processes, questions, and activities related to meeting employee requirements. Transaction-based activities might include the following.

- **Benefit-related activities:** Benefit changes, flex benefits, medical claims, beneficiary changes, and employee questions about policy and reimbursement.

- **Compensation/pay activities:** Stock-option paperwork, tax withholding, pension transactions (401 K), payroll (including voluntary deductions, W-2 filings, and W-4 mailings), processing timecards, vacation records and policy, environmental data (for example, policies specific to particular countries), and diversity statistics.

- **Development and learning activities:** Education assistance and training registration.

- **Corporate citizenship activities:** Matching gifts and United Way and other charity campaigns.

- **Records activities:** Relocation and address changes, title changes, travel reimbursement, food service, and recreation.

- **Staffing activities:** Application requests, company information, employment verification, job posting, and applicant flow, visa.

When National Semiconductor (NSC) created a shared services unit, most of its activities were transactions such as retirement updates, records (address changes and company forms, for example), payroll (including vacations), basic policy questions, training registration, and job posting. The NSC service center mission is "to provide highly accessible and flexible world class human resource services to all NSC employees."

The Northern Telecom service center focuses primarily on benefits and record keeping. This center serves 20,000 U.S.–based employees with thirty customer service representatives and eight specialists. The company estimates that this system has reduced its need for HR staff to handle such transactions from approximately seventy employees at seven locations to fewer than forty employees (including data process support and management) at one location. Northern Telecom estimates its savings at more than $1 million per year, after its initial investment of about $750,000. The company also discovered that about 50 percent of all inquiries could be managed without face-to-face interaction. Calls about employment verification, mortgage applications, and other routine matters were more effectively handled through a shared service center and an 800-number. By sharing services concerning HR technical issues (for example, compensation, training, and staffing), Northern Telecom also improved the firm's overall technical excellence. Rather than disperse technical competence throughout a series of business units, expertise was collectively shared, resulting in a more competent technical resource pool. Another company, finding that it had twenty-four separate registration systems for training programs, created a training shared service that consolidated the systems into one.

Centers of Expertise. Centers of expertise bring together technical experts in each HR area who would otherwise be distributed throughout a firm's business units, allowing ideas to be quickly developed and shared. Johnson & Johnson used to have training experts in each of its eighteen business units. Through reengineering, they created a center of training expertise, staffed by twelve training experts who contracted their services as needed to the different business units.

Centers of expertise often focus on transformation-based services or on HR activities that help implement strategy, create a new culture, or accomplish business goals. Transformation activities differ from transactions; thus they can be combined into *centers of expertise,* not into service centers. Centers of expertise combine individuals and teams who have deep knowledge and expertise in HR areas such as the following:

- **Staffing:** Sourcing candidates, succession planning, career planning, talent assessment, screening candidates, dual careers, and downsizing.
- **Development:** Executive development, action learning, personal development plans, competence modeling, performance management, developmental assignments, diversity, and organizational learning.
- **Compensation:** Pay for performance, job analysis, performance measurement, rewards and recognition programs, job evaluation, and gain sharing.
- **Organizational effectiveness:** Organizational change, process management, organizational diagnosis, culture change, and reengineering.

- **Communication:** Media management, meeting management, public relations, and human resources information systems (HRIS).

- **Organization design:** high-performing work teams and organization structure.

- **Employee relations:** Morale surveys, employee focus groups, psychological contract, work/family policies, and employee assistance.

- **Union relations:** Labor contracts and grievance procedures.

- **Security:** Physical security for employees, executives, and technology.

For each of these HR activities, centers of expertise combine talent (formerly distributed throughout a corporation) into a shared service; they then invite the firm's business units to use these resources to solve their business problems. Employees who otherwise would have been permanently assigned to a business now work in a center of expertise.

PPG, a company working in the chemical field, for example, is organized into ten centers of expertise, each designed to serve an HR strategic business unit (SBU) manager. SBU managers are the initial point of contact for each business unit's line managers. This HR professional's job is to identify current and future client needs and then to draw on resources from one of the ten centers of expertise to meet those needs. The ten centers established at PPG are listed below.

- Alternative rewards
- Productivity/employee satisfaction
- Measurement
- External factors
- Leadership
- Work processes/operating methods
- Safety and environment
- Work force skills
- Organizational structure
- Business strategy

HR professionals in centers of expertise consult with the business units. They must learn best practices in their technical area, translate best practice to their company-specific issues, and apply their knowledge to specific business problems. In complex, multinational companies such as Motorola, there may be multiple centers of expertise for a specific geographic area or business (for example, semiconductors, pagers, and satellite communication). These HR professionals also source and screen external vendors who might work for the company. As consultants, their influence depends less on corporate position and more on expertise. Managed from the corporate level, HR professionals in centers of expertise may also add value by knowing corporate strategies, culture, and history. HR professionals in centers of expertise also broker, screen, and provide technical expertise to the business units.

Shared services encompasses both service centers and centers of expertise. Each of these areas of operation has different purposes and operational processes as summarized in Table 4-5. Mixing service centers and centers

Table 4-5 **Differentiating Service Centers and Centers of Expertise**

	Service Center	Centers of Expertise
Focus	Employee transactions	HR practices that transform the company
Work Activity	Reengineer and get economies of scale	Centralize functional expertise so it can be allocated to businesses
Successful if . . .	1. Costs are reduced 2. Employees are served more quickly with better quality	HR practices help accomplish business goals in innovative, targeted ways
Role	• Customer service representatives • Policy experts	• Consultants/facilitators • Technical advisors • Troubleshooters • Screen suppliers • Coaches
Interface with . . .	All employees	Primarily through HR generalists in the field
Interface through . . .	• 800-numbers • Voice recognition • Kiosks • Customer service representatives • Information technology • Face-to-face contact	• Task teams • Consulting services

of expertise may result in confusion because of their different purposes and different organizational arrangements.

Integrated Solutions.   Integrated solutions bring technical experts together as resources to meet client needs. An integrated solution differs from a center of expertise in a number of ways. First, the integrated solution engages and enlists experts from multiple staff groups into teams that confront business problems within business units, unlike the center of expertise, though which HR experts independently contract with a business unit. When Sun Microsystems was building its European operation, the facilities, information technology, and HR staff groups formed a team to determine how to build the best infrastructure to support the European operation. Rather than have each staff area contract separately with the Sun European managers, these staff groups came together as an integrated team.

A second difference is that the integrated solution, either across the multiple functions of HR or across multiple staff groups, provides in-house consulting expertise on common business problems. Chase Manhattan Bank, for example, has established an acquisition task force to audit and integrate mergers that includes experts from HR, finance, facilities, legal, and information technology. This task force comes together when required to prepare Chase to accomplish its merger goals. On completion of a particular merger, members of the integrated solution team return to their functional centers of expertise. This resident, cross-functional capability adds enormous value to the firm. It enables the firm to transfer learning quickly from one incident (in this example, a merger) to another, and it simplifies the coordination of multiple staff activities.

Case study of the value-creation framework and delivery options: Amoco shared services

One of the most complex efforts at shaping a value-creation framework for delivery of HR and other staff services comes from Amoco Shared Services. Amoco Corporation, like other integrated oil and gas firms, operates in primarily three major businesses: Upstream businesses deal with the exploration and production of oil and gas; downstream businesses deal with the marketing, refining, and distribution of oil and gas products; chemical businesses deal with creating and marketing products that often use some by-product of the oil and gas resources. Traditionally, each of these three major businesses has its own dedicated staff.

In late 1994, the Amoco Strategic Planning Committee decided to create the Amoco Shared Services Corporation as a fourth business within Amoco. This Shared Services Corporation would pull scattered staff resources into fourteen staff groups, each of which would redefine its delivery mechanism by assessing and allocating its work. The HR shared services operation, for example, analyzed HR work and allocated it to the following sectors.

- **Corporate:** Policy-level HR work, effective across the organization and focused on long-term strategic issues or on the firm's senior executives.

- **Broker:** HR work that could be outsourced to a third party because, Amoco concluded, the work did not give the company a competitive advantage and the industry average on delivery was sufficient.

- **Service Center:** Routine, standardized, and administrative HR work that was similar across the three other businesses.

- **Center of Expertise:** HR work that required technical depth and expertise and could be contracted to the businesses by HR teams.

- **Business Unit:** HR work that aligned with the strategy of the particular business and that could be tailored specifically to the business's requirements.

- **Integrated Solutions:** HR work that could be woven together with work from other staff groups and then delivered to businesses.

From its conception Amoco Shared Services was a company with more than seven thousand employees and an annual operating budget of about $1 billion. Richard Flurry, the first senior vice president of Amoco Shared Services, worked with a shared services integrated team composed of the heads of each of the fourteen staff groups to articulate the new company's vision. They also developed the following criteria for effective delivery of shared services across Amoco.

- **Cost leadership:** Reduce cost of operations.

- **Customer focus:** Increase customer satisfaction with staff support.

- **Excellence:** Ensure state-of-the-art staff practices.

As each of these criteria was satisfied, discussions at Amoco shifted from who had power and authority over staff work to how staff work could add value to the particular business and to the corporation overall.

As demonstrated in the Amoco case, value creation occurs when the appropriate mix of all six delivery mechanisms–broker of services, service center, centers of expertise, integrated solutions, corporate policy, and business-unit representative–is applied. HR professionals as administrative experts define the appropriate use of these mechanisms to add value for their clients.

Framework 3: Define a value-creation process

The focus of value-creation logic is horizontal not vertical, process not function, and teamwork not individual. Horizontal focus implies that the long-debated vertical centralize/decentralize question is not only unanswerable, but irrelevant. It is less important who has hierarchical power than that the organization's resources flow to add value for customers. Process is more important than function. Process deals with how value can be added for the user of a service rather than paying attention to a function or to its leader. A shared service organization requires teamwork throughout the HR function. Service center and center of expertise employees must have the capacity to form dynamic teams to satisfy their customers.

Four steps describe the horizontal, team-based process of a shared service organization. (See Figure 4-3.) These steps make evident the importance of the customer and demonstrate that resources need to flow from the shared service organization to the customer.

Step 1: Customer Requirements.   A shared service organization begins with customer requirements, with *customer* representing the person next in the value chain. Ultimately, the external customer who pays for a firm's products must be considered in determining customer requirements, but the immediate customers for the HR shared service organization as a whole are the line managers and employees who use the firm's HR services. Customer requirements represent the client's expectations of HR services. The question that evolves from these requirements originates in the customer guarantee literature.[8] What does HR guarantee will happen within the business?

This question may be answered by HR and line managers working as partners. Discussion of HR guarantees represents the contracting process between HR and its clients. The answer ultimately defines for a given firm the value added of its HR practices to its business success. Chapter 2 outlined four generic deliverables from HR work: strategy execution, administrative

Figure 4-3 **Logic/Flow in a Shared Service Organization**

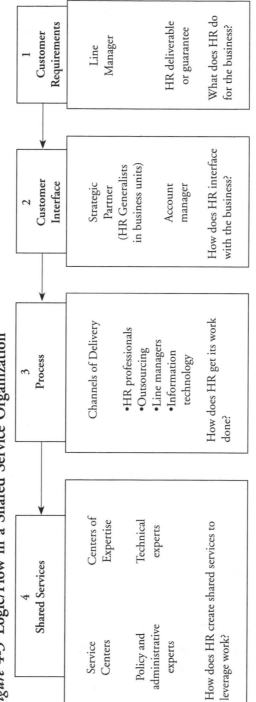

efficiency, employee contribution, and transformation/renewal. These deliverables become guarantees that HR professionals commit to the organization. Each deliverable may be contracted for as the first step in a value-creation process.

Step 2: Customer Interface.   To interface with business goals, HR professionals as strategic partners must become business generalists. In this capacity, HR professionals take responsibility for aligning HR practices with business goals, integrating diverse HR initiatives into common business foci, diagnosing organizational capability, and setting organizational priorities for competitiveness. HR professionals in these roles generally report to the business leader, serve on the business management team, and are deeply integrated within the business.

HR professionals also act as account managers for HR initiatives within the business. Activities related to people and processes within the organization become the responsibility of HR strategic partners. As the primary contact, or linking pin, for excellence in HR work, they translate HR initiatives into business results, becoming the owners of the organization's HR work and the dominant interface between shared services and business requirements.

These HR professionals, more generalists than specialists, have the obligation to assess quality work and to broker it into the business rather than to design and deliver quality work directly. Their job is not always to *do* the work, but to facilitate its accomplishment and to guarantee its quality.

Step 3: Process.   The HR business professional must not only diagnose what the business needs, but create a delivery mechanism to fulfill those needs. In traditional organizations, HR business professionals aligned resources with business strategies, but in shared service organizations, business partners deploy multiple delivery channels constituting the processes through which HR deliverables for the business can be accomplished. A typology of delivery mechanisms includes at least the following five delivery channels.

- **HR professionals dedicated to the business:** In the traditional organization, the majority of HR work was accomplished by HR professionals dedicated to the business. Even in a shared service organization, large and complex businesses may merit dedicated resources (for example, staffing, compensation, or training), but in general, use of this delivery channel is declining.

- **HR professionals in shared service roles:** As discussed, HR professionals in service centers and centers of expertise may be called on to meet business needs. In these cases, the HR business partner first defines the requirement and then assembles a team to meet the business's needs.

- **Line managers:** HR business partners use many approaches to involve and train line managers in HR work. Line managers for example, at Baxter Healthcare, do the primary compensation distribution; those at AlliedSignal do much of the quality training; and those at Sears take the lead in organizational change efforts.

- **Information technology:** Many companies are investing in HR information technology. Software, automation, and technology can help deliver HR services as simple as flexible benefits or as complex as succession planning. Information technology at Hewlett-Packard, for example, has been a key factor in the success of the HR professionals dedicated to the business, the shared service role, and the managers responsible for people.

- **Outsourcing:** A fifth means of delivering HR practices is to outsource them to vendors, consultants, or other third parties. IBM's Workforce Solutions, for example, outsourced many HR activities. Norrell, the temporary service agency, has developed a growing enterprise for outsourcing major parts of a business. Consulting firms are building large businesses based on long-term transformation projects, which are essentially outsourced organization change efforts. In large firms, outsourcing may be accomplished through insourcing. AT&T, for example, has created a resource pool of talented, full-time AT&T employees who move among the different AT&T businesses depending on demand.

Each of the above, plus other delivery channels, represents a means for providing HR services within a business. In many companies, the HR business professional has the obligation of facilitating selection of the particular channel that will best accomplish the guaranteed deliverables.

Step 4: Shared Services. The service centers and centers of expertise discussed above constitute the fourth step in achieving a shared service organization. These shared resources are consolidated for economies of scale but are dedicated to business requirements for customer service.

The flow of the shared service organization described in Figure 4-3 begins with identification of customer needs by the HR business generalists, who then specify the best delivery channel for fulfilling these needs. In many cases, effective delivery requires that both service centers and centers of expertise be used.

KEY SUCCESS FACTORS IN A SHARED SERVICE ORGANIZATION

While few firms have yet had enough experience with a shared service organization to fully evaluate its efficacy, some key success factors at each of the four steps can be identified.

Customer Requirements

Involve the customer in defining deliverables

At PPG, the HR function has articulated a mission and a set of principles on which the mission is based. Realizing, however, that if the HR customers (the line managers) don't engage in these deliverables they will not be committed to them, PPG's HR business partners conduct formal and informal discussions with their customers about HR's possible contributions to business success. These dialogues are not abstract, but concrete, in that they lead HR professionals to form contracts covering the line managers' expectations of the HR function.

To involve the customer in defining deliverables, the HR professional must clearly articulate who the customers are, what their goals are, and how HR can add value to these goals. One firm calls this practice "making our customers winners," and it encourages all HR professionals to work hard to make their internal clients winners through effective HR practices.

Help the customer see the importance of strategic HRM and the role of HR strategy

A key success factor in helping customers engage in HR processes is first to distinguish and then to connect strategic HR and HR strategy. *Strategic HR* is the process of identifying HR priorities based on the business plan. The dominant tool for this effort is organizational diagnosis (discussed in Chapter 3). *HR strategy* involves creating a mission, a vision, and an organization for the HR function (see Chapter 7 for a discussion of HR for HR). Line managers should be actively engaged in strategic HR because it affects their ability to accomplish business goals and because it determines the fate and role of the HR function.

Customer Interface

Select the right HR business professional

Perhaps the most challenging job in the shared service organization is that of HR strategic partner. This individual, both the primary HR representative within the business unit and a member of the business's management team, must have competence in business issues as well as exceptional knowledge of excellent HR practices to broker HR services within the business. At a personal level, such individuals need credibility with the business team, so that their ideas are valued, and with the HR community, so that requests for assistance are granted.

This key role in the shared service organization is filled by competent HR professionals who interface with the business. It is not a developmental assignment for a new hire, but a role for a seasoned, credible HR professional. It is not a short-term assignment—the time needed to fully know a business may require many years. HR business professionals, as partners, may become sources of continuity on the business team.

Be skilled at organizational diagnosis

A primary role for the HR strategic partner is leading organizational diagnosis. Organizational diagnosis leads to strategic HR; it is the process of translating a business's strategy into organizational initiatives and HR priorities. The deliverables that HR guarantees to the business should derive directly from this diagnosis.

Organizational diagnosis requires HR strategic partners to develop a model of capabilities necessary to successful organizations and to apply that model to their business. At Dial Corporation, for example, the consumer products division has a number of HR strategic partners, representing the diverse business lines, who employ a model that identifies six elements of a successful organization: shared mindset, competence, consequences, governance, capacity for change, and leadership. Each Dial HR strategic partner identifies HR priorities for the business by diagnosing the organization against these six capabilities, and these priorities become the foundation for the deliverables that each HR strategic partner ensures to his or her business. As this example shows, without organizational diagnosis, HR strategic partners cannot establish HR priorities for aiding their businesses' success.

Process

Define and use multiple channels of delivery

A key success factor for shared service processes is unlearning traditional channels of delivery. In many traditional HR organizations, the primary delivery mechanism for HR practices was the business's HR professional. In a shared service organization, multiple delivery channels can and must be used to deliver HR excellence. (See Table 4-6.)

New delivery channels refers to new ways of doing HR work. These delivery channels may include line managers doing traditional HR work, using technology to streamline work, contracting for work outside vendors, or asking employees to deliver traditional HR work. Such alternative delivery channels require time, attention, and money to set up, but they may save resources in the long run. Companies often fear that shared service organizations will result in a decline in the quality of HR services. This fear is unfounded: New channels of delivery, if firmly established, can maintain high service quality.

Table 4-6 Clients and Delivery Mechanisms for Shared Services

		Clients of Human Resources			
		Employees	Line Managers	Executives	External Customers
Roles Played within the HR Organization	Service Center	high	medium (personal)	medium (personal)	low
	Center of Expertise	low	low	high	medium
	Account Managers	low	high	low	high

Share information between customer and shared service and shared service and customer

In traditional HR organizations, information is shared on a need-to-know basis, and not everyone knows everything. In a shared service organization, information is also shared on a need-to-know basis, but it is acknowledged that everyone in the organization needs to know some critical factors. Everyone needs to know customer expectations (the deliverables expected from HR activities), the measures for the success of processes (how HR delivers against those expectations), and the delivery channels and rationale for services (how much shared services cost to deliver expectations).

In addition, shared service organizations must commit to sharing what they learn with other business units. Professionals in centers of expertise who consult with one business need to learn to share lessons across businesses. This sharing comes from technical experts working together on different projects, from co-location of center of expertise professionals, and from best practice forums and workshops. AT&T, for example, offers an annual award for business-partner best practices, developed either by individuals or in teams, that enables the company to publicize the HR professionals who contributed most to business success. Others in the company can then learn from these successful efforts.

Sharing information across the entire HR organization builds a shared mindset for the HR community. This shared mindset defines what a company's HR community "wants to be known" for, an identity that is then reinforced by the information shared within the community.

Shared Services

Remove boundaries within the HR function

Perhaps the greatest barrier to the success of shared service operations is the lingering mindset that builds boundaries around HR functions.[9] Boundaries make distinctions among people in the organization—generalist versus specialist, compensation versus development versus staffing, corporate versus field—and create hurdles for the flow of information, work, decision-making, and rewards.

Shared services will not work if boundaries dominate thinking. Boundaries may be removed, however, if individuals with different roles and responsibilities within the HR function develop a shared sense of the overall goals of the function. This can be achieved by creating a common goal that supersedes individual goals, by moving individuals to different roles within the function through career transitions, and by building incentives that encourage boundaryless behavior.

Clarify multiple roles within the shared service organization

The shared service organization represents a dramatic departure from the traditional HR organization. In most new organizational forms, participants want to find the comfort of the past rather than engage the demands of the present and future. A key success factor for achieving the goals of a shared service organization is thus to recognize the multiple roles required by the new organization that depart from past practices.

- The HR business professional cannot be a traditional generalist. While the HR business professional reports primarily to a senior line manager and represents HR within the business, this individual must act as a broker of services, a consultant to the management team, and a superb facilitator of change rather than as a traditional HR manager.

- Corporate HR professionals are no longer merely strategic. Some of the work done in the shared service organization continues to be strategic, for example, the work of the experts staffing centers of expertise. Much of the work at corporate shared services (for example, in service centers), however, is operational, with a focus on day-to-day efficiency rather than long-term strategy.

- Center of expertise professionals do not create and enforce policy; they share expertise. The heads of traditional functions (for example, compensation, executive development, organization effectiveness, or succession planning) focus less on creating corporate initiatives to be adopted by the business and more on consulting with businesses to adapt shared principles. Their job is to diagnose issues, participate on teams addressing issues, and help with the delivery of HR excellence within the business. They must know the business so that their applications add value.

With these new roles, a new set of competencies will emerge, including consulting skills, diagnosis, team work, and process management.

Co-locate members of the shared service organization

Members of shared service organizations generally function more effectively in a dedicated space. Without it, two problems will arise. The first is illustrated by a shared service organization that tried to leave the professionals assigned to its center of expertise in their existing physical locations, networked together through telecommunications. While they were formally assigned to a corporation-wide center of expertise, these professionals' housing within business units constrained their ability to serve the entire corporation. Users of their services from other business units found the HR professionals unresponsive and unavailable. By relocating the center of expertise members into a new, separate and distinct area, this organization sent a stronger message that these individuals served everyone. The second problem affects the center of expertise professionals themselves. They must become consultants to their corporation's business units, which makes it likely that they will spend most of their time moving from business to business, diagnosing problems and offering advice on implementation. Without a home base, these professionals can become isolated from their center of expertise and may have a hard time maintaining their shared skills and mindset.

In large corporations, multiple centers of expertise may arise. Digital Corporation, for example, has separate HR centers of expertise for training in Asia and the Pacific, Europe, and North America. These three centers are connected through technology, shared employees, and shared activities, but they are dedicated to the geographic area in which they are based. This reduces some costs and focuses training designs on regional needs.

Encourage and teach teamwork

Shared services organizations require teamwork. The HR strategic partner must be on both the management team and the HR team. Teams change as business needs change, so the ability to form and deploy teams rapidly and effectively is critical to effective service delivery by HR center of expertise professionals in shared service organizations. Experience has shown that teams are especially needed in Eastern Europe, China, Indonesia, India, and other emerging markets, in which a corporation's multiple businesses move simultaneously.

Service center professionals serve their organizations better when they form teams. Examples of the effectiveness of this strategy come from the new breed of 800-number insurance agencies, such as USAA and Nationwide. These agencies have made rapid gains in market share by using an 800-number rather than local agents for selling policies and servicing claims. These agencies were at first concerned that customers using the 800-number for claims would miss the personal touch and service formerly provided by field representatives. They found, however, that by assigning each claim to a team of claims processors, one of whom was made the primary processor responsible for handling the claim, the client's feeling of receiving personal service could be maintained. A customer calling in with an automobile claim, for example, is assigned to Person X on Team Y. Every time the customer calls in with questions or information, the call is transferred to Person X for handling, and the details are dutifully noted on a computer log. If at any time Person X is not available, the call is transferred to another member of Team Y who has worked with Person X and has access to the computer log describing the claim. The customer, as a result, feels that she or he consistently receives personal attention. USAA and Nationwide have found that by using this team structure their customer satisfaction rating continues to equal industry norms.

Service centers similarly handle employee problems or concerns (for example, processing benefits, answering pension questions, and so on). Concerns about losing the personal touch with a move away from field employee relations personnel to service centers can be forestalled by assigning each employee to a particular person on a particular service-center team. Having a primary contact allows the employee to feel a sense of having the personal attention of an HR professional even without face-to-face contact.

Get consolidations over as quickly as possible

A key success factor in almost any organizational change is to move quickly once the idea has been articulated and announced. The time between announcement and implementation should always be brief, even if many details and processes have not been completely worked out.

Establishing shared services means consolidating service center and center of expertise personnel. By sharing, fewer total employees are needed, which is a major force behind adoption of the concept. In most downsizing efforts, rapid, bold decisions enable employees to focus on the organization's future, not its past.[10] Likewise, in developing a shared service organization, it is better to create the service centers and centers of expertise speedily so that employees will know as soon as possible what their status will be within the new organization.

Define measures of shared-service success

Three factors may be examined to measure the effectiveness of service-center work. First, *customer value* may be assessed by indicators of customer satisfaction. In most cases, this means collecting data from managers and employees about the quality of the shared service work. Customer attitude data may come from surveys, focus groups, targeted interviews, or other customer-focused sources of information.

Second, *cost* of HR services may be assessed through productivity analyses. Establishment of shared services should reduce overall HR headcount and budget while maintaining or increasing the amount and quality of work. Users learning to make more informed decisions about HR services will lead to further reductions in costs. Shared services become an internal market in which costs for services used are made more explicit.

Third, HR can be evaluated in terms of reduced *cycle time* for HR services. Service center professionals should be able to answer employee questions and accomplish administrative work with dispatch. Center of expertise professionals should be able to design tailored HR initiatives without delay because they are knowledgeable about HR best practices and can move swiftly into business applications.

Techniques for measuring the success of shared services need to be established before the service center and center of expertise begin operations. Tracking benchmark measures may further indicate success or failure in HR delivery. Hewlett-Packard, for example, reduced its personnel staff by one-third between 1990 and 1993, decreasing its HR-to-employee ratio from 1 to 53 to 1 to 75. According to Pete Peterson, the HR head at the time, reductions in the department saved the corporation nearly $50 million over that time frame without a significant sacrifice in service.

To take another example, in the early 1990s, Intel launched a successful four-year plan to decrease its HR-to-employee ratio. In 1990, the ratio was 1 to 53; in 1991, 1 to 50; in 1992, 1 to 48; and in 1993, 1 to 45. Since then, however, cost-cutting imperatives have forced Intel to reverse this trend. Using a new four-year plan, they hope to increase the ratio to 1:100 by the end of 1996. Their method is illustrated by their new recruitment processes. Traditionally, Intel sent approximately two hundred operations managers to campuses to recruit students, bringing a number of them back to Intel for additional interviews. The new recruiting process relies primarily on six professionals for recruitment and screening, while one hundred to two hundred operations managers occasionally make on-site presentations, host job fairs, and sponsor open houses. The six recruitment professionals focus on screening and selecting talented students at different levels to work as interns. In 1992 and 1993, Intel offered seven hundred three-to-six month internships per year.

POTENTIAL PITFALLS AND THINGS TO WATCH OUT FOR

Power Shifts

With a shared service organization, power shifts from the corporate office to the field, and HR business professionals gain influence in the organization. Within corporate limits, they become the conduit through which HR practices are designed and delivered, the account managers for delivery of HR practices, and the HR representative within the business.

As shared service and business HR professionals collaborate as partners, they are able to anticipate and meet business needs. Creating a team of HR professionals with common interests, congruent business foci, and mutual respect requires dialogue and shared commitment among HR professionals.

Depersonalization

Some customers like using automatic teller machines and telephone and mail-in banking. Others feel that automated banking is a faceless, depersonalized experience; they prefer to visit live tellers. A similar sense of depersonalization may arise among employees using service centers. In lieu of seeing and knowing the HR professional who serves them, these employees may find their needs are being met through a combination of information technology and telephone transactions. Employee expectations from HR services must undergo a shift from valuing personal contact to valuing efficient delivery of quality services.

HR professionals working in service centers may also feel somewhat distant from the people they serve, especially those who went into human resources as a career because they "like people." The service center concept does not provide face-to-face personal contact; it represents a process for service. HR professionals who find the lack of face-to-face contact depersonalizing may, however, take comfort and pride from serving their clients efficiently and well.

Accountability

The shared service organization has more, not less, accountability for HR professionals working to deliver value to a business. Since this value may include complex issues (for example, strategy execution, administrative efficiency, employee commitment, and capacity to change), more is expected of HR professionals. Fulfilling their role effectively demands more than establishing policies and programs; these professionals must be contributing partners to business success, and their contribution will be measured by the extent to which they succeed in adding value.

HR professionals in centers of expertise are accountable for both technical excellence and consulting services. They must be knowledgeable in the best practices in their individual areas of expertise, and they must be able to communicate this knowledge to HR business partners. HR professionals in centers of expertise are measured by their ability to offer sound advice and to help in the implementation of corporate and business strategy.

HR professionals in service centers are accountable for delivering service in the most cost-efficient way. They are measured by their ability to respond to questions quickly, accurately, and courteously, and to solve employee problems with such things as medical payments, benefit distributions, diversity projections, and so on.

Shared Mindset

The greatest possible liability to an HR organization operating in a shared service mode is the failure to achieve a shared mindset across the organization's different functions and roles. A shared mindset is created by communicating the group's identity, purpose, and values to all involved in the shared service organization. The extent of a shared mindset may be assessed by asking this question: What are the top three things we in the HR function want to be known for? The responses of all HR professionals, regardless of where they work in the function, should show a 75 percent consensus. This overlap represents the unity that exists within the HR function, a unity that communicates and reinforces the department's sense of direction and focus. When HR professionals possess a shared mindset, the users of their services will absorb it as well.

Shadow Staff

Shared services means that line managers may no longer have HR professionals at their beck and call; often, the line manager's accustomed dedicated staff of HR professionals no longer exists. If, in response, line managers employ their own administrative assistants or turn to external consultants to perform organization/HR work, rather than using the HR shared services, a shadow staff may develop.

These shadow staffs defeat the purpose of the shared service organization. They lack expertise, and by using them, line managers add costs and disperse control. Shadow staffs create a bureaucracy that should have been avoided through effective development of the shared service organization. They emerge when the HR business partner has failed to deliver value to the organization.

SUMMARY: BECOMING AN ADMINISTRATIVE EXPERT

Administrative experts improve the efficiency of the work they perform. This chapter has focused on administrative efficiency within the HR function, but similar activities could be practiced for other functions and processes within a firm.

Being an administrative expert requires mastery of two phases of reengineering. In Phase 1, improving processes, HR professionals learn how to streamline, automate, and improve the efficiency of the HR practices. They apply the principles of reengineering business processes to reengineering HR processes. In Phase 2, rethinking value creation, HR professionals go beyond merely reengineering processes to rethinking how work is performed. Some of the innovations in shared services, aimed at value creation, not only improve processes but reframe organizational thinking. This thinking includes deciding what work is done and what is not done, where and how the work is done, and who does it.

Line managers can play a role in supporting HR reengineering and value-creation efforts through the following practices.

- Understanding and investing in reengineering all work processes.
- Redefining reengineering as the process of creating value.
- Creating appropriate shared services organizations, with delivery mechanisms and processes for action.

HR professionals, to become administrative experts, must learn how to:

- Reengineer HR work through use of technology, process reengineering teams, and quality improvements.
- Define the HR role in creating value for the firm.
- Create a shared services HR delivery mechanism.
- Measure HR results in terms of efficiency (cost) and effectiveness (quality).

Becoming an Employee Champion **5**

THE CHALLENGES FOR HR PROFESSIONALS acting as employee champions are many and complex, as the following anecdotes illustrate.

Remote Control

On a recent airplane flight, my seat mate looked over some of the material I was working on and started a conversation. When I said I was an HR professor and consultant, he wondered exactly what I did. He noted that his wife worked as a senior engineer at a large remote location of one of the companies for which I had worked. This company had received a great deal of public acclaim for its business results in recent years, to the point of being seen as a best practice company. My seat mate went on to say that this public perception was far from the day-to-day reality his wife experienced. In her engineering group, the work hours were awful, employees were demoralized, and many felt alienated from the company. The employees felt that the company was driven by numbers to the extent that their needs were ignored or slighted in the quest for profits. When I asked about how the HR professionals in the unit were responding, he laughed and said that according to his wife the HR professionals were always in some management meeting discussing topics far removed from the real issues facing employees. The employees in her unit felt that the HR professionals were wards of management rather than advocates of employees.

Real People, Real Needs

During two days spent discussing their strategy role with ten senior HR executives at a large U.S. pharmaceutical company, we examined their goals as business partners: understanding strategy, partnering with line managers, redesigning HR systems, and making strategic change happen. As these discussions neared completion, a woman who worked in HR at a plant on Long Island finally said that if she returned to her job and did only the strategic things we had talked about for the previous twelve hours, she would be a failure. She said that in her plant, with many immigrants, high turnover, low levels of employee education, and lots of real day-to-day issues, she had to pay very close attention to employee needs or the plant would close. She felt that much of her job as a business partner was to listen to employees, to help them help themselves with naturalization laws, and to be attentive to the real needs of real people.

Corporate Pressure Cooker

Discussions in a recent workshop with sixty high-potential managers from a successful global company turned to careers. Fifty percent of these managers (mostly in their thirties and early forties) did not think that they would retire from this company, not because of lack of opportunity but because of the enormous stress of their work and the high demands made by the company. Ninety percent of this high-potential group personally knew someone whom they felt was valuable to the company who had voluntarily left the company in the previous six months because of the increased work demands. When a workshop participant shared these comments with an executive the next day, the executive replied that a job at this company was a good job, that there were back-ups in place for anyone who did not want to work hard, and that discussions of work/life balance did not contribute to business results.

These vignettes share a common truth. In the face of downsizing, increased global competition, higher customer requirements, fewer layers of management, increased employee empowerment, and pressures exerted by almost every modern management practice, employees' work lives have changed, and not always for the better.

THE CHALLENGE OF FOSTERING EMPLOYEE CONTRIBUTION

Work today is more demanding than ever before—employees are continually being asked to do more, often with fewer resources. As firms move away from offering career or even employment security, employees find themselves rethinking their contribution and commitment to the firm.[1] If firms withdraw the old employment contract, which was based on security and promotability, and replace it with faint hopes of trust, employees will return in kind. Their relationship to the firm becomes transactional: they give their time but do not contribute their fullest efforts. Employees no longer try to exceed basic competence or to be completely invested in company actions.[2]

The effects can be seen at many levels. An executive at a firm that had recently experienced the trauma of downsizing feared that employees would give only their feet and not their minds to the business. He worried that because of the ill will caused by the restructurings, more employees would put their time but not their energy into company goals. Another executive was saddened when an employee, retiring after thirty-five years with the company, commented during his exit interview, "For the last fifteen years you had my body but not my mind." The employee went on to say that he had literally hundreds of good ideas on how to improve operation of the business, but since no one asked or seemed concerned about his ideas and opinions, he had kept them to himself. In an example from my own experience, I recently asked participants in a seminar how many present knew at least five ways to improve the operation in which they worked; one hundred percent raised their hands. But everyone likewise agreed that, since these ideas were neither solicited nor, if voiced, acted on, they now simply played the corporate game, keeping their bodies active and their minds closed.

Employee contribution becomes a critical business issue because in trying to produce more output with less employee input, companies have no choice but to try to engage not only the body but the mind and soul of every employee. Employee contributions go up when employees feel free to share ideas, when they feel that key individuals in the firm have their interests in mind, and when they feel they have a valid and valued employment relationship with the firm.

As business partners, HR professionals play a critical role in developing this employee-firm relationship. If no one listens to and represents the employees' interest, many who have choices outside the firm will act on them. If no one cares about employees' day-to-day needs, employee contribution suffers. If no one hears the voice of the employee, the voice may be silenced, to the detriment of the business.

HR professionals are business partners when they ensure that employee contribution remains high. In the past, this meant attending to the social needs of employees—picnics, parties, United Way campaigns, and so on. While the importance of these activities has declined, employee needs have not, and successful HR professionals must find serious replacement activities if they are to ensure employee commitment.

HR professionals alone do not own the responsibility for employee contribution and commitment. As Pete Peterson, the vice president of human resources for Hewlett-Packard, has put it, "Managers are responsible and accountable for people in their operation. HR professionals must help the manager do this duty."[3] This means that line managers have the primary accountability for many of the activities dedicated to assuring employee commitment. Many line managers would rather have it "the old way" and just let HR take care of all the people issues while they get on with business. HR professionals have worked hard through workshops, communications, and employee surveys to orient and train line managers to take responsibility for being the focal point of employee morale. The performance evaluations of all HP managers, for example, include trends in employee-attitude survey scores and in the quality of their action plans; survey scores and action plans are also subjects during major business reviews.

In many firms, as in the story related to me in the airplane, HR professionals have mistakenly defined business partnership as taking place exclusively in the strategic arena, not recognizing the importance of working with and for employee contribution.

A Framework for Understanding Employee Contribution

Success in being an employee champion requires a conceptual framework that helps define improvements HR professionals can make in employee contribution. I have found that the best framework for clarifying this organizational role happens to come from non-organizational theory and research.

Teenage Depression

Through my wife, a cognitive psychologist specializing in applying cognitive theory to family dynamics and, in particular, teenage depression, I have learned that in recent years teenage depression has become increasingly prevalent.[4] Today, 37 percent of adolescents are at least mildly depressed; suicide is second only to accidents in teenage death rates; and depression and suicide are equally prevalent across all socioeconomic groups. Recent theoretical explanations of the causes of teenage depression have focused on the imbalance between demands and resources facing teenagers.

Children entering their teenage years face many very real demands. Socially, they need to learn to mix with others outside the family. Physically, they must learn to deal with hormonal and other maturation changes. Cognitively, they must face academic and career expectations. These demands possess a number of comparable characteristics. First, they are inevitable. They affect every adolescent regardless of social status; avoiding or hiding from them is impossible. Second, they are real; they cannot be denied or discounted. Third, these demands are cognitive; adolescents perceive that they are linked to their own and others' expectations for their futures.

Demands may seem to cause depression, but they do not. Teenage depression does not result from high demands, but from demands that exceed resources (see Figure 5-1). Resources represent the energy-providing activities that help individuals cope with demands. At its simplest level, when teenagers feel "they just can't cope with it all," it is not the demand alone, but the inability to cope that causes depression. A number of resources increase the possibility of coping with high demands, including having friends among peers, among adults, and within the family; developing healthy habits in nutrition, exercise, sleep, and so on, that provide physical stamina and endurance; learning academic skills and abstract reasoning; learning to manage time and personal space; acquiring maturity in making decisions for the longer term; and developing a personal statement of morality, having faith in a higher order.

Figure 5-1 **Why Some Adolescents Get Depressed
and Others Do Not**

Depression occurs when D>R or R>D.

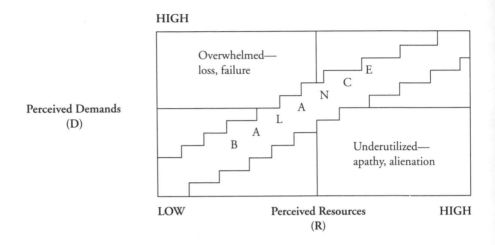

Such resources help teenagers cope with demands. The simple demand/
resource framework in Figure 5-1 helps explain teenage depression; it is
also a useful metaphor for employee contribution.

Employee Depression

The demand/resource frame for understanding teenager depression can
serve to frame the HR role in dealing with employee contribution. As more
is demanded of employees—to be more global, more customer-responsive,
more flexible, more learning-oriented, more team-driven, more productive,
and so on—firms must recognize that these demands are real and inevitable.
To be competitive, firms must demand more of employees, but the effects
of these demands cannot be ignored or discounted.

As these demands rise, employee depression may occur. Evidence of
employee depression includes a number of symptoms, some of which are
described in the assessment in Table 5-1. These symptoms may have an
underlying cause: Employees feel that the demands made on them exceed
the resources made available to them. They feel that they are being asked
to do more than they have the resources to accomplish. As with teenagers, the

Table 5-1 Assessment of Employee Depression

Symptoms of Employee Depression	Prevalence (1 = low; 4 = high)
1. Employees don't feel recognized or appreciated for the work that they do.	_____
2. Employees feel that their lives are out of balance, with too much energy focused on work and not enough on personal and family issues.	_____
3. Employees lament about how good work used to be.	_____
4. Employees feel that no matter how much they do, it is never enough.	_____
5. Employees feel unable to control the amount or quality of work they are asked to do.	_____
6. Talented and valued employees not only return calls from search firms, but leave.	_____
7. Employee stress-related health care costs rise faster than other health care costs.	_____
8. Employees feel that their bosses are out of touch with or don't care about the realities they face.	_____
9. Employees are embarrassed or reluctant to talk about personal issues at work (hobbies, family, and so on).	_____
10. Employees are short-tempered and argue over trivial issues.	_____
11. Employee morale is low.	_____
12. Employees spend more time thinking about protecting their own careers than serving customers.	_____
13. Employees rebel, merely following the rules and doing only what they are told to do.	_____
14. Employee disagreements and concerns are talked about more frequently in informal settings than through formal channels of communication.	_____
15. Employees don't have fun at work and talk about how difficult work is.	_____
16. Employees find it difficult to make commitments to getting work done.	_____
17. Employees feel that they have little chance of real career progression or that their career progression is outside their control.	_____

Table 5-1 Continued

Symptoms of Employee Depression	Prevalence (1 = low; 4 = high)
18. Employees are asked to do more, but they don't feel they have control over the resources required to do it.	_____
19. Employees feel caught in a rut or routine.	_____
20. Employees feel overwhelmed by all they have to do just to keep up.	_____
21. Employees talk about being burned-out by stress and pressure.	_____
22. Employees are cynical about new corporate initiatives and programs as just new ways to make them work harder.	_____
23. Employees don't see anything in it for them if they work harder.	_____
24. Employees don't know how to celebrate their successes.	_____
25. Employees leave work at the end of the day knowing they could have done or accomplished more but that they didn't have the resolve to do so.	_____
Total:	_____

depression does not come from high demands (because firm competitiveness requires that demands must be high), but from the lack of resources to meet demands.

HR professionals should be early observers of symptoms of employee depression during employee contacts, exit interviews, employee surveys, and employee relations activities. HR professionals as employee champions should also find ways to resolve the resource/demand imbalance. This is not as straightforward as it seems, however, because while some balance of demands and resources is necessary, complete balance is a mistake. Aspirations (a form of demands) should exceed resources.[5] Employees in a low demand/low resource state accept the status quo, with no opportunities for learning or improving.

When demands and resources are appropriately balanced, employees are able to contribute; they can commit themselves to improvement and can be competent enough to make the right improvements. HR professionals who guarantee employee contribution should be the observers, champions, and sponsors of balanced resources and demands, for both themselves and for the clients and employees they serve.

RESOLVING THE DEMAND/RESOURCE CHALLENGE

The demand/resource and employee contribution challenge has three possible solutions. First, reduce demands: Help employees find ways to do less and thus remain in balance with their current resources. Second, increase resources: Help employees find new resources that enable them to accomplish their work. Third, turn demands into resources: Help employees learn to transform demands into resources.

Reduce Demands

Among the many demands that teenagers feel are made on them, some are real or legitimate (for example, doing well in school) and others are not (for example, having a date every weekend). Helping teenagers sort the significant from the insignificant helps them to reduce stress.

Likewise, employees have many demands on them, some of which are more and some less important. Helping employees to separate the legitimate from the groundless—and then to the extent possible, removing the latter—can bring their lives into balance. HR professionals can take some specific steps to reduce demands.

Set priorities

Setting priorities among demands can reveal which, if any, are unnecessary. Most of us adhere to some degree to the adage, "Anything worth doing is worth doing well." This sentiment can become dangerous, Steve Kerr of GE notes, if it is taken, as it often is, to mean, "Anything worth doing is worth overdoing."[6] If Decision A requires a high-performing team, this reasoning goes, then every decision should be made by high-performing teams; if one group of employees benefited from a training program, then all employees must go through the same program. Such thinking processes and their conclusions overwhelm employees. By setting priorities, some activities will be revealed as worth doing well; others will be shown to be worth not doing at all.

At General Electric, the culture-change effort called Workout began with a focus on eliminating non-value-added work.[7] An assumption behind this focus was that work accumulates the same way clutter does in closets and attics: by piling up without much conscious thought or reason. Cleaning out closets requires discarding items that are no longer useful. Cleaning out work systems requires discarding work processes that are no longer adding value. To accomplish this cleansing at GE, for example, all bureaucratic processes— reports, approvals, procedures, measures, and meetings— were examined in light of the question "Is there a customer who gets value from this work?" If the answer was no, the work was eliminated. Other specific questions used to assess the value of work include the following.

Reports: Who uses the information in the report? How does the information improve decision-making? How accurate and up-to-date is the information? How much time is spent preparing the report?

Approvals: How often does someone say no? If requisitions (for example, for tuition waiver or travel approval) are always signed, then the required signature is more a bureaucratic form than a source of added value. Who is ultimately responsible for the action resulting from the approval? Does the approval process focus on this individual?

Measures: Who uses the measures being tracked? Do the measures reinforce desirable behaviors? Are the measures taken because they are easy to take or because they are important? How costly are the measures? Do the measures taken reveal lead or lag data?

Meetings: Why have the meeting? What would be the consequences of not having the meeting? What is the return on time spent for those who attend? Does the meeting serve as a communication or a decision-making tool?

Processes: How many steps are in the process? Can the process be streamlined to get things done more quickly?

These questions ferret out work that does not add value. As such work is discarded, employees have more time for activities that do add value and increase their contribution.

Focus

Demands on employees may be too high because of unfocused goals. Focus could be increased by eliminating multiple initiatives in favor of doing a few critical activities, but, unfortunately, in a high-demand world, quality, innovation, empowerment, customer focus, team building, productivity, and so on, are all necessary. Who would willingly forgo innovation to achieve high productivity? High-demand organizations win by pursuing multiple dimensions.

Focus, therefore, must be achieved by integrating multiple initiatives into overarching themes. In some ways, the particular overarching theme matters less than simply having one. George Fisher, the CEO at Eastman Kodak, for example, has selected quality as the overarching theme; Arthur Martinez, CEO at Sears, has focused on Sears's being a compelling place to work, shop, and invest; Irv Hockaday, CEO at Hallmark, has focused on product leadership.

Regardless of *the* theme, the contributing initiatives must be woven together to accomplish it. Steve Kerr suggests that integrative themes are like train locomotives pulling many different cars. The individual boxcars (initiatives) may change, but the locomotive pulls them along the same track. HR professionals help employees both to set priorities and to focus.

Reengineer

Many good texts discuss the general principles behind reengineering work.[8] The approaches used to reengineer work processes that enhance employee contribution by reducing demands include streamlining, automating, and simplifying. Simplifying complex processes reduces demands on employees. The following two examples illustrate this effect in action.

Dale Carnegie, in designing management training programs, found that the process time for a new program, from concept to delivery, was about six months. Through serious reengineering efforts, during which employees examined the decision points for new programs, the steps to creating materials, the necessary and unnecessary activities, and so on, Carnegie was able to reduce the cycle time for a new program to twenty days.

Camco, the General Electric Appliance business unit in Canada, reengineered its distribution system so that customer orders could immediately be turned into products. Instead of building to inventory, they built to order, significantly reducing inventory costs, eliminating much unnecessary work, and shifting employee focus from non- to high-value-added work.

HR professionals can help reduce demands on employees by understanding and applying reengineering principles to work and business processes. Even with thoughtful efforts to set priorities, focus themes, and reengineer processes, demands on employees will continue, and, in many cases, will increase. Regardless of how many demands are removed or reduced, competitive realities continue.

Increase Resources

Not all demands can be reduced, particularly if business demands accompany the desire to compete in tough markets. In many cases, walking away from the competitive market would equal failure. Globally competitive firms inevitably experience high demands. The resources available to HR professionals responding to such demands include values, practices, and actions, among them the strategies described below. (These ten strategies are summarized as an assessment tool in Table 5-2.)

Control

In a classic management-science experiment, employees on an assembly line were given control over the line's speed. Initially afraid that employees would take advantage of the situation and slow down production, management found to its surprise that employees actually worked faster when they controlled their own work.

Many companies have learned the value of sharing control with employees, giving them a say in how they accomplish and cope with increased demand. A hotel chain working to increase the productivity of maids wanted to raise the standard from cleaning eighteen rooms per day to cleaning nineteen rooms per day. Rather than merely raise the standard, the management experimented in a number of hotels by forming high-performing work teams of five maids who were responsible for cleaning ninety-five rooms per day (the new standard). Each team, however, was given complete control over how they organized themselves to get the work done on time and within quality standards. One team decided that four of its members would clean and the fifth would watch the kids of all five. This approach gave management what it wanted—increased productivity and continued quality—and employees what they wanted—flexibility and autonomy.

Control takes many forms. It may be control over work schedules. Flextime has helped a number of firms maintain employee commitment. In Microsoft's early days, the computer programmers faced enormous pressures and demands in preparing the thousands of lines of code needed for the new operating system. These programmers controlled their work

Table 5-2 Demand/Resource Diagnostic

Resources To what extent is my work unit characterized by the following:	Score seldom = 1; often = 10
Control: Employees control key decision-making processes about how work is done.	
Commitment: Employees have a vision and direction that commits them to working hard.	
Challenging Work: Employees are given challenging work that provides opportunities to learn new skills.	
Collaboration/Teamwork: Employees work in teams to accomplish goals.	
Culture: The work environment provides opportunity for celebration, fun, excitement, and openness.	
Compensation: Employees share gains for work accomplished.	
Communication: Employees enjoy open, candid, and frequent information-sharing with management.	
Concern for Due Process: Each individual is treated with dignity and differences are openly respected and shared.	
Computers and Technology: Employees have access to and use of technology that makes their work easier.	
Competence: Employees have the skills to do their work well.	
Score (total)	

schedules: They had no time clock and no one monitored their work. Giving these employees control over how they met the demands placed on them was a key part of Microsoft's success.

Where work is done may also be a control issue. Arthur Andersen Consulting lets employees live where they choose, as long as they are able to travel to meet client demands. Rather than traveling to clients four days a week and to the office on the fifth day, consultants may now spend the fifth day working out of their homes or another location. This autonomy over workplace does not mean that standards are any less rigorous, merely that employees control where their work gets done.

By sharing power and giving up control, managers express implicit trust in their employees' ability to do a good job and the motivation to do it well. Sharing control demonstrates trust and builds employee contribution. HR professionals seeking means for using control creatively and flexibly should start by considering the following questions.

Where is work done?

How is work done?

What work is done?

When is work done?

Who does what work?

As long as employees understand and are committed to their firm's goals, decisions over the means of accomplishing those goals may be shared.

It is not surprising that many employees who start small firms after leaving large ones, either voluntarily or involuntarily, end up working longer hours and enjoying it more. One reason for this increased work satisfaction despite the longer hours is that the owners of a business (a restaurant, a consulting service, or whatever) have control over their work. They and no one else decides how much work to do and when to do it.

Commitment

When employees feel personally committed to a project or a company, they are more likely to work hard to accomplish their goals. When employees are asked to recall a time when they faced enormously high demands (for example, a tough schedule or a difficult customer) and to articulate their feelings about working to accomplish those demands, almost unanimously they cite their sense of commitment to a common vision. Employee commitment often comes from a leader who shares a clear vision that passionately communicates an agenda and intent. Executives with such visions provide employees with direction and resources that increase their resolve to cope successfully with increased demand.

A demonstration of senior management commitment also translates into added resources for employees. When George Fisher became chairman of Eastman Kodak, one employee commented that Kodak had for years undertaken many quality improvement and efficiency initiatives, but that Fisher really was serious. This employee's feeling was that while the language remained the same, the passion and dedication behind it were new. He also commented that many other employees were excited and energized by the new leadership dedication.

Challenging work

Boring work is draining; lots of boring work is deadly. Asking employees to do increasing amounts of boring work is self defeating. There are numerous ways to make work challenging.

Baxter Healthcare, for example, creates more challenging work by connecting employees directly with customers. One criterion of employee effectiveness has become the degree to which customers see and use the work done inside Baxter. In one instance, Frank LaFasto, vice president in Human Resources, spends a large portion of his time team building with hospitals who are Baxter customers. His hard work is immediately challenging and has direct customer payback.

Amgen, one of the world's leading biotech firms, provides another example. Constantly searching for new genes and biotechnology that can be turned into products, Amgen asks its scientists to excel in all areas: research, application, and product-introduction time. These scientists' motivation is continually stimulated by extensive technical support, up-to-date laboratories, and extremely challenging work. Scientists at Amgen know that they are working on cutting-edge research that will add value to science as well as to Amgen's portfolio.

Collaboration/teamwork

Teams often can turn modest individual efforts into extraordinary successes. Studies of high performing teams[9] provide clear evidence that teams can often leverage average individual talents into superior collective achievements. When faced with high demands, teams often find better ways to solve demands than do individuals working in isolation.

Boeing provides an example of teamwork in action to meet extraordinary demands. The Boeing 777 air frame, the foundation of Boeing's twentieth-century fleet, was created under exceptionally difficult demands. It had to be completed (from design to delivery) in less time than previous models had been; it had to be produced at less cost and be fuel efficient beyond any aircraft in the air; it had to meet very high customer performance expectations; and it had to please the pilots who would fly it. These demands did not have clear, or in some cases, even available answers. More than two hundred teams participated in the design, engineering, manufacture, and assembly of the Boeing 777, however, and the results redefined not only the Boeing fleet, but the process by which air frames could be delivered.

Teams are often accused of being slow to come to decisions. Actually, in many cases, the opposite has been true. In situations of high demand, where answers and solutions are not readily available, teams used as resources can focus members' attention and more rapidly resolve issues than can individuals. Hallmark has established itself as the standard for greeting cards; as competition grew from American Standard and other brands, however, Hallmark executives knew they would have to rethink how work was accomplished. These executives, under the leadership of Irv Hockaday, the CEO, embarked on the development of a product leadership strategy to define the distinct brands and products to be distributed to its different and diverse outlets. Creating this strategy took enormous time and energy, as it necessitated changing many assumptions and processes that had already been reengineered at Hallmark. A key to the effective execution of the Hallmark strategy was the formation of the North American Management Team (NAMT), composed of the firm's twelve senior executives. Meeting regularly, these key decision-makers struggled to make the strategy work. Exerting peer pressure on each other, and under Hockaday's leadership, the group made disciplined, rigorous, and tough decisions in order to execute the product leadership strategy. NAMT improved both Hallmark's decision-making and its strategy implementation and served as a resource for meeting increasing business demands.

Teams can be formal corporate bodies, such as Hallmark's NAMT, or task forces, such as the hundreds of Boeing 777 teams. They can also be less formal support groups, which offer individuals emotional and intellectual support during periods of high demand. Coopers & Lybrand found that a host of informal, collegial teams helped employees find outlet for their demands and provided arenas for discussing problems and finding creative solutions outside the formal hierarchy. Support groups, clubs, social activities, professional associations, minority groups, and other informal teams increase the coping resources available to individual employees.

Finally, collaboration may take the form not of a large group but of a formal or informal mentor relationship. In the U.S. Army during the Vietnam era, many of the younger officers became disillusioned about the older officers' lack of commitment to sharing their experience. These young officers formed a mentor program through which the officer who had previously held a given position would spend time observing his or her replacement in simulations or other realistic settings. Although army regulations prevented officers from officially mentoring those under his or her command, the outgoing officer, who had experienced many of the challenges and concerns facing the new officer, provided unofficial, off-the-record comments on how to improve performance. This mentoring system has been credited with improving leadership quality as it provided a resource for current officers that helps them to cope with their responsibilities.[10]

Culture of fun in work setting

Imagine being involved in a competitive event that requires you to work very hard for a long time (for example, a sports event, forensics meet, debate, music competition, and so on). Imagine your feelings, then, if you win the award. Now, imagine that you cannot celebrate that success but must quietly accept the award and immediately begin preparation for the next round of competition. Does it sound like fun?

Too many work settings have taken the fun out of winning. Setting, striving for, and accomplishing stretch goals should be energizing, exciting, and worthy of celebration.

Some companies have maintained the fun culture. Southwest Airlines requires employees to take very seriously the airline's rules and regulations, but it also asks them to go out of their way to help passengers enjoy flying on Southwest.[11] Flight attendants have been known to sing, dance, climb into overhead bins, and in other ways entertain passengers while performing their required duties. Sam Walton performed a hula dance on Wall Street after his company exceeded stretch goals; his performance was fun for employees, but it also showed them that Walton would go to great (and humorous) lengths to reward employees for delivering results.

A fun work culture can be epitomized in other ways. Employees, for example, can be encouraged to live the company's values. A Harley-Davidson employee is more likely to wear a Harley T-shirt and a pair of Levi's to work than more formal office attire. Harley employees often attend rallies where they ride their bikes, or bikes loaned to them by the company, and join their customers in the Harley experience. The staffers in Hallmark's creative department are encouraged not only to develop innovative cards but to have fun in the process. They decorate their work stations, have brainstorming sessions, meet with customers, and seek other ways to provide outlets for their creativity and personalities.

Creating a culture where successes are celebrated helps employees to cope with increased demands.

Compensation: Shared gains

The concept of compensation as a resource is clear to any dual-career couple. When both partners have careers, demands within the relationship increase. Extra income can serve as a buffer to the effects of busy schedules by providing funds for eating out more often, hiring house-cleaning services, taking better or more frequent vacations, or providing other resources that help cope with the increased demands on the family.

A similar process occurs in work settings. In a recent workshop, I spent two hours talking about all the exciting things happening at the company. Company executives were articulating a vision, producing new and exciting products, reducing cycle times for product introduction, and serving customers. At the end of this presentation, a workshop participant who had been listening quietly commented, "This is all well and good, but what's in it for me?" Great question! At some point, working hard for great causes must be rewarded on a personal level. Almost no one is totally altruistic; we want to touch, see, and feel rewards for what we do. For most people, compensation becomes a scorecard for success.

Companies are learning that sharing the economic gains of reaching targets works and helps employees stay motivated to reach increasingly difficult goals. PepsiCo has instituted a program called Sharepower that makes all employees (not just a select group of senior executives) working at least 1500 hours per year and employed by Pepsi one year or longer eligible for stock. For Pepsi, this means 500,000 workers in 195 countries. Such gain-sharing is not altruistic; it is intended to increase the employee commitment to the company's success. Stories abound at Pepsi about how employees have gone the extra mile to serve customers. This is at least partly attributable to the employees' awareness of the impact of customer service on future stock performance.[12]

When HR professionals help employees see that a particularly demanding project or exercise will result in economic payback for the employee, the employee is likely to work harder. With a clear line of sight between work and reward, employees may cope better with increased demands.

Communication: Never too much

The results of almost every organization capability or employee attitude survey that asks about communication suggest that not enough information is shared. Even after weeks and months of presenting and communicating a new strategy, many employees will not understand it. The fact that communication is difficult, however, does not undermine its importance as an employee resource.

If employees understand why something is being done, they will more readily accept what is expected. Too often, managers focus on the *what* and not the *why*, making descriptive statements about the program to be instituted: reorganization, reduction in cycle times, increased quality, reengineered processes, and so on. Employees are exposed to the program but not to the principles behind it, with inefficiency and resentment the result. In contrast, employees who are given knowledge of the business, to the extent that they are able to communicate business goals to external stakeholders (for example, customers, investors, suppliers, potential employee groups, and so on), see this communication and information as resources and become committed to the change.

When Hallmark introduced a new organization that would increase the demands on and expectations of almost the entire workforce, the executive team worked diligently to communicate to employees the intent and implications of the changes. They held a series of "all hands" meetings at which executives explained the new organization and goals and answered employees' questions. Hallmark prepared press releases that provided employees' families with a sense of what was happening within the company. Summaries of executives' remarks were released in briefings, newsletters, and question-and-answer columns. Employees with further questions were encouraged to contact their managers for answers. This extensive communication plan became a major resource for the new Hallmark organization. Employees throughout the organization not only knew what was happening, but why, and they knew how changes would affect their jobs and careers.

Communication requires symbols as well as words. When Sears was developing its vision of becoming a compelling place to shop, work, and invest, Barbara Lehman, the director of transformation communications, worked with her staff to create a symbol for this vision: a triangle that incorporated the three components of their balanced scorecard. One of the tangible forms of this symbol was a paperweight with a base setting out the shared beliefs that Sears wanted to foster—performance leadership, people add value, and passion for the customer. Each side represented one of the stakeholders in this effort (customers, employees, and investors). At the Chairman's Conference at which the vision was first presented and discussed, each participant left with one of these paperweights as a memento and symbol of the new Sears. Participants also received a gyroscope, which, of course, spins and balances. These mementos, which may seem somewhat trite to outsiders, became symbols that communicated and sparked memories of the new strategy.

When HR professionals help produce clear, consistent, and concise information, communication becomes a resource for meeting increased demands.

Concern for individuals and due process

Being busy is often not an option; it is a given. Some of our ancestors were pioneers who left the comfort of established homes and moved, with relatively few possessions, to new settings. Today's pioneers meet the challenge, not of new geography, but of limited time; they must learn to forge a path through many activities and to deal with endless lists of things—they must become pioneers of time.

Some companies provide employees with resources to help them cope with these demands on their time. The corporate office complex of 3Com, for example, includes space leased to a bank and fitness center and to small businesses that provide services, such as video rental, dry cleaning, and film developing, and products, such as flowers, cards, gifts, and toiletries. A Starbucks, a travel agency, and a general store are among the other businesses 3Com employees find useful and convenient. The company's reasoning is that if employees can use their time before, during, and after work to accomplish errands more efficiently, they will have more time to focus on the demands of their work and of their personal lives. This concentration of services also helps to create a sense of community among 3Com employees.

In some of their senior executive training programs, Cargill invites trainees' spouses and other life partners to attend sessions in which the challenges facing the business are discussed candidly. These events help families to become more involved with and committed to business expectations. Federal Express has institutionalized grievance procedures that enable employees who have a conflict with their managers to get a hearing from senior managers. Motorola ensures employees that anyone who has been with the company ten years or more will not be terminated without a personal review by a member of the Executive Committee.

Policies such as these help increase employees' perceptions that resources are available to help them cope with increasing work demands.

Computers and other technology

New technologies may impose a demand (the necessity of learning how to do things differently) or provide a resource (the ability to do things differently). As a resource, technology can remove barriers by helping to share information and by simplifying work processes. Computers, for example, can often remove or replace routine, standardized transaction work.

A technology resource may also restructure how work is done. In an internal study, AT&T found that a high percentage of work activity could be done from remote locations through telephone, fax, and modem connections. Instead of facing the demands of traffic, parking, and going to the office every day, employees were given the option of and resources for telecommuting, working from remote and distributed locations. Virtual offices, the boundaries of which are not geography but information, are becoming more frequent at other companies, as well.

National Semiconductor personnel have examined ways to use technology to make employees' work lives easier.[13] An internal product, Groupware, now allows employees to communicate anytime and anyplace. It was developed in response to research that revealed four prevailing basic communication settings, with varying needs for innovative technological solutions.

1. **Same time/same place.** Employees working similar hours in common locations rely on traditional gathering procedures, such as meetings, focus groups, classes, and forums.

2. **Same time/different place.** Employees working in the same time zone but at different locations (for example, different buildings or facilities) can communicate face-to-face, but only with expenditure of time. Technology, including telephone and conference calls, video confer-

ences, and electronic mail (for example, *Lotus Notes*), is therefore used to ease the communication demand.

3. **Different time/same place.** Employees who work in the same location but at different times (for example, on different shifts) communicate through bulletin boards, log books, or overlapping schedules.

4. **Different time/different place.** Employees distributed across locations and time zones communicate through electronic voice mail, local– and wide–area networks, and video and text databases.

Regardless of the distribution of employees in time and space, technology offers effective ways for them to achieve a feeling of community in their interactions.

HR professionals who understand technology (for example, video conferencing) may use it as a resource to save employees' time and to share information in ways that are easy for employees (for example, by making it possible for them to work from home).

Competence: Training and development

As demands on employees increase, skills to cope with those demands must be found, and many companies invest heavily in helping employees to do this through development and learning activities.[14]

Four types of development activities are in general use. First, many companies invest in systematic management curricula to develop employees at each level of their careers. At General Electric, the Crotonville Development Center has prepared courses for employees at every level, from entry through company officer. These courses, tailored to the requirements of employees at each stage of their careers, ensure that they have the skills needed to do their work.

Second, many companies structure developmental experiences through which employees can acquire necessary skills; these include job assignments, task forces, apprenticeships, and job rotation. These developmental assignments are based on the assumption that individuals learn from doing and that employees who are given new work challenges, will learn from the experience.

Third, employees may acquire competence through action-learning training activities. Action learning occurs when intact work teams attend training activities focused on a real business problem. The outcome of the development experience is not merely a set of skills, but the ability to apply those skills.

Finally, employees who need to work in teams may enhance their competencies by discussing not only the business projects at hand but also the nature and mechanics of teamwork. Many teams use outward bound activities to improve their members' competence for working in teams.

HR professionals weave together all four types of development experiences, thus ensuring that employees have the competence to meet increased work demands.

Turn Demands into Resources

At times, what might be seen as a demand may be turned into a resource. Activities that turn demands into resources have the potential for providing the most powerful leverage of any of the techniques discussed in this chapter.

Exit interviews

Employees leaving a firm may be the best source of information about what is really happening there. HR professionals performing exit interviews have the opportunity to recognize how company policies or management actions translate into demands on employees. By collating data gathered from exit interviews, HR may find ways to reduce these demands on other employees. But as valuable as these interviews might be, they are still a lag indicator of employee attitude and may be done too late to have meaningful impact.

New manager assimilation

New managers often raise the demands on employees. Employees reporting to new managers, and uncertain about their expectations, work styles, and behavior, experience increased levels of stress.

General Electric has instituted a systematic assimilation process for new managers to help overcome this uncertainty and to smooth employees' transitions to working with new managers. In this half-day workshop, employees and the new manager remove any barriers to their working together. Among the exercises used are the following.

1. Employees meet as a group and list any questions they have about the new manager (for example, background, work habits, expectations, and so on).

2. The new manager meets with employees and responds to the questions as openly and candidly as possible.

3. The new manager shares concerns and questions he or she has about working with the group.

4. The group shares expectations about work processes, such as decision-making, conflict resolution, goals, and roles.

Investing time up front on these issues saves time and resources by changing the demand of altered leadership to the resource of an effective working relationship. HR professionals can help by designing and facilitating opportunities for assimilation.

Consider the impact of company policies on extended employee personal relationships

Work demands often become family demands. HR professionals may turn work demands into resources by considering issues that affect families. Marriott Corporation and Cargill invite spouses or partners to participate in some executive development experiences. Partners do not attend just to visit the city but to hear about and discuss business strategies and the personal and family implications of these strategies.

Family-friendly organizations also sponsor policies and practices that engage employees' families. These take many forms. Some companies invite partners and children on interview trips to help them become comfortable with the possibility of relocation. Adequate family-leave policies—for childbirth, illness, parent care, and so on—help relieve employee stress. On-site or corporate-supported child-care program help employees deal with the work/family balance. Corporate-supported family vacations, outings, extracurricular activities (for example, sports leagues and community events), and events (for example, a father-daughter day) help employees integrate work and home. In firms that are increasing their global presence, family training programs may help both the employee and the family adapt to global conditions and relocation to a foreign country.

While not applicable to all employees, this array of family-focused corporate activities may help some employees to modify work/family demands by helping their families to better understand and su requirements.

Involve employees in key decisions

Demands can be turned into resources by involving employees in decisions that affect them. Involving employees in a decision generally means sharing with them its context and rationale. Employees who participate more fully in the decision-making process—framing the decision, collecting information, generating alternatives, making recommendations, and implementing and acting upon the decision—become more engaged and committed to the outcome.

Involving employees in the full range of the decision process can reduce their sense of being controlled and increase their sense of being committed. Employees involved in screening applicants for the position of their own supervisor (laying out criteria, interviewing, voicing an opinion) become more committed to the supervisor who is ultimately hired. Employees who are able to voice their opinions about product introductions become more committed to the new product. Employees who have a voice in where a new plant or facility will be established become more committed to their own relocation. Employees who participate in the dialogue about new strategies become more committed to making them happen.

Involvement can range along a continuum from sharing information and voicing ideas and alternatives to sharing decision-making authority and the consequences of the decisions made. The higher the level of involvement, the more the employee will feel a part of the decision and the more involvement will become a resource rather than a demand.

HR professionals who understand these concepts work to involve appropriate people in business decisions. They must decide who should receive information, participate in the task forces that generate information for decisions (for example, benchmarking), help draft and implement recommendations, and follow up on decisions. These important elements of the involvement process make it possible to transform decisions that might have been demands on employees into resources that enhance their contentment and commitment.

Manage redeployment

Downsizing is one of the most stressful events for any business. Redeployment creates demands both for employees who leave and for those who stay. If the typical redeployment process can be improved, however, it can become instead a resource for all employees.

For a number of years, Intel has used redeployment to upgrade the skills of its workforce. By laying off unproductive employees and asking those remaining to be more productive (what Intel called the 125 percent solution), Intel took a somewhat traditional approach to redeployment.

To upgrade the redeployment process while maintaining employee commitment, Intel's HR professionals initiated a series of changes. They created a redeployment fund of $10 million to be used for outsourcing, retraining, or relocation of laid-off employees. They worked to move people between divisions rather than letting them go. They taught employees to own their employability by taking control of their careers. They shared honest messages with employees about the need for continuous improvement, high performance standards, and requirements for increased productivity. They created an infrastructure for moving people around within the company through job posting, automated internal sourcing, and candidate slates that spanned company boundaries. They engaged in workforce planning to anticipate workforce numbers and competencies needed in the future. They helped employees to assess their skills and match them with the company's present and future needs. As a result of these efforts, 92 percent of Intel employees in a recent survey stated that they felt they "owned their own employability."

Intel turned redeployment from a demand into an employee resource. Through this process, employees saw executives face tough issues head-on and make decisions that were for the good of both the company and the individual. A potentially heavy demand had been transformed into a significant resource.

Summary: Becoming an Employee Champion

HR professionals who work as employee champions focus on finding the right balance between demands and resources. They help legitimate demands on employees, and they help employees to deal with demands by learning to focus and set priorities. They also find creative ways to leverage resources so that employees do not feel overwhelmed by what is expected of them.

To become an employee champion, HR professionals must demonstrate to employees the confidence and trust of ministers, the sensitivity of psychologists, the creativity of artists, and the discipline of pilots. In working to build employee contribution, HR professionals work with managers and employees to ensure that employees can meet their expectations. They develop credibility with employees by listening, respecting their confidences, and being trustworthy.

Line managers should pay attention to employees' needs and ensure employee contribution through activities such as the following.

- Articulating a new employee contract for all employees within the business.

- Setting stretch goals, but supplying the resources that make it possible to reach those goals.

- Reinvesting in employee contribution.

HR professionals complement the line managers' work by undertaking the following tasks.

- Being the employees' voice in management discussions.

- Assuring employees that their concerns are being heard.

- Defining and providing resources that help employees meet the demands made on them.

These activities will help employees to contribute more fully because they will have the competence to do a good job and the commitment to do it right.

Becoming a Change Agent

6

To ADAPT A POPULAR PHRASE, "Change happens." The pace of change today—due to globalization, customer demands, technological innovation, and information access—is both dizzying and dazzling. Steve Kerr of General Electric has captured the challenge of change in his saying "Don't be surprised that you are surprised." His point is that both winners and losers will face increasing amounts of change that cannot be fully predicted, anticipated, or controlled. A primary difference between winners and losers will *not* be the pace of change, but the ability to *respond* to the pace of change. Winners will not be surprised at the unanticipated changes they face; they will have developed the ability to adapt, learn, and respond. Losers will spend time trying to control and master change rather than responding to it quickly.

The necessary range of a firm's responses to change must expand as the pace of change outside a firm increases. Three general response types may be identified: initiatives, processes, and cultural adaptations. *Initiative changes* focus on implementing new programs, projects, or procedures.

Such initiatives (for example, implementing a new organizational structure, customer-service agenda, quality-improvement effort, or cost-reduction program) occur annually in most firms. Through strategic planning, specific initiatives are identified as necessary and are implemented as part of an evolving management-improvement process. *Process changes* within a firm focus on the ways in which work gets done. Firms first identify core processes and then try to improve those processes through work simplification, value-added assessments, and other reengineering efforts. Cultural changes occur within a firm when the fundamental ways of doing business are reconceptualized. The identity of the firm is transformed both for employees and customers.

All three types of change are important. Initiatives that upgrade management quality are equivalent to the daily nourishment a body needs. They replenish the organization with new ideas, insights, and approaches. Processes that change how work is done are like the bodily systems (respiratory system, nervous system, and so on) that keep the body alive. Process improvements redefine the infrastructure of the firm. Cultural changes permeate the soul and mind of the organization. They change how the organization thinks and feels about itself.

HR professionals as change agents build a firm's capacity to handle all three types of change. They make sure that initiatives are defined, developed, and delivered in a timely manner; that processes are stopped, started, and simplified; and that fundamental values within the organization are debated and appropriately adapted to changing business conditions. While the intellectual commitment to change is easy to make, the practical efforts involved in change are difficult. Successful HR change agents replace resistance with resolve, planning with results, and fear of change with excitement about its possibilities. With thoughtful support from HR professionals, many firms have successfully accomplished all three types of change. The following two case studies, from General Electric and Sears, show HR change agents in action: driving initiatives, reengineering processes, and framing cultural transformation.

General Electric

Much has been written about the General Electric (GE) transformation effort since the early 1980s.[1] The early part of the transformation focused on initiatives that restructured the business mix, including both buying and selling businesses and significantly reducing the workforce. By the late 1980s, GE was strategically strong, with thirteen major businesses, each lean, globally positioned, and number one or two in market share.

Since the latter part of the 1980s, GE's management has focused on more fundamental culture change. Under the rubric Workout, a number of initiatives involved GE employees in dismantling bureaucracies, making faster decisions, moving more quickly to serve customers, and getting rid of unnecessary work. Through town-hall meetings in which employees worked with managers to identify and eliminate unnecessary work, GE worked to incorporate the values of speed, simplicity, and self confidence into the organization's culture.

As these new values took hold, work processes needed to be modified. Under the direction of a corporate business development group, six critical processes were identified: order fulfillment, new product introduction, quick market intelligence, productivity, globalization, and supplier management. In each of the major GE businesses, these processes were audited to find areas for improvement. The consequent process reforms resulted in improvements in cash flow, customer service, and employee morale.

The HR function played a major role in all of these GE changes. As businesses were divested and acquired, HR professionals on the restructuring teams helped to determine the value of assets and quality of management of the businesses and to develop an integration or separation process appropriate to each. As Workout spread throughout the organization, many HR professionals became facilitators for and exemplars of the new culture. As business processes were improved, HR professionals identified HR processes (for example, staffing, compensation, training, and communication) that needed to be modified to implement the improved business processes.

When William Conaty became GE's senior vice president of human resources in 1994, he continued the legacy of change. He quickly found that HR employees needed a new vision to help them sustain the commitment to change. The HR function established the following statement of purpose: "To be a credible, visible, value-added business partner." Conaty also articulated four roles for HR professionals at GE, described in Table 6-1, of which managing change was held to be one of the most important. Conaty has described the HR role this way.

Table 6-1 **General Electric's Vision and Roles for Human Resources**

Credible: Relationship of trust with other departments; predictable, dependable service required from all HR professionals, regardless of level, position, function, or activity

Cell	Visible (what HR does)	Value-Added (what HR accomplishes)
Management of Strategic Resources (strategist)	• Design organization • Diagnose organization • Prioritize HR initiatives	Make initiatives real
Management of Firm Infrastructure	• Reengineer HR processes • Ensure HR efficiency • Provide invisible support	Increase service and quality Reduce cost
Management of Employee Contribution	• Champion employee needs • Be the voice of the employee • Provide resources to employees	Make sure employees are committed
Management of Transformation and Change	• Change • Manage processes • Act	Make initiatives happen

I think what's key from a human resources standpoint is anticipating the business needs and trying to define and create what really adds value to business performance. I have no problem getting to the leadership table. And when at the table, you're expected to add some value.[2]

Sears

The face of the retail industry has changed dramatically over the past fifteen years. Small local stores have been replaced by large stores; mall foot-traffic has declined significantly; technology has modified inventory controls; and customer demands for time, reduced cost, and improved quality have become more intense. WalMart embodies the new re-tailer—a high volume, technology-driven service store with low costs. Other stores, even those with long traditions, have had to adapt or fail.

Sears, in the 1990s, has been engaged in a fundamental transformation or cultural change. In 1993, *Business Week* published an article about organizational dinosaurs, firms operating under old assumptions and likely to become extinct. It highlighted Sears, IBM, and General

Motors. While the article may not have garnered total favor among Sears executives, it certainly galvanized their attention.

Under the leadership of Arthur Martinez, the president of Sears Merchandising, many changes were initiated.[3] Unprofitable operations were closed, including the core catalogue business, which had forged the Sears identity for more than eighty years. Product merchandising changed; product brands such as Sony, General Electric, Levi's, and Nike appeared alongside Sears's brands. Sears divested itself of Allstate, its insurance business, to concentrate solely on retailing. It began global expansion by opening stores throughout North America. Its advertising began to focus on the softer side of Sears with a focus on apparel and accessories. Finally, customer service became a major theme through the creation of a positive sales environment among all store associates.

Through all these initiatives, Sears underwent a turnaround. Profits rose dramatically; the stock market responded extremely well; and Sears outperformed its competitors. Sears executives recognized that the turnaround did not equal transformation. Turnaround focused on results; transformation focuses on mindset. Turnaround emphasized short-term activities that affected the balance sheet; transformation focuses on long-term behaviors that affect the thought processes of how Sears works. Turnaround emphasized winning; transformation points out why winning occurs. Turnarounds could be one-time events; transformations have to be on-going processes.

To help architect the Sears transformation, Anthony Rucci, the senior vice president of administration (including human resources), established and chaired a team comprising senior managers from the stores and from the store support organizations (for example, credit, automotive, apparel, brand central). This team crafted the transformation. It focused on creating a vision around 3-Cs: compelling place to shop, compelling place to work, and compelling place to invest. They then integrated initiatives that were underway into this vision. Strategies for becoming a compelling place to shop included consistent in-stock performance, customer-service training, brand-name merchandise, competitive prices, and better advertising (The sales theme, "a softer side of Sears," for example, was developed at this time.) Strategies for becoming a compelling place to work included better communication, education, training, and employee suggestion systems and involvement of all sales associates in decision-making. Strategies for becoming a compelling place to invest included reducing inventories, lowering administrative costs, strategic sourcing, better cost-accounting, and store remodeling.

The senior managers on the transformation team endeavored to make the vision a reality through town-hall meetings where managers and associates discussed the vision and identified actions that they could stop, start, or simplify to make the vision happen in their work units. The team integrated subcommittee work on a total performance index (TPI) that would measure each of the three Cs and provide benchmarks for tracking Sears's performance. TPI scores would serve as indicators of managerial effectiveness and would be tied to long-term incentives. The team structured communications processes (for example, newsletters and employee correspondence) and communications events (for example, an annual chairman's conference) to keep the transformation theme fresh and alive for all employees.

The Sears turnaround was evident in visible short-term results; its transformation will be evident in how associates and customers think and feel about the company. This vignette captures the essence of the transformation effort.

> It is Saturday morning before Christmas. A shopper wakes up hoping to "almost" finish his shopping on this day. His first thought is that Sears will be his primary store for most of his holiday gift purchases. This is a logical conclusion because he has had such positive experiences in recent visits to Sears' stores, high quality merchandise, displayed creatively, and sold with exceptional service.

This vision indicates that the transformation of Sears is not an event or activity, but an image or mindset owned by the customer and created by the associates who serve the customer.

CHALLENGES TO SUCCESSFUL CHANGE

In most studies of whether change works, results lag behind expectations.[4] Answers to the following questions demonstrate the extent to which change often fails to produce change:[5]

1. What percent of people reach their target weight in Weight Watchers?

2. What percent of people maintain their target weight forever?

3. What percent of people stop smoking and never start again?

4. What percent of people stop smoking and never start again after a major physical crisis?

5. What percent of reengineering (or quality) efforts are judged to be successful?

Answers to these questions are often lower than people expect. Five percent of Weight Watchers clients reach their target weight; one-half of one percent maintain it forever. Seventeen percent stop smoking and never start again, and forty-three do so after a major physical crisis. Individual change is difficult. Most New Year's resolutions fall prey to old practices; habits are hard to change and seldom do. If individuals find change difficult, it is not surprising that organizations do too. Twenty-five percent of all reengineering efforts are judged to be successful. Understanding why changes fail may be a first step in overcoming failure. Table 6-2 offers my list of the top ten reasons why changes don't produce change.

While many people and organizations recognize the need for change, few are able to sustain successful change efforts. Many want to change, but few are capable of really accomplishing it. HR professionals as change agents must turn desire into competence by recognizing the challenges to successful change and by building plans to overcome those challenges.

HR professionals can be champions in making change happen. For *initiative and process changes,* HR professionals can create a change model

Table 6-2 **Why Changes Don't Produce Change**

1. Not tied to strategy.
2. Seen as a fad or quick fix.
3. Short-term perspective.
4. Political realities undermine change.
5. Grandiose expectations versus simple successes.
6. Inflexible change designs.
7. Lack of leadership about change.
8. Lack of measurable, tangible results.
9. Afraid of the unknown.
10. Unable to mobilize commitment to sustain change.

pplied to any change initiative or business process to reduce
ssary for and increase the quality of the change. For *cultural*
HR professionals can create the architecture and actions that lead
to new cultures.

INITIATIVE/PROCESS: BUILDING CAPACITY FOR CHANGE

As discussed above, generally only about 25 percent of change initiatives (for example, reorganizations or quality or customer-service improvement projects) are judged to be successful, with success measured in results and the time needed to accomplish those results. HR professionals as change agents, helping their businesses both to meet new objectives and to do so quickly, should consider taking the following steps: (1) identify key success factors for building capacity for change; (2) provide the extent to which these key success factors are being managed; (3) identify the improvement activities for each success factor; and (4) see review of the seven key factors as an iterative process, not an event.

Step 1: Identify Key Success Factors for Building Capacity for Change

Many studies have identified the key factors for successful change.[6] These factors may be categorized according to the type of change targeted: individual change (for example, changing personal habits),[7] team change,[8] organizational change, and societal change. In 1992, General Electric's Management Development Center at Crotonville commissioned a team to examine research and theory on change and to synthesize this research into the key success factors for successful change.[9] This team studied more than one hundred articles, chapters, and books on change and identified the following seven critical factors for success.

- **Leading change:** Having a sponsor of change who owns and leads the change initiative.
- **Creating a shared need:** Ensuring that individuals know why they should change and that the need for change is greater than the resistance to change.

- **Shaping a vision:** Articulating the desired outcome from the change.

- **Mobilizing commitment:** Identifying, involving, and pledging the key stakeholders who must be involved to accomplish the change.

- **Changing systems and structures:** Using HR and management tools (staffing, development, appraisal, rewards, organization design, communication, systems, and so on) to ensure that the change is built into the organization's infrastructure.

- **Monitoring progress:** Defining benchmarks, milestones, and experiments with which to measure and demonstrate progress.

- **Making change last:** Ensuring that change happens through implementation plans, follow-through, and on-going commitments.

These seven critical success factors in change are fairly obvious, and not in and of themselves terribly useful. In fact, most managers can derive most of them with ten minutes' reflection.

Change presents a paradox: If so much is known about it—the key success factors of change can quickly be identified—why do "we" do so poorly at making change happen? HR professionals who act as change agents must resolve this paradox. They must turn knowledge about change into know-how for accomplishing change. They must turn key success factors for change into action plans for accomplishing change.

The first step for resolving this paradox (making what is known improve what is experienced) is to have a clearly defined change model. A model identifies the key factors for a successful change and the questions that must be answered to put the model into action. Table 6-3 summarizes the seven key success factors noted above and lists some of the specific questions that can be used to diagnose the extent to which these factors exist within a company.

Step 2: Profile the Extent to Which These Key Success Factors Are Being Managed

Resolving the paradox of change means turning the seven key success factors from an academic exercise into a managerial tool. Dale Lake, president of Human Systems Development, has brought a personal insight to the

Table 6-3 Seven Key Factors for Success in Making Change Happen

Key Success Factors for Change	Questions to Assess and Accomplish the Key Success Factors for Change
Leading change (*who* is responsible)	Do we have a leader . . . who owns and champions the change? who publicly commits to making it happen? who will garner the resources necessary to sustain it? who will put in the personal time and attention needed to follow through?
Creating a shared need (*why* do it)	Do employees . . . see the reason for the change? understand why the change is important? see how it will help them and/or the business in the short- and long-term?
Shaping a vision (*what* will it look like when we are done)	Do employees . . . see the outcomes of the change in behavioral terms (that is, in terms of what they will do differently as a result of the change)? get excited about the results of accomplishing the change? understand how the change will benefit customers and other stakeholders?
Mobilizing commitment (*who else* needs to be involved)	Do the sponsors of the change . . . recognize who else needs to be committed to the change to make it happen? know how to build a coalition of support for the change? have the ability to enlist support of key individuals in the organization? have the ability to build a responsibility matrix to make the change happen?
Modifying systems and structures (*how* will it be institutionalized)	Do the sponsors of the change . . . understand how to link the change to other HR systems, for example, staffing, training, appraisal, rewards, structure, communication, and so on? recognize the systems implications of the change?
Monitoring progress (*how* will it be measured)	Do the sponsors of the change . . . have a means of measuring the success of the change? plan to benchmark progress on both the results of the change and the process of implementing the change?
Making it last (*how* will it get started and last)	Do the sponsors of the change . . . recognize the first steps in getting started? have a short- and long-term plan to keep attention focused on the change? have a plan to adapting the change over time?

Note: These processes have been developed in work with General Electric and a design team including Steve Kerr, Dave Ulrich, Craig Schneier, Jon Biel, Ron Gager, and Mary Anne Devanna, outsiders to GE, and Jacquie Vierling, Cathy Friarson, and Amy Howard, GE employees.

conception and use of these seven factors. Lake is a pilot. Early in his flight training he learned the importance of rigorously completing the preflight checklist prior to each and every flight. After hundreds of hours in the air, nothing in the preflight checklist is a surprise to him; he knows every item on the list. He has learned, however, that checking *every* item, *every* time improves the probability of a successful flight.

The pilot's checklist provides a metaphor for using the seven factors of change. Considered as a "pilot's checklist" for managing change, these key success factors must be managed in each initiative or change effort. By reviewing *each* factor, *each* time, the probability of achieving successful change increases dramatically.

By thus using the seven factors systematically, in keeping with the pilot's checklist metaphor, the capacity for change in a given organization can be profiled, using the profile tool in Figure 6-1. The corresponding questions for completing the profile are listed in Table 6-4. As those who have the task of accomplishing the change discuss these questions with the attentiveness given a pilot's preflight checklist, they ensure that the resources necessary for making the change happen will be available.

The profiling tool shown in Figure 6-1 has been used in more than one thousand change efforts.[10] In these cases, the profiling questions have served as a diagnostic for assessing the probability of successful change. By answering them, those faced with the task of implementing a change recognize which change factors need work (for example, a shared vision has yet to be developed or systems and structures need to be aligned, and so on); they can then focus their energies on improving these particular factors.

HR professionals as change agents do not carry out change, but they must be able to *get the change done.* By identifying and profiling key factors for change, HR professionals can lead teams through the steps of increasing capacity for change. One organization's management team, for example, having voiced a commitment to "valuing diversity" as one of its priorities for the subsequent year, found in the press of business that the diversity initiative received less action than rhetoric. The HR professional for this business asked the team members to spend two hours profiling where they felt the diversity initiative stood on each of the seven critical success factors for change. The collective profile, shared with the team, led to a useful discussion that eventually moved change forward. This profile is shown in Figure 6-2.

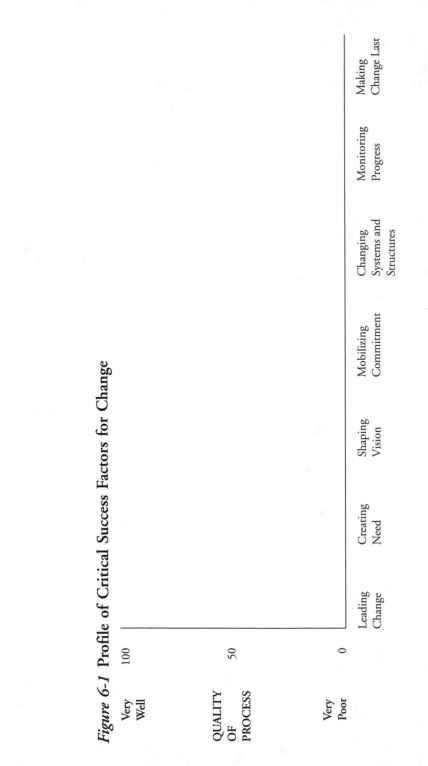

Figure 6-1 Profile of Critical Success Factors for Change

Table 6-4 **Summary of Profiling Questions Regarding Capacity for Change**

Success Factors	Key Question
Leading Change	To what extent does the change have a clear champion, sponsor, or other leader who will support the change?
Creating a Need	To what extent do the people essential to the success of the change feel a need for change that exceeds the resistance to the change?
Shaping a Vision	To what extent do we know the desired outcome from the change?
Mobilizing Commitment	To what extent are key stakeholders committed to the change outcomes?
Changing Systems and Structures	To what extent have we institutionalized the change through systems and structures?
Monitoring Progress	To what extent are indicators in place to track our progress on the change effort?
Making Change Last	To what extent do we have an action plan for getting change to happen?

Their discussion and profile revealed that the diversity initiative would not be likely to succeed without intensive work. The overall scores on the profile were so low that no one should have been surprised that the diversity initiative was flagging. The profile also indicated where attention should be directed. The responsible team had high scores on leading change and monitoring progress. Team members knew who was sponsoring and who was responsible for the diversity initiative, and they knew the measures that would be used to track the initiative. On the other five factors, however, team members recognized that they were far below required minimums. The profiling tool revealed the work that needed to be done and the questions that needed to be answered.

- Create a need for diversity—Why are we seeking diversity? What will be the benefit to the business and its customers?

- Shape a vision of diversity—What would diversity look like? What is the ideal form of diversity for this company?

- Mobilize commitment to diversity—Who needs to be supportive and involved in making the initiative real?

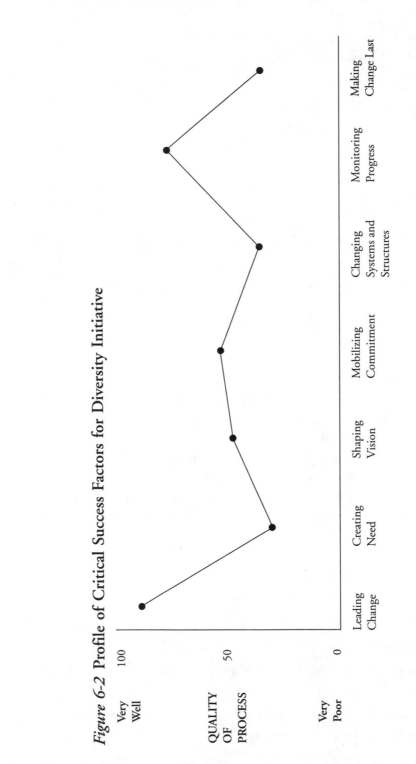

Figure 6-2 Profile of Critical Success Factors for Diversity Initiative

- Change systems and structures to support diversity—How do we institutionalize diversity throughout our management practices (for example, in staffing, hiring, training, performance review, and communication)?

- Make it last—How do we build an action plan for creating and maintaining diversity?

An HR professional, after spending two hours with the management team, was able to assess where the team stood on the change effort, to identify what more needed to be done, and to suggest resolutions for moving forward.

The probabilities of implementing *any* initiative improve dramatically when these seven success factors are assessed, profiled, and discussed. What matters most in the profiling process is not the score but the discussion used to derive the score. HR professionals leading the change should ask questions that point up underlying assumptions. Why did you score this factor this way? What is your evidence? What is the source of your perception?

Step 3: Identify the Improvement Activities for Each Success Factor

After using the profiling exercise to identify the probability of success in a change initiative and to focus the work needed to improve the change effort, the HR professional may help the group to identify activities that will improve performance on those factors that received a low rating. Again, the *dialogue* about the seven factors is generally more important than any "right" answer. The questions in Table 6-4 may be used to discuss action plans for each of the seven success factors.

In the diversity example above, the HR professional used the following discussion topics to focus on the four success factors that most needed attention and the responses to which would constitute an action plan for achieving diversity.

- **Create a need for diversity.** How can we build a business rationale for investing in diversity? What data can we collect to show where our diversity efforts need improvement? What data would communicate to key individuals that we need to make a change?

- **Shape a vision of diversity.** What is the vision or goal of our diversity initiative? What will be different if we accomplish our diversity goals? When will we be able to say that our diversity effort has been successful?

- **Mobilize commitment to diversity.** Who needs to be involved in the diversity effort? How do we get key individuals committed to making it happen? What network of support can we create to enhance the diversity initiative?

- **Change systems and structures to support diversity.** How do we build diversity into our hiring, training, and appraisal processes? What is the communication plan for diversity?

By leading the executive team through discussions of these detailed questions, the HR professional helps derive an action plan for making change happen. One mistake often made by HR professionals as change agents is to believe that they have to own all the actions to make change happen. Not so. The primary job of an HR professional as change agent is to guide those charged with making a change into choosing smart actions. Using the pilot's checklist in Table 6-4 to profile and audit change helps businesses to overcome the paradox of change. Profiling transfers what is known about successful change into what can be done to make change successful.

Step 4: See the Seven Key Factors as an Iterative Process, Not an Event

On any given initiative, the seven key factors for change do not need attention at one stage only. As Sears, for example, began work on transforming its culture, they profiled themselves on the seven factors and identified work that needed to be done. As they proceeded with the transformation, they realized that the work necessary for each of the seven factors was evolving. For example, as shown in Table 6-5, the dominant leadership agenda early on was to identify the change sponsor or champion. Over time, leadership remained critical, but making everyone own leadership responsibility for the transformation became more important than having a single sponsor or champion. Also, in shaping a need and creating a vision, the challenge over time became to enlist and engage the sales associates in the transformation.

Table 6–5 Change at Sears: The Next Generation

	Leading Change	Creating a Shared Need	Shaping a Vision	Mobilizing Commitment	Changing Systems and Structures	Monitoring Progress	Making Change Last
Round 1 Turnaround	Having a sponsor and champion	Seeing the need for trying something new	Articulating the future	Getting key people to participate	Changing management systems	Putting monitoring measures in place	Building action plans
Round 2 Transformation	Making everyone a leader	Making the need for change real to everyone	Making the vision real to everyone	Overcoming resistance to change by gaining everyone's commitment	Rethinking all management practices	Creating new monitoring measures that touch everyone	Learning by doing

HR professionals who act as change agents recognize that periodically revisiting the seven factors for change keeps the change agenda moving forward.

Summary: Initiative/Process: Building Capacity for Change

As organizations make plans, they create initiatives for improvement. HR professionals can be change agents when they rigorously and systematically apply a change process to business initiatives and processes. Following the four steps described above should result in a higher proportion of initiatives that not only happen, but happen faster and more successfully.

CULTURE CHANGE: CHANGING MINDSET

Initiatives for change often evolve quickly from identifying and trying to implement new programs, practices, or processes to more fundamental, or transformational, change. Transformational change differs from change initiatives in that it deals with the fundamental identity, values, and culture of a firm. Known variously as renewal, reinvention, transformation, or reengineering, such fundamental alterations produce what Robert Quinn calls "deep change," that is, change in which deeply held values, beliefs, and assumptions are challenged and modified.[11] In the examples that introduce this chapter, General Electric and Sears were engaged in transformational change. While they worked to change many company practices, the cumulative effect of these changes led to a fundamentally new culture or corporate identity.[12]

HR professionals trying to change an organization's culture face a difficult challenge: Few, if any, mature companies have successfully undergone a complete culture change. To make the GE Workout program a success, for example, the company drew on the expertise of a group of academics and consultants who were assigned to work with the different GE businesses to bring about the targeted overall corporate culture change.[13] This group met quarterly during 1989 to plan and review the progress of the culture change effort in each GE business, with the intention of pooling the various experiences of group members to provide a foundation for the overall GE culture change effort. Discussions during one of the first meetings revealed much about the concepts and practices of large-scale culture change then current. In casual after-dinner conversation, someone asked the experts what companies had successfully engaged in or completed a culture change without a business crisis, so that the GE teams could study and learn from their experiences. In the room were experts with many years of consulting experience, the authors of more than twenty-five books and hundreds of articles. Yet, when these authorities tried to identify companies that had transformed their cultures, the resulting list was very short. Several companies were named that had created *new* cultures—for example, Nike, Apple, Intel, and Microsoft—but, for the most part, these companies had *started* with the new cultures, not created them by transforming something else. Other companies named had come back from the brink of disaster (for example, Harley-Davidson) with a new competitiveness, but these companies' achievements were more turnarounds than transformations. The concept of culture change, propounded by academics in the 1980s, had not yet been fully exploited in businesses.[14] While executives talked and academics wrote about culture change, neither group had yet experienced it.

Since 1989, commitment to and experience of culture change has dramatically increased. No longer is it an abstract form of "non-imitable competitive advantage," discussed in academic circles, but it is at the heart of what many chief executives define as their primary mission. Leading executives such as John F. Welch at General Electric, Lawrence Bossidy at AlliedSignal, Arthur Martinez at Sears, William Weiss at Ameritech, and Michael Walsh at Tenneco talk at length about the importance of culture change for their firms and for their personal success as CEO.[15] A number of consulting firms (for example, Index, Gemini, Andersen, and McKinsey), in responding to their clients' attempts at culture change, have expanded exponentially their change management practices. One consulting firm claims it will need to hire twelve thousand additional consultants primarily to deal with its clients' demands for consulting advice on culture change.

Much has been learned in the last few years about culture change and about how HR professionals play a central role in its accomplishment. In a simplistic way, five steps reflect the essence of the HR professional's role in successsful culture change: (1) define and clarify the concept of culture change; (2) articulate why culture change is central to business success; (3) define a process for assessing the current culture, the desired future culture, and the gap between the two; (4) identify alternative approaches to creating culture change; and (5) build an action plan that integrates multiple approaches to culture change.

Step 1: Define and Clarify the Concept of Culture Change

There are as many definitions of business culture as there are writers about the topic. Some definitions represent culture as unchangeable, that is, in terms of the underlying values embedded and rooted in a firm's history.[16] Others describe culture as totally malleable, in other words, as no more than the behaviors and practices of a firm's employees.[17]

Discussions of business cultures generally begin with a simple premise: Organizations don't act; people do. Understanding an organization's culture requires discerning the shared mindset of the individuals within that organization.[18] Shared mindset represents the automatic thoughts common among the individuals within the organization.[19] Automatic thoughts lead individuals in organizations to act and think without conscious action or thought. Such unexamined acts and thoughts are automatic; they are part of the "way things are done."

Automatic thoughts may be embedded in four organizational processes: work flow, communication/information flow, decision-making/authority flow, and human-resource flow. (See Table 6-6 for a summary of these four processes.) *Work flow* deals with how work is distributed and performed within the organization. *Communication/information flow* deals with how information is created and shared within the organization. *Decision-making/ authority flow* deals with how decisions are made and where authority resides in the organization. *Human-resource flow* deals with how people are treated within the organization.

Shared mindset concerning each of these four processes (and others) comes from information and behavior. Information provides employees with data about the automatic thoughts expected. The more information an employee has, the more likely that the employee will demonstrate a shared mindset. Information may come from a variety of sources, ranging from formal HR systems to informal discussions with fellow employees. The more credible and consistent the information, the more likely that the mindset will be shared. At Harley-Davidson, for example, when Richard Teerlink, the chairman, speaks about the importance of creating a learning organization, he is credible—Rich is the chairman—and consistent—he constantly reiterates the same message and builds it into his training and performance-management programs. As a result, Harley employees share a mindset about creating a learning organization to a greater degree than do employees in other organizations.

Behavior signals to employees what actions are expected. Consistent behavior follows from a shared mindset. Action to change behavior can occur through formal HR practices or informal meetings. Rich Teerlink at Harley-Davidson has institutionalized his commitment to learning by forming Harley University, where leadership development courses translate his values into action; by establishing a Performance Effectiveness Program, through which the value he places on learning is applied to individual performance reviews; and by molding a new organization, in which shared learning is the glue that holds the employees together.

Shared mindset may also exist at different levels of an organization, for the organization as a whole as well as for any entity within it (a division, business, function, and so on). Mindset may be shared both inside the organization, among employees, and outside, between employees and customers or suppliers. A fully shared mindset exists when employees inside and customers or suppliers outside the organization embrace similar automatic thoughts about the organization's processes.

Although difficult to accomplish, a shared mindset may be changed, as it was built, by using information and behavior. The effect of a shared mindset is to commit employees and others concerned to think and act in accordance with the needs and values of the organization. To change a shared mindset, executives must send new information signals and/or change employee behavior.

Step 2: Articulate Why Culture Change Is Central to Business Success

Two assumptions frame the rationale for cultural change: first, that culture affects the performance of a business[20] and second, that old ways are not new ways. Employees who share a culture are more likely to be unified in their actions, and such unity affects performance. It helps a business to focus its resources, to penetrate its markets, to meet customer requirements, and to accomplish strategic goals. In general, the more thoroughly a culture

Table 6-6 Core Organizational Processes Constituting Organizational Culture

Core Processes	Key Questions and Issues to Determine Processes
Work Flow	• Does the organization encourage work as individuals or as a team? Some organizations instill automatic thoughts about individuals working independently, while others attempt to build teams within divisions, across units, and across boundaries. • To what extent does the organization have the capacity to change? Some organizations respond quickly to change; some try to buffer themselves from it. Employees within the organization usually evolve a set of automatic thoughts about how quickly changes are made. Changes may be made in organizational structures, reporting relationships, product developments, technologies, or working patterns. The issue is the capacity of an organization to adapt to change. • How does the organization deal with waste and productivity? Some organizations create automatic thoughts that accept waste and current standards of productivity as givens; others become obsessed with eliminating waste and continuously improving productivity. • How does the organization deal with work priorities? Some organizations try to be all things to all people for fear of excluding or not including an individual or division. Other organizations' work processes encourage public prioritization of projects and activities.
Communication/Information Flow	• How much information is shared in the organization? Some organizations are very open about their plans, directions, and processes. Other organizations keep plans numbered so no one without authorization will see them. Employees come to derive automatic thoughts about information sharing within the organization. • What are the information-sharing patterns within the organization? Some organizations share information one-way, from top to bottom; others develop accepted ways of sharing information so that it moves in all directions: side-to-side, top-to-bottom, and bottom-to-top. The information-sharing pattern of an organization may reflect employees' automatic thoughts about how work gets done. • What is the means of communication flow? Some organizations share information primarily face to face; others through electronic mail, memos, or other secondary means. The means of information sharing often communicates how the organization gets work done.

Decision-making/Authority Flow	• Where are critical decisions made in the organization—at the top or bottom levels? The location of decisions about resource allocation, strategic direction, hiring, budgets, firing, and other critical decisions are indicators of an organization's shared means for doing work. Some organizations have automatic thoughts that most, if not all, decisions are entrusted to top managers and that middle managers and employees are primarily responsible for making recommendations and carrying out plans. Other organizations have more distributed authority and decision-making, with employees carrying more responsibility and ownership for decisions. The extent of employee participation and involvement in formulating decisions may become an automatic thought process among organizational employees. • What is the speed of decision-making? Some organizations have automatic thoughts and accepted norms that decisions, once identified, can be made quickly; others take months of debate, discussion, and dialogue before arriving at a decision. Organizations are often characterized as bureaucratic or open on this dimension of automatic thoughts. • How does the organization balance short- and long-term implications of decisions? Some organizations operate at either extreme: some focus exclusively on short-term decisions and consequences; others primarily on long-term. Most organizations find some balance between the short- and long-term implications of decisions. • How does the organization ensure accountability for decision-making? An organization over time develops expectations for how accountable individuals are for the decisions they make. Some organizations absolve individuals of accountability; others highlight it. Employees are likely to develop a set of automatic thoughts about the extent of accountability.
Human Resource Flow	• How does the organization deal with managerial or employee failure? Does it allow employees to take risks and fail, or does it punish failure and limit risk-taking? One senior manager has argued convincingly that how an organization deals with managers who fail is a critical indicator of the "culture" of the organization. He argued that an organization can be too lenient, not imposing any consequences for failure; or be too strict and "kill the messenger." He argued that either extreme was a strong indicator of the company's overall willingness to change and adapt to new ideas. A parallel issue to failure is success. How does an organization manage an employee's success? Does the organization reward the individual or the team? Does the organization publicize and laud success or quietly accept them as part of business practice?

Table 6-6 Continued

Core Processes	Key Questions and Issues to Determine Processes
Human Resource Flow (continued)	• What is the source of the organization's employee competence? Some organizations generate competence primarily by buying talent from other firms; others generate competence by training and developing their employees. The means of generating competence is often an indicator of an organization's people flow.
	• How effectively does the organization encourage and manage diversity? One critical people-flow issue relates to the ways in which the organization encourages diversity. Diversity may be revealed in obvious ways, such as race or sex, but it also may emerge in issues such as cultural diversity, global diversity, philosophical diversity, and so on. Some organizations try to identify diversity, then quickly eliminate it; others encourage diversity.
	• How does the organization treat individuals? This is a rather generic process, but organizations develop unique automatic thoughts about the "treatment of individuals." Some organizations tend to treat individuals as replaceable parts that can and should be bought or sold as commodities. Other organizations treat individuals as long-term critical investments to be nurtured and maintained.
	• What is the commitment of the employee to the organization and of the organization to the employee? Employees have choices about what firm they join and stay with. Employee commitment to a firm may be based on some combination of economics (this organization pays more), relationships (this organization is a fun place to work, and I like my colleagues), or vision (this organization is an exciting place to be). The basis of an employee commitment indicates an underlying sense of the processes used for getting work done within the organization.

is shared, the more likely that the business will be successful; the cultural consensus and performance curve, however, is more complex than a mere linear relationship.

Figure 6-3 illustrates the relationship between cultural unity and performance. It shows that a firm may have a strong (unified) culture, and yet a drop in performance (Path B), while another firm with a strong culture sees its performance rise (Path A). These different courses illustrate that mere cultural consensus is not enough: It must be the *right* culture. Firms on Path B—more consensus, lower performance—may have wrongly focused their culture on honoring and maintaining traditions, rather than on changing to new norms; they may have focused too heavily on internal processes and have encouraged a one-size-fits-all approach to customer needs. Firms on Path A—more consensus, more performance—may have focused their culture on responsiveness, meeting changing customer expectations, valuing diversity, reinventing the corporation, and constantly reassessing and rebuilding culture. It is easy to brand and dismiss firms that have fallen into Path B; stuck in their past, they fail to renew themselves for their future. In contrast, executives of firms following Path A are con-

Figure 6-3 **Cultural Unity and Performance**

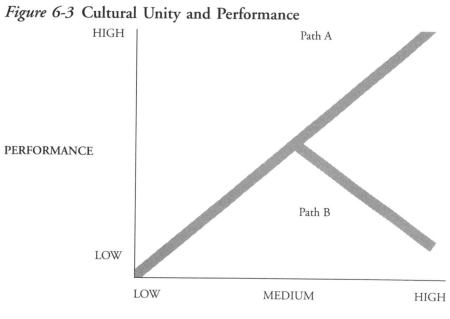

sumed with renewal, with change, and with creation of new cultures. Rich Teerlink at Harley, for example, sees one of his primary responsibilities as the creation of a learning organization that practices old values to maintain integrity with Harley's past while learning new values that will predict and form Harley's future.

Cultural unity also affects performance because it focuses employee attention *on the right issues.* Cultural unity around the wrong values is like setting out for a party and arriving at the wrong house. When a firm's culture aligns with customer expectations, its employees are focused on the right issues, and business performance will improve. At Digital Equipment Corporation, for example, the "hub" cultural statement for decades was to "value differences." This cultural hub permeated management processes. Rather than depend on rules and procedures to guide decision-making, managers disagreed, debated, and explored alternatives to ensure that differences were valued. This worked for Digital because of the market in which it operated. It would not work for the Federal Aviation Administration (FAA), for example, where the cultural hub has always been stability, precision, and rigor. The FAA culture of discipline and dedication to rules and accuracy fits its business requirements as well as Digital's more open culture suits it.

Because of the unity provided by a strong culture, such a culture can become the fingerprint of an organization. These fingerprints become the means by which customers, suppliers, employees, and investors identify an organization, and they provide it with marketplace recognition and acceptance. In the computer industry, these cultural differentiators have been called brand equity; one study provided the following examples.

Apple	simple, easy, friendly
Bull	challenger
Fujitsu	Japanese, reliable, multiactivity
Hewlett-Packard	quality, value
IBM	safe choice, tried and true
Microsoft	creative, easy to use, successful
Sun Microsystems	hot, powerful

John Scully, formerly of Apple, in another example, described PepsiCo and Apple's mission as one of creating "share of mind" not just "market share";

that is, the Apple and PepsiCo cultures were intended to define and distinguish their companies in the marketplace. Cultural fingerprints offer employees identity, a feeling of pride in the way they work for their companies.

Cultures and fingerprints are unique to each firm. Competitors that try to mimic or copy cultures generally end up as also-rans, with little identity. In competitive markets, businesses are always looking for new ways to differentiate themselves from their competitors. When businesses have reached technological parity, and one business can copy another's technology; when businesses have reached product parity, and one business can copy another's product features; when businesses have reached financial parity, and one business can gain equal access to capital—the cultural fingerprint comes to the fore as a viable source of differentiation.

The second assumption for culture change, that old ways are not new ways, also has implications for both a company's internal and its external relations. If businesses existed in static worlds, cultures could be formed and formalized. In reality, businesses exist in increasingly complex and dynamic worlds. As a result, cultures that matched old business needs must give way to cultures that reflect current market trends. The greatest challenge with company cultures is not defining or molding them but in constantly adapting them. At Digital, the valuing differences hub culture was viable during a period of dynamic growth. In the early 1990s, when the global computer market declined and consolidated, this valuing differences culture was augmented by an accountability focus, in which Robert Palmer, the chairman in 1992, encouraged all Digital employees to be accountable to customers, employees, and shareholders. While not denying the importance of valuing diversity and of Digital's legacy, Palmer brought the culture forward to meet changing business conditions.

A key to culture change is to recognize that the new culture must fit changing business requirements. New business cultures are not easy to instill. Employees are much more comfortable falling back into familiar habits. Old shoes fit better than new shoes; old work patterns are more comforting than new ones. A major rationale for cultural change—the need to throw away old shoes that may feel good but that are damaging one's feet—is the replacement of old, comforting ways of working with new, competitive ways of working. Just as people's closets and attics may be stuffed with mementos of sentimental value, organizations may preserve old cultures that feel cozy but become burdensome by failing to respond to change. Closets must be cleaned; attics must be seen to hold remnants of the past; and organizations must learn to let go of old cultures when new ones become necessary.

Step 3: Define a Process for Assessing the Current Culture, the Desired Future Culture, and the Gap Between the Two

The extent to which a mindset is shared may be audited in four steps. First, within the entity to be examined, ask a group of employees (either top management only or an employee cross section) to answer this question: What are the top three things (as a firm, department, or function) we want to be known for by our customers? This question highlights the essential ingredients of a mindset—what we are *known for* by our customers. Second, after collecting the answers from the employee group, cluster the similar responses; the relative numbers of answers in each cluster will provide a measure of the degree of "sharedness." The rule of thumb is that 75 percent of the responses should be in the top three clusters. In the many times my colleagues and I have done this exercise, with many firms, we have seldom found such high (75 percent) consensus. Third, ask a similar question of customers (of the firm, department, or function): What would you like your supplier of choice to be known for? Finally, compare the answers of those inside and outside the firm.

The above exercise audits the shared mindset. It reveals what the mindset is and whether it is shared among employees and customers. At times, employees may share a common mindset, whereas customers do not. This exercise also identifies any gap between present and desired culture. The desired culture is best framed in terms of what customers want the firm to be known for. If cultural alignment begins with customers and then shifts to how employees should perceive the firm, consistent with the customer mindset, unity will follow. Gaps may exist among employees (when they do not share a common mindset) or between employees and customers (when employee and customer mindsets differ).

Step 4: Identify Alternative Approaches to Creating Culture Change

Once a mindset is audited and gaps are identified, the mindset can be changed. Making culture change happen has become less magical and more practical in recent years as more firms have embarked on a wider variety of culture change efforts. Based on experiences at a number of firms, three types of culture change efforts can be distinguished. (See Figure 6-4.) HR professionals working to describe best practices for creating shared mindsets should be aware of all three approaches, of how they interact with each other, and of when to use which approach.

Top-down—directive

One type of culture change effort is directed and driven from the top of the organization down throughout the organization. These forms of culture change initiatives are often sponsored by the senior executives and implemented through a mix of various HR processes (for example, training programs, reward or compensation programs, and corporate-wide communication efforts), and from there they cascade throughout the organization.

Many companies used this type of culture change to implement a quality-focused culture. Xerox, for example, wanted to instill a greater commitment to quality throughout the organization.[21] Under CEO David Kearn's direction, the program Leadership Through Quality was implemented. The

Figure 6-4 Types of Culture Change

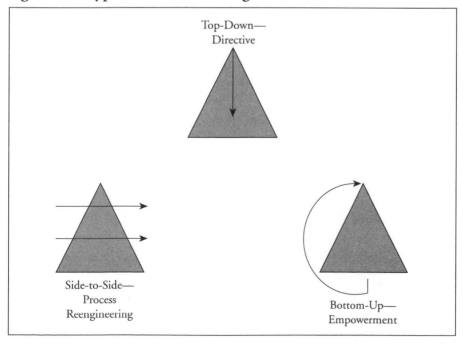

program cascaded throughout the organization following a LUTI model: in this model, managers at one level *l*earn the tools of quality, *u*se the tools in their business, *t*each the tools to the level below them, and, finally, *i*nspect others' work to make sure that the tools were used. In theory, no one could attend the quality program before one's supervisor, because the supervisor was the program teacher.

Many programs attempt culture change through top-down directive initiatives. Boeing has put thousands of its managers through its World-Class Competitiveness program to communicate the changing competitive rules in the airframe business. Motorola's Six Sigma initiative uses training and performance management initiatives to communicate the standards of its new quality-driven culture. AlliedSignal's Total Quality initiative exposed all 85,000 employees to a quality framework. Pepsi's compensation program, Sharepower, aims to increase employee commitment by ensuring that every employee has some form of stock ownership in the firm.

The good news about these programs is that they offer consistent, corporate-wide messages about the importance of the new culture. They also institutionalize the new culture through HR practices that share information and attempt to shape employee behavior. The challenge to these mandated initiatives, however, is that they are often seen as isolated events during which employees are dipped into the new culture for a period of time (the duration of the training) but are not fully converted to it. A series of isolated events may add up to cynicism rather than culture change. In one company, middle managers who were constantly exposed to new corporate programs began to call them AFPs (Another Fine Program); they failed to realize and cooperate with the intended changes in the company's mindset.

Side-to-side—process reengineering

In the early 1990s, a popular approach to culture change developed, an approach based on examining and reengineering business processes for doing work rather than on top-down programs.[22] Process reengineering examines how work is done, then systematically improves the processes for doing work by streamlining operations, leveraging automation, reducing redundancies, and improving the line of sight between work flow and customers.

Process reengineering has been used with dramatic results in a number of firms. Pepsi identified sixteen core processes within the organization (for example, ordering, distributing, and so on) and then worked aggressively to streamline those processes. As work was done more efficiently, faster, with fewer resources, and with greater customer pay-off, enormous cost-savings were realized. Process reengineering has been applied to HR processes as well as business processes. Northern Telecom, through process reengineering, has consolidated many administrative duties into a service center where employee needs are met (with very high standards) through a shared set of resources. This center reduced the duplication of resources, streamlined the organization, and saved money for the company while ensuring that employees (customers of the process, in this case) continued to have their needs met.

Process approaches to culture change assume that as processes are examined and reengineered, the new processes will bring with them a new culture or mindset. The advantage of the process approach to culture change is that the changes become relatively permanent, the new processes provide clear business deliverables, and the processes elicit new information for and behavior from employees. The downside of process improvement is that it takes an enormous amount of time to complete. To map and change even seemingly simple processes requires considerable management attention. The process improvements also may require extensive time to complete before employees see and feel results. Reengineering efforts often rely on technical experts (perhaps outside consultants) who have the technical skills to map a process and then improve it.

Bottom/up—empowerment

A third type of culture change occurs when the desired culture is quickly translated into employee action. This approach to culture change may be illustrated with a simple metaphor. If you were going for a walk and a mosquito landed on your arm, what would you do? The top-down approach to making sure that mosquitos did not attack would be to set up a government program to train people to avoid mosquito-infested areas, to wear long sleeves, and to study the causes of the mosquito problem. The process approach would be to reinvent and reengineer efforts to drain the swamps, spray for mosquitos, and prevent mosquito attacks. The empowerment approach would be to kill the mosquito when it landed on your arm.

Empowerment approaches to culture change are not new, but they have received increasing attention through recent efforts at companies such as General Electric. GE's Workout program lays out the company's desired mindset. Jack Welch, the chairman, wants GE to be known by its customers and employees in all lines of its businesses for speed, simplicity, and self-confidence. To make this happen, he empowered thousands of employees to take out "low-hanging fruit"—work that was counter to the new culture. Bureaucratic reports, meetings, approvals, and measures, for example, were often counter to the new culture. Through town meetings, GE employees identified items that could be changed immediately (killing the mosquito) and made more consistent with the new culture.

Successful empowerment approaches to culture change are more than gripe sessions in which employees come together to complain about what is wrong with the firm. They are built on the principle "no blaming, no complaining," which means that an employee who identifies a problem can't blame someone else or simply complain about it but must move to fix it. Empowerment efforts are more than suggestion systems in which employees offer random suggestions for improvements; they are focused on translating a specific mindset into specific employee behavior. They are more than a series of isolated discussion groups, each offering different opinions about how to improve work; they are integrated sets of activities that empower employees to act based on the new culture.

Step 5: Build an Action Plan that Integrates Multiple Approaches to Culture Change

None of the approaches to culture change is pure; no firm uses one to the exclusion of the other two. Many firms, however, focus on one and may miss the benefits of using multiple approaches. Executives acting to change cultures may begin with any of the three approaches, but they need to learn quickly to use the other two, thus taking a holistic approach to instilling the desired new mindset. When the three approaches are used in parallel, employees receive information and behavior is shaped, leading to sustained culture change.

To build an action plan for implementing culture change, the seven critical success factors for change should be considered.

- **Leading Change:** Identify a sponsor for the culture change effort.
- **Creating a Shared Need:** Ensure that the rationale for the culture change is tied to business results and that a clear reason for a culture-change effort exists and is articulated.
- **Shaping a Vision:** Articulate the desired outcomes of the culture change.
- **Mobilizing Commitment:** Identify key stakeholders who need to accept the desired culture.
- **Changing Systems and Structures:** Realign and redo HR practices to be consistent with the desired culture.
- **Monitoring Progress:** Track and measure the new culture.
- **Making Change Last:** Take specific actions, assign accountabilities and time frames, and integrate multidirectional activities (top-down, side-to-side, and bottom-up).

As HR professionals help executives work through these success factors, they will create an integrated culture-change action plan.

Summary: Lessons Learned About Culture Change

If the meeting held at GE in 1989, discussed on pages 168–169, were to be reconvened today, how would participants' conclusions about the possibility and nature of successful culture change have altered? A number of lessons can be synthesized from the extensive experience with culture change at many firms in the last few years.

First, culture change must add value to a firm's customers. Implementing culture change merely to increase employee commitment is not enough. Culture change must improve a firm's competitive position in the market by changing its identity to accord with customer needs. Culture change at Sears will be complete when its customers have a new image, when they think differently about shopping at Sears.

Second, as with most business lessons, the old concept of equifinality holds.[23] *Equifinality* means that there are many ways to approach and accomplish culture change. No one has discovered a magic checklist or recipe, but effective approaches have been formulated. HR professionals need to think top-down, bottom-up, and side-to-side to architect culture change.

Third, many of the sacred truths of culture change (for example, that CEO commitment or training or participation is key) are myths. As Joe Miraglia, former senior vice president of human resources for Motorola, has noted, culture change has more myths than realities, but culture can be changed through continual management attention to the desired new culture.[24]

Fourth, HR professionals may play a central and critical role in culture change. Their changed agenda requires new competencies and commitments, but the pay-off can be commensurate with the effort. Companies that leverage HR professionals are more likely to change cultures.

Fifth, managing culture change has become one of the new sets of expectations held for HR professionals. Traditional HR practices (for example, staffing, training, performance management, and so on), must today be supplemented with practices ensuring culture change. As HR professionals design and lead culture change, they help their firms achieve transformation.

Finally, it is time to build confidence in the emerging understanding that culture change can and does occur. It matters. It can be defined. It can happen.

HR PROFESSIONALS AS CHANGE AGENTS

If HR professionals are going to be change agents and design and manage both capacity for change and culture change, they need to master four agendas.

Catalyst/Champion/Sponsor

Frontier Communications found that a cultural transformation was necessary for it to compete in the changing telecommunications marketplace. To effect this transformation, Ronald Bittner (chairman, president, and chief executive officer) affirmed a vision of Frontier as the "premier telecommunication company in the world," with a focus on products and customers. He articulated this view in the following statement.

> No vision can be achieved without an able and dedicated employee body. . . . We've undertaken a fresh, critical assessment of the skills and competencies each of our employees must have to move forward.

Where we lack that expertise, we're committed to move it in from the outside.[25]

To help facilitate the cultural transformation, Bittner hired a senior HR executive, Janet Sansone, who was given the explicit task of championing the change effort, with responsibility for ensuring that culture change was part of every management discussion, that models for culture change were created and implemented, and that executive attention on culture change remained high (see pages 54–55). Similarly, at GE and Sears, senior HR professionals were expected to add value by being change agents and champions of cultural change.

Facilitator

In addition to being the champion of change, HR professionals must help facilitate change. This was a primary role for HR professionals involved in GE's Workout program. Three stages of HR facilitation were defined in Workout: external support, internal transition, and management ownership.

External facilitation support was central to the initiation of GE's Workout activities. The external team leaders and team members helped create a receptive climate for Workout. With the political backing of the CEO, they built relationships across levels in the organization and framed Workout goals for each business. This role was an important catalyst in Workout's early stages. As the program moved into a more institutionalized phase, however, the need for external facilitators was reduced, and this role was replaced by that of internal facilitator.

HR professionals supported the external facilitators. They offered technical support that helped external facilitators acquire insight into GE procedures. They offered political insight that helped external facilitators understand relationships and power distribution within the business. Finally, they offered cultural insight that shaped the efforts of the external facilitators by revealing elements of the firm's history and by helping to find areas in which the existing culture was open to change.

Facilitators of internal transition helped GE employees to assume responsibility for examining, managing, and implementing new work processes. Internal facilitators identified and changed work processes and helped task forces reduce cycle time, improve engineering efforts, reduce engineering design time, and examine purchasing times. They participated in on-going team meetings as process observers, and they served the teams as experts in process skills.

Over time, as internal facilitators replaced external facilitators, cultural change was increasingly owned by GE employees. HR professionals played two roles with regard to internal facilitation. First, HR professionals who had business acumen, process skills, and worked well with management teams were at times included in the pool of trained internal facilitators that included high-talent employees from the various professional departments and functions, for example, finance, engineering, marketing, and research. Second, HR professionals were centrally involved in the development of internal facilitator training. This was coordinated and designed centrally by the HR professionals at the Crotonville facility and adapted and implemented at all other locations by the business unit HR professionals. In both cases, the HR professionals were experts in designing and delivering the training programs that could supply a cadre of internal facilitators.

Management-owned facilitation, with each GE manager becoming his or her own facilitator, was the final stage of facilitator focus. Each manager had the ability to diagnose problems; to implement proceedings to examine problems; to demonstrate competence in work-flow assessment, simplification, and improvement; and to build commitment among team members. When the manager became the facilitator, Workout was greatly nourished; the external and internal facilitator crutches were removed, and managers walked the Workout talk. They became owners of Workout, and Workout became an on-going way of business.

HR professionals helped develop management's competence in self-facilitation. They trained managers (again either centrally, through Crotonville, or within each business). They helped to assess current managers' capabilities at facilitation and to select future managers who had facilitation competencies, and they offered counsel and advice for improvements.

Designer

In the cases of GE and Sears, HR professionals redesigned HR systems, thereby playing a major role in company-wide cultural transformation. Staffing, development, appraisal, rewards, organization design, and communication practices were redesigned to allow managers to understand and own the cultural transformation. Designing new systems required HR professionals to move ahead of the culture-change curve, devising and implementing innovative and exciting HR practices.

Demonstrator

The final, and perhaps most critical role for HR professionals assisting culture change is to demonstrate the change within their own function. As Sears, for example, underwent dramatic culture change, Tony Rucci, the executive vice president of administration, worked hard to make the HR function a leading example of effective reengineering and change. He spent an enormous amount of personal time ensuring the commitment of senior HR talent to the effort of reengineering the HR function. By setting the example, other managers have come to respect the HR function as one that "has its own house in order."

Rather than preaching culture change to the choir, HR professionals need to become part of the choir. They need to be able to live and experience first hand the lessons of culture change.

SUMMARY: BECOMING A CHANGE AGENT

Change happens. It always has and always will. If anything, it is happening more quickly now than ever before. To help organizations respond to change initiatives, process changes, and culture change, line managers and HR professionals must master both the theory and the practice of change. In particular, as champions of change, line managers should be responsible for fulfilling the following goals.

- Align internal culture to desired market identity.
- Understand the process for creating a shared mindset.
- Have a model of change that is used throughout the business.
- Keep the pressure on the business for responding to change, even in the midst of creating new strategies.

HR professionals play a critical role as change agents when they perform the following functions.

- Lead transformation by doing it first within the HR function.
- Serve as a catalyst for change, a facilitator of change, and a designer of systems for change.
- Use the pilot's checklist for change with line managers.

By understanding the theory and applying the tools of change, HR professionals and line managers can begin to see change as a friend, not a foe; as an opportunity, not a hazard; as a competitive advantage, not an obstacle; and as a source of value, not a hurdle.

HR for HR

THE FOUR ROLES or deliverables for HR described in the previous chapters—management of strategic HR, firm infrastructure, employee contribution, and transformation and change—require new ways of thinking and
doing HR. Too often, human resource professionals are the cobbler's unshod
children: they design systems, give advice, and help others, but they fail to
apply HR principles to themselves. If HR professionals are to become
partners and play the four roles described, they must champion HR principles within their department. This means building a strategic intent for
the HR function and creating an HR organization to deliver that strategy,
in other words, what Wayne Brockbank has called "doing HR for HR."[1]
In doing HR for HR, three separate but related aspects of the job need to
be understood: strategic HR, HR strategy, and HR organization.

Strategic human resources refers to the process of linking HR practices
to business strategy. Strategic HR is owned, directed, and used by line
managers to make HR strategies happen. Line managers invest in the HR
function through strategic HR. Strategic HR creates a process for moving
from business strategy to organizational capability to HR practice. HR

planning often describes the processes whereby business strategies result in HR actions. Strategic HR serves stakeholders of the business (investors, customers, and employees) who want the business to deliver results.

HR strategy refers to building an agenda for the HR function. HR strategy creates a purpose and focus for the HR function. HR strategy serves HR professionals who want to add value to their business, and it defines the mission, vision, and priorities of the HR function.

HR organization refers to the process of diagnosing and improving an HR function to deliver HR services. It creates a process that ensures HR strategies happen and, like HR strategy, it serves HR professionals in adding value to their businesses. HR organizations are investments by HR executives in HR professionals.

These three issues are related because all focus on helping a business to be more successful. The definitions of and differences among the three concepts are laid out in Table 7-1. Confusion among the three approaches sometimes occurs, as, for example, when HR professionals building organizational capabilities to accomplish business strategies (strategic HR) forget that the HR organization also needs attention (HR strategy). On the other hand, HR professionals may be so invested in making HR operate productively (HR organization) that they forget to provide the organizational and HR processes (strategic HR) necessary for the success of business strategies.

This chapter presents tools and examples of strategic HR, HR strategy, and HR organization—the three components of doing HR for HR. Its goal is to show HR professionals how to translate strategy into results and to build the HR functional capability to meet business plans, which means doing HR for HR.

STRATEGIC HR: TURNING BUSINESS STRATEGIES INTO HR PRIORITIES

Chapter 3 laid out the purpose and processes of turning business strategies into HR priorities through organizational diagnosis. This chapter lays out the process of moving from a business strategy to an HR plan. Many HR executives maintain that this is their primary strategic challenge. Bruce

Table 7-1 **Differences Among Strategic HR, HR Strategy, and HR Organization**

Dimensions	Strategic HR	HR Strategy	HR Organization
Purpose	Translating business strategies first into organizational capabilities and then into HR practices	Building a strategy, organization, and action plan focused on making the HR function or department more effective	Crafting, designing, and improving an HR function to deliver HR services
Owner	Line managers	HR executives	HR executives
Measures	Business results through use of HR practices	Effectiveness and efficiency of the HR practices	Effectiveness and efficiency of HR function
Audience	• Managers who use HR practices for business results • Employees who are affected by HR practices • Customers who receive the benefits of effective organizations • Investors who reap the rewards of organization capabilities	• HR professionals who design and deliver HR practices • Line managers who use HR practices	• HR professionals who work in HR function
Roles	• Line manager as owner • HR professional as facilitator	• Line manager as investor • HR professional as creator	• Line manager as investor • HR executive as leader

Ellig, corporate vice president of personnel at Pfizer, says that Pfizer's personnel function does not create stand-alone HR plans but helps make business plans happen.[2] Anthony Rucci, executive vice president of administration at Sears, says that in his first year on the job he never thought about creating an HR plan; what he wanted to do was to create a business plan that worked, which in turn required the adoption of certain HR practices.[3] In both cases, these HR executives engage in doing strategic HR, turning business strategies into results through HR practices. Traditionally, strategic planning can be divided into two phases: strategy formulation and strategy implementation.

Strategy Formulation without Implementation: Unfulfilled Promises

Strategy formulation serves three purposes. First, it articulates a future direction for the business. This direction may be called a vision, an intent, a destination, a mission, or a foresight, but regardless of the label, it articulates a point of view about the business's future. This point of view generally positions the business relative to its broader business environment of customers, regulators, technology changes, and investors.

Second, strategy formulation allocates resources. Organizations have resources, which may be focused on various purposes (for example, reducing costs, serving customers, improving quality, and so on). Since few organizations have sufficient resources to be all things to all stakeholders, resource allocations must be made. Strategy statements often reflect the outcomes of debates about what priorities should be set and where resources should be allocated.

Third, strategy formulation enunciates promises that reflect commitments made through strategy formulation discussions. Promises may be made to multiple stakeholders. To employees, promises may be made about work opportunities, management actions, or corporate governance. To customers, promises may be made about products, markets served, or value created. To investors, promises may be made about profitability, performance, or shareholder value.

Through strategy formulation processes, executives develop a vision of the future, allocate resources to realize that vision, and make promises to stakeholders about attaining it.

Strategy implementation generally follows formulation. Implementation occurs when organizational practices are aligned with the business strategy.[4] Too often, more strategies are formed than are implemented. Strategic plans are created, but implementation fails to follow. Vision or mission statements are drafted, published, and lauded in executive speeches, but they do not change either organizational practices or individual behaviors. Aspirations are established that articulate a brighter and more competitive future, but these aspirations are never realized. As espoused initiatives falter, resource allocations are never fully instituted. Promises made through strategy discussions are not fulfilled.

Strategic HR and Fulfillment of Strategic Promises: Defining Capabilities

Overcoming the formulation-without-implementation conundrum becomes one primary purpose of strategic HR work. A strategic HR effort attempts to ensure that all strategies are accompanied by clear plans and actions for accomplishing them. An important step to be added to the traditional two-step, formulation-to-implementation process, is the "organizational capability" step. As discussed in Chapter 3, a firm's organizational capabilities represent the processes and practices necessary to make a strategy happen. Many in the strategy field argue that capabilities become *the* important missing link between formulation and implementation.[5]

Strategic HR often connects business strategies to HR actions by defining the critical capabilities required for an organization to succeed. The case study, from Eastman Kodak, illustrates a move from strategy to action through focus on capability.

Strategic HR: Eastman Kodak Company

When George Fisher became chief executive officer at Eastman Kodak in 1994, he was committed to changing not only the performance, but the underlying culture of the company. He revised the company portfolio by selling non-core businesses, and he adapted the corporate culture to fully integrate Kodak's five core values: respect for the individual, uncompromising integrity, trust, credibility, and continuous improvement and personal renewal.

Part of the effort to change corporate culture focused on defining the people strategy to which all Kodak managers would be committed and for which they would be responsible. With the guidance of Michael Morley, senior vice president of corporate human resources, a corporate HR strategy was derived using the following six foci.

- **Performance-driven culture:** Kodak will be a company in which performance standards and accountability to meet those standards pervade all actions and in which employees experience differential consequences determined by their performance.

- **Marketplace competitiveness:** Kodak will be a leader not only on products and services, but on attraction, retention, compensation, and motivation of employees.

- **Valuing differences:** Kodak recognizes diversity as a business imperative. All Kodak employees will learn not only to appreciate but to value gender, race, culture, and other differences; in particular, the Kodak employee population will reflect the global marketplace in which the company operates and the communities in which its facilities are placed. (In the United States, for example, 70 percent of the buyers of Kodak products are women.)

- **Continual learning and development:** Kodak will provide employees with opportunities for education and growth, per employee, a minimum of forty hours per year, and in return Kodak employees will commit to ongoing education and learning.

- **World-class leadership:** Kodak will become known for world-class leaders who can compete in changing global markets.

- **Environment:** Kodak will continue to create a safe and healthy work environment.

These six points formed the backdrop for Kodak's strategic HR work at all levels. They were defined and owned by all senior executives, beginning with George Fisher, the chairman, who had his own personal objectives to work toward in each of these areas.

With the backdrop of this corporate HR strategy, Morley also helped craft a strategic HR planning process for each business. This process answered the following three basic questions.

- **Business issues:** What are the major business issues we face?

- **Organizational capabilities:** What are the organizational capabilities required to meet out business goals?

- **HR practices:** How do we leverage our HR practices to create, reinforce, and sustain these needed capabilities?

These three questions led to a three-step process for the strategies of each of Kodak's business units. The application of this model to the Health Sciences Division, for example, illustrates the general concept and the specific application (see Table 7-2). Kodak's experience shows that between strategy formulation and implementation of HR practices, a definitive set

Table 7-2 Eastman Kodak Company: Business Unit Human Resource Strategy

Business Issues	Organizational Capabilities	HR Practices
General Concept		
What are the major business issues we face?	What are the organizational capabilities required to meet business goals?	How do we leverage our HR practices to create, reinforce, and sustain the capabilities?
Application to Health Sciences Division		
Declining profitability in medical business Technology substitution for traditional products Dramatic health-care policy changes Significant growth potential in underdeveloped countries Changes in customer decision-makers and criteria Customer need for business solutions	The ability to anticipate and respond to change faster and better than anyone else Flexible people, processes, structures, and systems	Staffing and selection Appraisal Rewards Training/development Communications Organization design

of organizational capabilities for moving strategy to action can be articulated, improved, and measured. They constitute a critical ingredient for making strategic HR happen. As Morley has stated,

> In all of our seven businesses, we've assigned HR strategic business partners who work as members of the business management team just as the financial person, or the marketing and sales person, or the production person might. As the business strategy evolves, the HR strategy evolves along with it. It doesn't develop in a vacuum.[6]

HR STRATEGY: SHAPING THE HR FUNCTION

While strategic HR ensures that a company has the resources necessary to accomplish its business goals, HR strategy defines the value created by the HR function. An HR strategy articulates a point of view for the HR function, defining how the work done by HR professionals adds value to a business. HR strategy shapes the HR function by defining the deliverables or outcomes that result from investing in it, justifying the resources it consumes, and helping to set its priorities.

A number of firms have done innovative work on HR strategies. At Clorox, Janet Brady, the vice president of human resources, has worked to create an HR vision. A task force of senior HR leaders and line managers worked with focus groups composed of HR professionals from all areas of the company to draft the following HR vision.

> Ensure improved business performance and competitive advantage by enabling managers to build, develop, and manage employees. We are direct participants in this effort because we are *credible, responsive,* and the products and services we offer *add value and build organizational capability* to meet strategic objectives.

Embedded in this vision statement are the goals of the function, the responsibility for accomplishing these goals, the identity or mindset the HR function wants to establish, and the outcomes or deliverables that the function supports.

At TRINOVA, Debby Schaefer, director of corporate human resources, worked with a team of HR leaders to create an HR strategy or strategic architecture. This HR architecture was established to advance TRINOVA's vision for its HR function, to define how the HR function added value to the business, to reveal any gap between the present and the desired state for each of the deliverables, and to set priorities for effective allocation of HR resources. Table 7-3 summarizes TRINOVA's HR strategic architecture.

TRINOVA's HR architecture has served a number of purposes. A similar strategic architecture had previously been created for each business unit, and by creating a similar architecture for itself, the HR function demonstrated its business credibility to the line managers. In addition, the HR professionals derive from it a focus on what they must do to succeed. The four deliverables—management capability, employee commitment, organizational effectiveness, and administrative efficiency—become definitive results for which the HR function strives, and the architecture sets the priorities that help HR professionals accomplish the deliverables.

Hallmark, too, has established processes for creating both a human resource plan for the corporation, which is owned by the CEO, and a human resource division business plan, which is owned by the vice president of HR within the division. The corporation's human resources plan is designed to identify HR priorities for business strategies, for both the overall corporation and for business units within the corporation. The HR division business plan is designed to identify the priorities and direction for the HR function to ensure that it adds value to the overall business, creates leverage across different business units, and can be measured as a value-adding business unit. Ralph Christensen, Hallmark's vice president of human resources, felt that both plans were necessary because they served different purposes. Table 7-4 summarizes his thinking. This table shows different purposes of and audiences for the two planning efforts. Line managers must own the Hallmark's organization and people strategy, while they are investors in the Hallmark division HR plan. The Hallmark work focuses more on asking the right questions than on providing answers.

Clorox, TRINOVA, and Hallmark show the variety of approaches to HR strategy. Some HR strategies focus more on visions and direction, as at Clorox; others focus more on plans for moving forward, as at TRINOVA; and still others focus more on the processes used, as at Hallmark. Regardless of their focus, HR strategies provide an internal point of view about a company's HR function. These points of view typically include some or all of the eight concepts described in Table 7-5.

Few HR executives create HR strategies that include all eight elements, but many HR strategies include most of them. I am often asked for a formula for devising an HR strategy. While it is tempting to propose a blueprint to which only a few dimensions and details need to be added, such an approach will not produce the most useful HR strategies. More useful results come from identifying the potential elements of an HR strategy and then having these evaluated by an HR executive who takes into account what best suits the company's unique business environment. The closer an HR strategy matches a business approach to strategy, the more likely it is to be perceived as credible within the business. At TRINOVA, for example, the framework for a strategic architecture has been well accepted, so when Schaefer and her colleagues created their HR strategy, they used this framework. At Hallmark, the steps used to created Hallmark's organization and people strategy are the same steps used to create an HR division strategy.

While it is helpful to identify the elements that may be combined to create an HR strategy, it is also useful to see what the products of HR strategies have been. Table 7-6[7] summarizes the HR strategies of thirteen

Table 7-3 TRINOVA's Human Resources Strategic Architecture

Vision: Partner with our business to attract, motivate, develop, and retain the best people who will accomplish the TRINOVA mission

Future Situation

Management Capability
Managers are
- customer focused;
- strategic and results oriented;
- change agents;
- intelligent risk takers;
- possessors of global business acumen;
- people builders;
- team players;
- continual learners; and
- respected by others.

Employee Commitment
- Employees have access to resources to meet needs.
- Employees contribute to organization outcomes.
- Employees take initiative.
- Employee contribution recognized and shared.
- Individual differences and talents leveraged and valued.
- Opportunities provided for feedback, dialogue, and open communication.
- Compensation and benefits competitive.
- Safe work environment provided.

Organizational Effectiveness
- Organization fulfills mission, strategies, and goals.
- Processes are tied to strategies and performance.
- Processes are flexible and adaptable.
- Organization possesses capacity for change.
- Resources are leveraged across organization.
- Work teams are used effectively.
- Compensation systems are flexible.
- HR information system is interactive.

Administrative Efficiency
- 100% fulfillment of commitments.
- Efficient and timely delivery of HR services.
- No non-value-added services or duplication.
- Continuous improvement of processes and reduction of variability.
- Compliance with policy, laws, and regulations.

Strategic Direction

Guiding Principles
- TRINOVA strategy core values.
- Partnering with operating units to support strategy initiatives and business goals.
- HR processes must add value.

People
- Right people, right jobs
- aligned workforce
- communications
- teaming for results
- diverse workforce

Performance management process
- results-driven
- fact-based and documented
- infrastructure
- 360 feedback

External Influences
- Globalization
- Rapid technological change
- Demanding customer requirements
- Innovation

Strategic Direction (Continued)			
• Fast, flexible, and cost effective delivery of programs and services. • Maintain priorities. • Provide continuous learning opportunities.	Continuous learning • education/training/development Compensation/Benefits/Recognition • linked to results and strategy • competitive	Infrastructure • HRIS • Service centers Centers of expertise	• Fast pace of change • Partnering with suppliers • Increasing competition • Capital markets • Sourcing talent • Changing labor relations • Government regulation/policy
Current Situation			
Management Capability Managers are • more internally focused; • momentum-driven; • more short-term oriented; and • working to be more global. Analytic base is growing. Underdeveloped pool of talent.	Employee Commitment • Employee safety a growing priority. • Employees have access to training. • Employees focus effort to educate on EEO. • Employee commitment receives limited measurement. • Rewards principally compensation-focused. • Linkages of merit increases to performance inconsistent. • Performance management inconsistent and non-evident.	Organizational effectiveness • Transitioning to understanding processes. • Moving from hierarchical to flatter organization. • Company-, division-, and function-focus. • Focus on filling positions more than building talent resources. • Compensation systems are rigid and not tied to strategy. • HRIS is narrowly focused.	Administrative Efficiency • In process of consolidating HR services to reduce cost and to share services. • Process in place to reconcile and consolidate HR services. • Efforts to measure and improve effectiveness and timeliness and to reduce variability. • Compliance with policy and laws. • HR data fragmented and not easily accessible.

Table 7-4 **Hallmark's Organization and People Strategy and HR Division Plan**

	Hallmark's Organization and People Strategy	Hallmark's HR Division Plan
Purpose	• To leverage HR practices across the organization • To integrate the separate business unit HR practices • To translate corporate strategy to action	To set priorities for the HR division To articulate a mission/vision for the HR division
Audience	Line owned, HR designed	Line invested, HR owned
Outcomes	HR priorities for the business	Stronger HR division
Step 1: Business Environment	Competitors Customers/consumers Hallmark employee principles Hallmark employee contract for 　Individual dignity 　Performance 　Feedback 　Development 　Consistency	Labor market Internal/external Business plan Hallmark culture
Step 2: Strategy	Business priorities; resource allocation	Mission/vision/aspiration of HR
Step 3: Capabilities	What are the critical things our organization has to be able to do to meet strategy? • Capacity for change • Innovation/creativity • Shared vision • Performance orientation	What are the critical things our HR function must do to meet commitments?
Step 4: Individual Competencies	What are the knowledge, skills, and abilities our individuals need to achieve competence?	What are the competencies required of the HR professionals to make the capabilities happen?
Step 5: HR Architecture	• Workplace: Work flow, relationships, processes, organization, effectiveness, change • Work force: Staffing, development, careers, diversity • Work process: performance management, HRIS, rewards, benefits	Apply workplace, work force, and work process efforts to the HR function itself.
Step 6: Priorities	What should we focus on first to make things happen?	Where should the function allocate its collective attention?

Table 7-5 Issues for Building an HR Point of View

Concept	Definition	Key Question	Outcome
Vision	Quick, energizing statement of why function exists	What is HR trying to accomplish as a function?	**Tag line** (e.g., "HR: part of the solution"; "HR: dynamic business partner")
Mission	Statement of what HR does to add value to the enterprise	What can HR do to add value for and guarantee service to customers of the HR function?	**Deliverables from HR** (e.g., competitive advantage, strategy execution, administrative efficiency, employee commitment, capacity for change)
Values	Statement of what HR believes in as a function	What does HR believe in as a function?	**Principles on which function is built** (e.g., integrity)
Stakeholders	Statement of who HR serves	Who are the major constituents served by HR?	**Clients and their expectations** (e.g., managers, employees, shareholders, customers)
Initiatives	Statement of what programs and services HR could offer	What practices or systems *could* HR design and deliver to add value?	**Organizational diagnosis** (e.g., pillars, 7-S, star diagnostic framework)
Priorities (Goals/ Objectives)	Statement of the top two to four priorities HR will sponsor and champion	What practices or systems *should* HR design and deliver to add value?	**Organizational priorities** for resource allocation
Actions	Statement of an action plan for implementation	What practices or systems *will* HR design and deliver to add value?	**Action plan** (e.g., 7-step pilot checklist)
Measures	Statement of what HR is accountable for	What measures will HR use to indicate its success?	**Benchmarks and tracking indicators**

Table 7-6 Summary of HR for HR: Examples of Directions

Company	Vision	Mission	Values
Anheuser-Busch	". . . enabling employees at all levels to better understand their company and the role they play in its success."	"Our goals are to . . . • maintain our reputation for the highest-quality products and services; • market our products aggressively, successfully, and responsibly; and • increase our share of global beverage sales through quality products."	
AT&T	"We share a passion for delighting customers and for achieving business results through innovation, continuous learning, and empowerment. . . . We are respected and admired worldwide as the key source of competitive advantage. We make AT&T a very special place."	"We are dedicated to being the world's best at bringing people together, giving them easy access to each other and to the information and services they want and need anytime, anywhere."	"Common Bond: • respect for individuals, • dedication to helping customers; • highest standards of integrity; • innovation; and teamwork."

Initiatives	Priorities	Actions	Measures
"Our products and people . . . • quality as the cornerstone • business and personal integrity • pride in all levels of business. Our work methods . . . • a sense of urgency • teamwork • long-range planning • innovation and creativity • learning • full debate, close ranks. Our working conditions . . . • encouraging employees • motivating employees • caring for employees • honest expression by employees"			
"• leadership, and education, and training • workplace and work force of the future • globalization • inventing the next generation of human resources"	"• Transformation of leadership, workplace, work force, and global talent • Transformation of talent with HR systems and levers: • rewarding talent • education of talent • staffing talent • surplus of talent • diversity of talent • health of talent • human side of quality"		

Table 7-6 **Continued**

Company	Vision	Mission	Values
Banc One	"National leadership; Line of business orientation; Commitment to excellence; and Quality customer service."	"HR serves its customers in meeting business and strategic objectives through people."	"HR services imperatives. . . • achieve fairness, • consistency, high • performance, and responsiveness • reduce administrative costs • align services with national strategy • support corporate culture of new BancOne"
Delco Chasis	"To become a dynamic 'learning organization' where people are enthusiastic partners in attaining organizational objectives."	"To provide an HR presence which accentuates the achievement of business objectives. To provide employees with a balanced work environment so their success translates to customer enthusiasm and organizational success."	"We believe in . . . • customer enthusiasm; • commitment to excel; • a supportive work environment; • continuous improvement; and • employee involvement."

Initiatives	Priorities	Actions	Measures
"• Functional revitalization • Benefits project • Payroll consolidation • Staffing/employment reengineering • Employee development project • Compensation standardization"		"• Future senior management are responsible for people development. • Future employees form a relationship with Banc-One that is explicit, dynamic, and flexible. • Future HR teams are skilled consultants who partner with management to develop and deliver HR management. • Future HRIS is user-friendly, integrated, and accessible."	
"What we must establish to be winners: • customer-driven functions, processes, and actions • feedback processes • effective selection, career development, relationships, diversity, global experience • effective training and participatory culture • understanding of leadership • HR processes at each organizational level • benchmarking • target compliance			"• Customer feedback process • Reduced supervisor spans • Diversity measures • Reduced absenteeism • Employee survey results • Increased productivity"

Table 7-6 **Continued**

Company	Vision	Mission	Values
First of America	". . . to develop, implement, and administer HR policies, practices, and programs which are responsive to and support the strategic direction of the Corporation and which will create a competitive advantage within FOA's greatest resource in its employees."		"This will be accomplished through the establishment of programs that will attract, motivate, reward, and retain employees of the highest caliber such that superior rate of return will be generated for our shareholders."
Fortis	"Enhancing the effectiveness of Fortis people . . . together."	"We will enhance the effectiveness of Fortis people by working with them to help Fortis become a recognized leader in the financial services and insurance industries."	
Frontier Communications	"Consistent with corporate vision: premier company in telecommunications industry."	"By providing products, services, and applications that delight our **customers**; by being a team of qualified **employees** committed and accountable to that vision; by delivering exceptional returns to **owners**."	

Initiatives	Priorities	Actions	Measures
"• select and retain the best people • create a climate of continuous learning and improvement • develop current and future leaders • promote health and wellness • promote understanding through open communication"		"We strive to work hard, add value, and have fun!"	
"• Create core competence model of managerial behavior • Provide standards, measures, rewards based on business results (pay for performance) • Perpetuate leadership of the company • Unify corporate staffing • Establish corporate pipeline			"• Business unit measures • Employee survey results • Assessment of high potential talent • Reducing in staffing costs • Integration of new acquisitions • Productivity"

Table 7-6 Continued

Company	Vision	Mission	Values
Frontier Communications *(continued)*			
LaFarge Corporation	"HR's goal is to develop the people, programs, and organizational structure with the characteristics to lead the company through this and future change. HR's role is to emphasize the People and Organizational aspects of accomplishing the company's business objectives."		
Public Service Gas & Electric (PSE&G)	"The mission of HR is to be a partner in creating the organization that supports PSE&G's vision and that gives us a sustainable competitive advantage in the energy service industry."		"It is the goal of the HR community to partner with clients to create a workforce with a sense of urgency."

Initiatives	Priorities	Actions	Measures
"• Provide corporate with tools to drive change • Utilize and enhance communication as a lever for change"			
"• Responsive and accountable matrix • Create competence • Consistent, coordinated visions and programs around safety • Provide information quickly"			
"• Adapt to change and leverage change • Encourage, recognize, and reward contributions from all associates • Execute business decisions • Have high level of commitment and excitement about company and have responsibility for business results."	"• Build shared mindset • Attract qualified diverse workforce • Enhance performance management system • Nurture work force environment • Design new organization"		

Table 7-6 **Continued**

Company	Vision	Mission	Values
Quantum	"Drive organizational and people capability to inspire breakthrough performance."	"As a valuable resource to our business partners, HR . . . • provides innovative systems, tools, and programs for capability • addresses strategic needs • supports managers in developing environment of learning • efficiently executes and delivers"	
Raychem	"Orchestrate peoples' talents for competitive advantage"	"In partnership with Raychem's businesses, design and maintain integrated state-of-the-art HR systems and programs to contribute to the overall effectiveness of the organization."	"Delight the customer; continuous improvement of Raychem values."
Sony	"To be the best in the world at identifying, acquiring, developing, and retaining human competencies required for Sony's competitiveness and customer satisfaction."	"We want Sony people to feel respected, treated fairly, listened to, involved, and committed. We must create and maintain a company culture in which people have the opportunity to contribute, learn, grow, and increase their wealth."	"Sony HR people need to demonstrate . . . • toughness and discipline • pride • ability as self-starters and team players • integrity, trust, and fairness."
Suncor	"We consistently deliver outstanding achievements in Canadian petroleum and related business."		"The ideal workplace is challenging, stimulating, and fair, a place where each employee has the opportunity to grow and accomplish;

Initiatives	Priorities	Actions	Measures
"HR key processes . . . • communication • process focus • staffing/diversity • training/develop-ment • performance man-agement • organization/team development • total compensa-tion and recogni-tion programs"			• Establish product development teams • Sourcing/recruit-ment • Alignment • Drive for excel-lence • Leadership devel-opment • Upgrade core HR processes • Cultural Rein-forcement • Education
"STRATEGIES: • Partner with man-agement teams; • Guide change pro-cess; • Enable leadership development; • Share and Reward success."	"Development: cre-ate a continuous learning organiza-tion. Management: make management re-sponsible to moti-vate and develop employee."	"Enact policies on . . . • people develop-ment • compensation • equal opportunity • ethics • safety/environ-ment • communications"	
"• Seize opportuni-ties • Capitalize on ex-isting core assets • Ensure excellence in execution of all businesses"		"Industrial Rela-tions: union, safety, health issues. HR Development build talent of work-force at local level. Personnel Services:	

Table 7-6 Continued

Company	Vision	Mission	Values
Suncor *(continued)*			a place where commitment is freely given and the desire to outperform competitors is strong."

companies, using various materials that they have circulated internally and made available to the public. As this table shows, many companies work hard to define the vision, mission, and values of the HR function. It is not surprising that HR strategies suffer some of the same shortcomings that strategic HR efforts do: More time is spent anticipating a future than creating an operational plan for getting there. This leads to the third component of HR for HR, the need for organizational diagnosis to ensure that HR strategies happen.

HR ORGANIZATION: ORGANIZATION DIAGNOSIS TO BUILD HR INFRASTRUCTURE

An HR strategy sets the destination toward which the HR function is headed; an HR organization provides the road map for getting there. An HR organization may be strengthened by following the organizational diagnostic process outlined in Chapter 3 for becoming a strategic partner.

Step 1: Define an Organizational Architecture

The architecture presented in Table 3-5 describes six factors that can be used to create a stronger HR organization.

- **Shared mindset:** The extent to which the HR function possesses a shared mindset, or common identity.

Initiatives	Priorities	Actions	Measures
• Earn exceptional loyalty in all relationships • Set and attain aggressive standards • Encourage individual and • collective contribution		Do administrative work (e.g., benefits). Communications: share information. Commitment: engage employees.	

- **Competence:** The extent to which the HR function is staffed by individuals who have knowledge, skills, and abilities to perform their current and future work.

- **Consequence:** The extent to which the performance management system used by HR professionals focuses on the right behaviors and outcomes.

- **Governance:** The extent to which the HR function has effective reporting relationships, communications, decision-making, and policies.

- **Work processes/capacity for change:** The extent to which the HR function learns and adapts, and thus understands and improves processes.

- **Leadership:** The extent to which effective leadership permeates the HR function.

These six factors represent the building essential building blocks of an HR organization.

Step 2: Create an Assessment Process

An HR organizational diagnosis turns an HR architecture into an assessment tool. As such, the factors identified in the architecture suggest assessment or audit questions for probing the strengths and weaknesses of the HR organization. Table 7-7 demonstrates how the six factors of the organizational architecture can be used as diagnostic tools for examining an HR function. In this table, the six factors, listed at the left, have been turned into assessment questions that focus on the extent to which the factor helps

Table 7-7 Assessment of HR Organization-Capability Architecture

Strategy: Given our HR organization's strategies and expected capabilities, how would we rate ourselves on each of the following management actions necessary to accomplish our strategy?

	Question	Rating (1–10)	Best Practice
Shared Mindset	To what extent does my HR organization have the right shared mindset (culture)?		
Competence	To what extent does my HR organization have the required competencies (knowledge, skills, and abilities) to reach future goals?		
Consequence	To what extent does my HR organization have the right performance management system (measures, rewards, and incentives) to reach future goals?		
Governance	To what extent does my HR organization have the right organizational structure, communication, and policies to reach future goals?		
Work Process/ Capacity for Change	To what extent does my HR organization have the ability to improve work processes, to change, and to learn in order to reach future goals?		
Leadership	To what extent does my HR organization have the leadership required to reach future goals?		

accomplish HR strategy. The rating column suggests using a simple metric (1 = low, 10 = high) for the evaluation. The precise numerical score assigned each factor is less important than the discussion evoked during the assessment process. The Best Practice column provides space for identifying targeted improvements in practices.

As in assessments of organizational capability, the assessment process may be undertaken in an informal or a formal way. Informally, for example,

HR executives may use the assessment tool in Table 7-7 when they create their HR strategy. More formally, it may be used to collect data about HR performance relative to strategy from HR professionals, line managers, customers, employees, and other stakeholders. The assessment may be done by a task force of HR professionals within the firm, by external consultants or advisors to the firm, or by clients within the firm.

Step 3: Provide Leadership in Improvement Practices

Improving the HR organization requires modifying management practices that the organizational audit has identified as weak. By pursuing the activities described below, the HR function applies to itself model HR practices. When this happens, these practices become the building blocks of the HR organization.

Shared mindset

A shared mindset within the HR organization is reflected by a unity in answering the question, "What do we, as an HR function, want to be known for by our customers?" As when calculating the shared mindset within a business, HR organizations should strive for 75 percent in their internal shared mindset. The shared mindset should include both HR employees and their customers.

In work with many HR departments, I have found that the shared mindset exercise often follows a predictable track. Each HR professional is asked to provide three answers to the question, "What do you want to be known for by your customers?" After the responses are collected and tabulated, the percent of answers clustered into the three most common categories is determined. This number, divided by the total number of answers, yields the degree of shared mindset among participants. I generally find that even HR groups with a clear vision and mission show agreement only in the 35 to 60 percent range. These HR professionals want to be known for many noble and good qualities—for example, they strive to be proactive, aggressive, innovative, risk takers, credible, and so on—but they lack a *shared* mindset about what they want to be known for.

The discussions that follow this revelation center on the importance to the HR community of having a common mindset or identity. I often encourage the HR professionals to think about their function as though they were its stakeholders: "What would make *you* excited about using your services? What image would you like implanted in the mind of your customers about who you are? What would you like to tell new recruits in the function about your identity in the company? What image of HR would you like top executives to present the board of directors?" These questions generally lead participants to a consensus about the mindset they want to create for their function.

Competence

Research has revealed four major categories of HR competencies: knowledge of business, delivery of HR, management of change, and personal credibility.[8] After an organization has assessed its competencies and identified any gaps between current versus required competencies, it must select one of three options for improvement: buy, build, or borrow.

Buying competencies means hiring talent from outside the organization. Some HR organizations have done this quite dramatically. Don Redlinger, the senior vice president of HR for AlliedSignal Corporation, replaced a large portion of his senior HR staff with HR professionals from outside Allied, who brought with them many new perspectives. Buying competence may also be done in a more targeted way. A system proposed by Warren Wilhelm,[9] who consults widely in HR, involves hiring key individuals into visible positions from which they can influence the overall direction of the HR organization. When Tony Rucci became the executive vice president of administration at Sears, he did not instigate a wholesale outsourcing of the existing HR staff, but he did hire a handful of key senior HR executives from outside Sears to set a new tone for the entire function.

Building competencies results from upgrading the skills and knowledge of current HR professionals through training and development. Skill improvement may take place through formal training, job assignments, career mobility, task-force assignments, or other forms of development. A number of companies have invested in the development of their HR professionals to build their HR talent base.

Borrowing competencies involves forming a joint venture, partnership, or alliance between the HR function and a group outside it. A common type of partnership consists of a contract between a consulting firm and an HR function, under which the consultants deliver HR services to the HR function and to the firm of which it is part. Such outsourcing arrangements give firms competence without the obligation of owning it.

Consequences

Consequences represent the standards and measures that HR professionals must meet. The key to this aspect of the HR improvement process is ensuring that HR professionals have a performance management system that encourages behaviors consistent with desired business outcomes.

HR professionals are often their own worst enemies when it comes to performance management. Although they design and advocate their company's performance management process, they often fail to apply it within their own department. Successful application of performance management requires meeting the following three goals.

1. Set standards for expectations from HR professionals. These standards may be behavioral (what HR professionals should do) or involve outcomes (what HR professionals accomplish). They should be understandable, controllable, significant, and supported by a convention of shared commitment to their accomplishment.

2. Make rewards contingent on meeting standards. Rewards motivate HR professionals just as they do everyone else. HR professionals should get paid according to their performance. Nonfinancial rewards—celebrations, opportunity to do interesting work, and so on—should be used in the HR function as well as in other parts of the business.

3. Collect and share feedback on results. Feedback on how well HR professionals attain standards can be monitored. Some of the best feedback comes from self-monitoring using the HR professionals' own tracking indices. Receiving timely, helpful, and candid performance reviews helps HR professionals set and accomplish goals.

An effective performance management system for HR professionals demonstrates that consequences exist for good or bad behavior. By identifying the more competent and capable HR professionals, their performance standards are reinforced.

Governance

Governance deals with the organization structure for delivering HR (see Chapter 4) and the infrastructure required to make delivery work. An important and often underutilized infrastructure process is communication. Individuals in many HR functions do valuable work that is never acknowledged because no one in the company knows about it. Communication of

HR agendas, goals, activities, and results does not mean bragging and overselling what is not there. Effective communication of HR practices and policies involves sharing messages about implementation of innovative HR practices, about how HR professionals add value to the business, and about how HR functions are helping meet business goals. HR for HR means that HR professionals spend some time marketing their success, packaging the work they have done so that managers and employees throughout a firm can appreciate it.

Governance also implies the fair and equitable administration of policies. The HR function should represent a model for how to treat employees. Formal corporate policies regarding discrimination, sexual abuse, child care, absenteeism, leave, telecommuting, and so on, should be innovatively modeled within the HR function, as should informal policies concerning treatment of employees, valuing differences, work flexibility, and so on.

Improving governance within the HR function may involve restructuring how work is done, focusing on communication and marketing of ideas, and on fairly applying policies within the function.

Work processes/capacity for change

An HR function may conceive of its work as a series of processes designed to help the business compete (see Chapter 4 for examples). Too often, HR functions are seen as lagging behind in innovation, flexibility, and change, as the caretakers of tradition, embodied in policies and procedures, rather than as trailblazers.

To improve the HR function's speed, agility, and responsiveness, HR professionals must take risks, experiment with new programs, seek new ideas and approaches, and move ideas rapidly into action. Using the following simple diagnostic exercise, an HR department can assess its speed in responding to shifts in market and business and HR strategies.

- **Question 1: What is the pace of change in your industry?**
  Generally, using a scale of 1 to 10, the score for this item is very high. Most HR professionals recognize that customers, technology, regulation, globalization, and other environmental forces are changing quickly.

- **Question 2: What is the pace of change in your business's strategy?**
  Again, on a scale of 1 to 10, this item scores high. Companies articulate new business strategies almost as rapidly as the external environment changes.

- **Question 3: What is the pace of change in your firm's HR practices to accomplish those strategies?**
  On this question, scores generally plummet. HR practices often outlive the environments and strategies for which they were created. While the environment and strategy changes are evident, the HR responses lag.

Improving the HR function's speed, agility, and responsiveness requires taking risks and understanding the processes necessary for making change happen quickly (see Chapter 6).

Leadership

Creating HR leadership is not a trivial task. Some HR search firms have struggled for months to fill top HR jobs, not because of a lack of commitment on the part of the hiring firm but because of a perceived lack of the talent needed to fill the job. These jobs have salaries that exceed almost all other staff salaries.[10] The individuals in these positions report to the CEO or president and are given the challenge of creating and transforming organizational cultures. These are exciting jobs. They go unfilled because the talent to meet these requirements is scarce.

Leadership of the HR function requires top-quality HR professionals who can wear multiple hats. As members of senior management, they participate fully in business decisions and can ensure the success of their businesses. As leaders and managers of the HR function, they must be both visionaries and realists.

Step 4: Set Priorities

Step 4 of organizational diagnosis requires setting priorities, focusing the attention of the HR function on a few critical issues. Using the criteria established in Chapter 3—impact and implementability—the HR function can set priorities for developing HR practices. These practices build the infrastructure of the HR function making possible effective delivery of HR strategy and implementation of strategic HR.

CASE STUDY: STRATEGIC HR, HR STRATEGY, AND HR ORGANIZATION AT AMOCO

Amoco, a large, diversified oil firm, operates in three primary areas: upstream (exploration and production of oil and gas), downstream (refining, distribution, and marketing), and chemicals (products related to oil). One of the world's largest fully integrated oil companies, it has operations around the world.

Amoco's HR function was traditionally divided into three parts: corporate HR, operating company HR, and business unit HR. Corporate HR had a strong voice in setting policies, defining the corporate HR agenda, ensuring dissemination of management philosophy and practice throughout the firm, and delivering centralized services. Operating company HR created HR practices and agendas for the company and oversaw implementation of corporate HR efforts. Business unit HR implemented policies, supported unit business strategies, and provided HR services to the business unit.

In the late 1980s, Amoco executives, under the direction of Larry Fuller, the president (and now chairman), and Wayne Anderson, senior vice president of human resources, felt that the firm needed to change its traditional culture and mindset to become more competitive. With other line executives, they embarked on a renewal process throughout the company. This process began in earnest in 1988 at a senior management conference at which top executives gathered for four days to talk about people-related issues. Participants agreed that optimizing the productivity and creativity of Amoco's people was critical to the organization's long-term competitive success. As a result of this meeting, a number of HR initiatives, including the following, were instituted.

- Redesign of the existing performance appraisal system into Amoco Performance Management (APM), a more comprehensive process for setting standards, establishing development activities, giving feedback, and allocating rewards based on performance.

- Development of a recognition and reward process (R&R), which highlighted and rewarded employees and teams for extraordinary performance.

- Reengineering of the recruiting process to focus selection on a combination of defined skills and behavioral values.

- Development of employee surveys to monitor and assess attitudes about the organization's values, performance, and effectiveness.

Again, the intent of investing in these initiatives was to create an Amoco organization that could anticipate and respond to changing business conditions and beat the competition.

In 1990, the corporate mission, vision, values, strategies, and goals were articulated. The mission, vision, and values were designed to weave together in one framework both business and organizational initiatives for renewing the company. The goals included a focus on creating organizational capability throughout Amoco, in support of which point Anderson made a presentation to Amoco's board of directors.

Along with a major communication of the mission, vision, and values, Amoco in the early 1990s invested heavily in diversity, learning and development, career management, and compensation. The company encouraged diversity in all personnel decisions and emphasized diversity awareness through the formation of diversity councils. Amoco managers, to ensure their alignment with Amoco's strategic direction and renewal process, attended the new Amoco Learning Center for instruction in basic and cutting-edge management concepts and practices. A career management process emphasized each employee's responsibility for managing his or her career. And, finally, the company instituted a compensation philosophy that incorporated incentive pay practices and stock ownership, and that later evolved into a market-based pay concept, under which people inside Amoco were paid commensurately with what employees at other firms in the industry were paid.

At the 1993 Worldwide Senior Management Meeting, discussions centered on Amoco's goal of becoming a strategically managed company, meaning that the corporation wanted to find ways to synergize work across the firm. A study of corporate centers was initiated, which led to a major reorganization of Amoco in 1994. Amoco's three operating companies were replaced by an organization that distributed operating accountability to seventeen business groups. A shared services organization now combined staff groups from the three operating companies and fourteen corporate departments into a function that acted as a partner, providing staff expertise to each of the business units (see Chapter 4). Corporate departments were downsized, and their responsibilities were focused on corporate strategy and policy rather than providing service support to business units. Three small sector organizations were created to serve as a liaison between the business groups and corporate executive management.

These structural changes were accompanied by a major shift in culture from centralized and controlled to decentralized, with the focus of activity shifting from corporate to the business groups, supported by Shared Services and corporate units.

To support these changes, a leadership philosophy calling for increased accountability, continuous improvement, and coaching was developed, articulated, and disseminated throughout Amoco. Successful leaders at Amoco would henceforth stress downward delegation, teamwork, flexibility, trust, and collaboration. Under this philosophy, each employee was to become a leader.

While the corporate centers study was taking place, a task force composed of HR and line managers was working to develop a set of people strategies for the company. In late 1993, the Strategic Planning Committee and the Board of Directors committed Amoco to the key people-strategy action steps listed below.

- Build an organizational-capability assessment process into the strategic planning process for all business units.

- Develop specific action plans to build and maintain required organizational capabilities, including individual competencies.

- Implement a people-strategy framework.

- Reexamine people policies to provide greater flexibility to business units to maximize cost-to-value ratio.

- Develop and communicate a global vision, assess required organizational capabilities, and develop needed capabilities to become more global.

- Complete and communicate an employment philosophy.

More specifically, Amoco created its people-strategy framework to complement its operations and financial strategies. Essentially, Amoco's traditional people philosophy had been based on establishing uniform policies for managing people, viewing people as costs versus investments, expecting a lifetime employment commitment, and being in the middle of the oil company pack in terms of pay, benefits, and employment policies. The new Amoco philosophy encouraged more flexibility, a focus on the value created by its employees, global work processes, strategy-driven people practices, and a more aggressive HR function.

One major result of this people-strategy effort was identification of organizational capability requirements for each business strategy. Table 7-8 outlines the strategic management process steps for all Amoco businesses and demonstrates the utility for Amoco executives of the organizational-capability assessment step. An HR organization-capability

Table 7-8 **Amoco's Strategic Management Process**

Strategy Creation	Visioning	Create picture of desired future
	Situation analysis	Assess strengths, weaknesses, opportunities, and threats
	Strategy development	Determine direction for each business (e.g., strategic alliance/joint ventures, responsiveness to market, cost leadership, buy/sell assets, customer focus, global expansion)
Organizational Capability Assessment	Identification of capability requirements	Define organizational capabilities (i.e., structure, work processes, individual competencies, and reward/ measurement systems)
	Gap analysis	Assess current vs. desired state
Strategy Execution	Implementation planning	Identify steps to implement the strategy and develop required capabilities
		Assign accountabilities
		Develop measures
Measurement and Feedback	Evaluate progress and improve	Assess progress toward achievement of strategic milestones and development of required capabilities
		Make adjustments to improve

Source: Reprinted with permission of Wayne Anderson at Amoco Corporation.

group was formed to help business units to define and assess capabilities and to define actions to develop capabilities. The corporate senior executives modeled these steps and identified capabilities critical to the success of Amoco's corporate strategy. The application of this framework is shown in Table 7-9.

The organization-capability assessment process also represented a methodology for establishing HR priorities based on business strategies. In addition, Chairman Fuller articulated four major expectations for the HR function, listed below.

- HR must have a knowledge of the business.

- HR must have a knowledge of HR.

- HR must have an ability to lead any change process.

- HR must have the leadership ability to influence the organization.

To accomplish these expectations, HR's mission and vision were reviewed and its responsibilities for implementation were defined. This HR mission directed HR to develop people strategies and to recommend policies, programs, and practices in support of those strategies. Simply stated, if an HR practice or proposed practice did not align with Amoco's values and business strategy, that practice would be discontinued or would not be implemented. Management's role then became to approve, take ownership of, and determine the timing of the people strategies and corresponding policies, programs, and practices. The HR function became accountable for providing the needed tools to help management effectively implement the people component of Amoco's business strategy.

Anderson and the HR senior management defined four roles for Amoco HR professionals: strategic people-planning, people acquisition and development, organization design and development, and administration of people policies, programs, and practices. In addition, they defined three strategies for shifting HR focus from administration to consultation and development work (see Figure 7–1).

To help make this shift, Amoco's HR invested in itself. The HR organizational structure was changed by moving much of HR into Shared Services. Performance standards were made clear and aggressive, and HR professionals were given greater accountability for meeting

Table 7-9 **Revised People Strategies Driven by Amoco Strategic Framework and Organizational Capabilities Required to Execute Business Strategies**

External and Internal Environment	• New competitors (foreign national oils, well heeled independents) • Weakened demand • Loss of oligopolistic control • Fewer "good opportunities" • Decisions need to be faster and closer to the material • Poor recent financial performance • Limited funds for reinvestment • Declining productivity • Domestically focused businesses • Centralized decision making • Strong technical skills
Operating Strategy	• Build better customer relationships • Better manage response to supply/demand cycles • Manage costs through cost reduction and reengineering • Increase investment outside North America • Use joint ventures to increase assets with limited investment • Acquire and divest assets to improve operating efficiency
Organizational Capabilities	• Rapid consensus-building and decision-making • Effective negotiation and deal-making • Investment/divestment opportunities identification • Rapid deployment of resources • Rapid development of appropriate products and services • Relentless focus on costs • Understand cost/value relationship • Create/sustain relationships • Integrate/manage cultural diversity • Understand/anticipate customer requirements
People Strategies	Strategy 1: Improve Amoco's organizational capability to act quickly and decisively (speed and agility). Strategy 2: Build and deploy critical people competencies (competence). Strategy 3: Increase the return on investment in people (cost effectiveness).

Source: Reprinted with permission of Wayne Anderson at Amoco Corporation.

Figure 7-1 HR's Role—Conceptual Framework

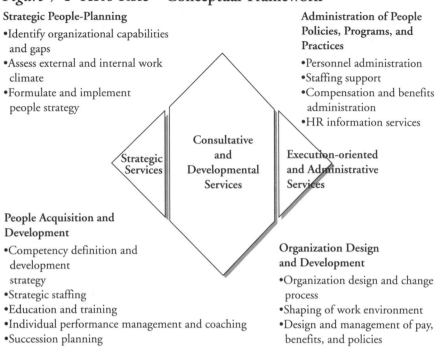

Strategic People-Planning
- Identify organizational capabilities and gaps
- Assess external and internal work climate
- Formulate and implement people strategy

Administration of People Policies, Programs, and Practices
- Personnel administration
- Staffing support
- Compensation and benefits administration
- HR information services

Consultative and Developmental Services

Strategic Services

Execution-oriented and Administrative Services

People Acquisition and Development
- Competency definition and development strategy
- Strategic staffing
- Education and training
- Individual performance management and coaching
- Succession planning

Organization Design and Development
- Organization design and change process
- Shaping of work environment
- Design and management of pay, benefits, and policies

Source: Reprinted with permission of Wayne Anderson at Amoco Corporation.

those standards. HR processes were improved. Some HR activities were outsourced (for example, medical-plan administration, savings-plan administration, compensation and other surveys, long-term disability, dental-plan administration, relocation, retirement calculations, and benefits delivery). These outsourced activities created measurable value for Amoco—more than $11 million in cost savings. In addition, through an increased use of preferred provider organizations and health maintenance organizations and the shared costs of managed care, Amoco's health-care costs are $36 million less than would be expected given the industry average for major oil companies.

Amoco HR also adopted a set of operating principles for developing and implementing its people practices.

- Remember that one tight policy does not fit all.

- Focus on cost-to-value of people.

- Develop a global perspective.
- Focus on developing a mutually beneficial employment relationship.
- Ensure that business strategies drive people policies, programs, and practices.

Amoco's HR operating guidelines for daily activities focus on the following goals.

- Know the strategies and goals of both your business unit and Amoco.
- Set annual HR goals that relate directly to the business goals and strategies.
- Tie the value of each HR policy, program, or practice to customer business strategy.
- Market HR's expertise.
- Be a problem-solver, not a policy/practice controller.
- Provide customers with more than they asked for.
- Make decisions/recommendations more quickly—don't make customers wait on HR.
- Provide frequent feedback to customers—both good and bad.

The Amoco HR function also invested in itself through two workshops designed to increase the competence of its professionals. Human Resources Development Workshop I (HRDW-I) focused on understanding the concept of organizational capability. From 1990 through 1993, eleven sessions were held, with 330 HR employee participants. HRDW-I emphasized HR's role in creating a competitive organization through development of organizational capability. Topics covered included the following.

- Shared mindset
- Change management
- Teamwork
- Legendary customer service
- Diversity
- HR practices
- Leadership

HRDW-II focused on understanding HR strategy. This workshop, attended by more than 300 HR professionals between 1993 and 1995, had as its key objectives ensuring that each Amoco HR professional gained the following abilities or knowledge.

- Identify how HR work fit with business strategy

- Understand Amoco's people-strategy framework

- Apply the organizational-capability assessment process

- Understand the financial implications of people strategies

- Align HR practices with business strategy

- Learn best practices in handling current and emerging HR issues (organization design, rewards, change and so on)

- Prepare a personal action plan for applying the people-strategy framework to the organization each participant supported.

In summary, the HR function at Amoco came to play an integral role in helping the company develop its ability to manage strategically. Each Amoco business strategy now includes assessment or oganizational-capability requirements; priorities are set for each HR practice based on business strategy requirements; and the HR functional roles, competencies, structure, and processes have been assessed and improved to better support business needs. The net result is an HR function that clearly adds value to the business.

SUMMARY: HR FOR HR

Too often HR professionals focus more on helping others than on helping themselves. The HR principles that help businesses, when applied to the HR function itself, will improve it. HR for HR requires that HR professionals manage the following three sets of activities.

First, the professionals must do *strategic HR*, turning business strategies into organizational capabilities and organizational capabilities into actions. Strategic HR helps fulfill the promise of strategic decisions, and fulfilling promises helps organizations to develop successful relationships with their employees, customers, and investors.

Second, HR professionals must do *HR strategy*, crafting a point of view for the HR function. A point of view may be defined through an explicit vision, mission, mindset, or other descriptor. It sets the direction for the HR function and helps those both inside and outside the function to understand its purpose.

Third, HR professionals must do *HR organization*, using HR strategy to strengthen the function. This process includes undertaking organizational diagnosis of the HR function itself, followed by any necessary improvements in hiring, training, compensating, organizing, and delivering HR work.

As HR professionals model the principles they preach, they gain credibility in their companies and increase the probability that they will be successful business partners.

What's Next?

NO ONE CAN PREDICT the organization of the future. No one can predict the future course of the HR profession. No one can predict how HR practices will change in the future. Thinking about the future, however, helps us to prepare for it. Thinking about the future may lead to innovative insights. Thinking about the future of HR may help to change today's HR practices in positive ways.

In this final chapter, I focus on the future of HR by addressing three questions: "What's so?" "So what?" and "Now what?" (These three questions derive from a learning framework used by Steve Kerr at General Electric.) The answers to these three questions should help predict *what's next* in the development of HR issues and the HR profession.

WHAT'S SO?

In many cases, human resource issues are the next venue for corporations seeking to create value and deliver results. Business theorists have proposed a number of foci for conducting the ongoing search for competitiveness, including manufacturing,[1] business strategy,[2] marketing and service,[3] financial management,[4] technology,[5] reengineering,[6] and quality.[7] While all of these approaches are valid, innovation in the search for competitiveness must continue, and new concepts must be created to complement and replace current ideas and practices.

In recent years, increasing attention has been paid to the organizational components of competitiveness. Organization as a source of competitiveness has been defined in terms of the organization itself,[8] the core competencies within the organization,[9] the people within the organization,[10] the organizational culture or shared values,[11] and knowledge or learning.[12] My belief is that this array of organizational factors has moved to occupy the center of the successful search for competitiveness, for the reasons described in Chapter 1: globalization, the value chain, growth, capability focus, change, technology, intellectual capital, and transformation. These challenges have given rise to a renewed focus on how organizations can build competitiveness. The nature of the competitive challenges outlined in Chapter 1 suggests that creating value is no longer exclusively an economic equation leading to a financial outcome. Dealing with what has traditionally been the softer side of management and organization has now become the harder and more demanding part of most executive jobs. The importance of organization is increasingly accepted by executives[13] and academics.

My focus on human resources as the dominant lever for creating value and delivering results is not universally accepted. In fact, many HR consultants and theorists shy away from using the term *human resources* because it conjures up an image of stodgy personnel departments that deal only with policy-making, policing, and transacting. My view is that this image is outdated and dysfunctional. Few would dispute that the keys for creating competitive organizations are how people are treated, how organizational processes are governed, and how an organization's work is coordinated. I would argue further, however, that the tools for creating competitive organizations come from redefining and upgrading human resources.

Human resource practices (for example, staffing, training, development, performance management, rewards, communications, organizational design, culture change, and so on) can, should, and must be modified to align with and anticipate business strategy. Human resource departments can, should, and must find ways to accomplish necessary transaction work (for example, payroll) while focusing aggressively on work that executes strategy, increases employee contribution, and transforms organizations. Human resource professionals can, should, and must become partners with other senior managers by creating value and delivering results.

Ignoring the present and future world of human resources in the quest to build competitive organizations is like an architect ignoring the basic systems necessary in a modern house. A house, however elegant its design, however wonderful its layout and space, will not be functional without appropriate heating, lighting, and plumbing systems. Innovations in heating types and equipment (for example, new thermostats, gauges, and standards of efficiency), in lighting (recessed, computer-controlled, and so on), and in plumbing (water and energy efficiency, instant hot water, and so on) should be evaluated and, where appropriate in the budget-design tradeoff, integrated for the maximum pleasure and comfort of the prospective residents. Ignoring these systems may result in a house that appeals on the outside but that does not function well on the inside.

Likewise, those who argue that human resources can be ignored as virtual, boundaryless, and global organizations of the future are created may design an elegant organizational morphology, but it will lack sufficient infrastructure to sustain itself. Human resource systems present organizations with the tools they need to ensure that people, processes, and practices are governed in ways that create value and deliver results. HR systems need to be retained and constantly upgraded and changed: People will always need to be hired and trained; processes will always need to be created and upgraded; cultures will always need to be established and transformed.

Some firms separate the HR department from other staff groups with responsibility for knowledge transfer, quality, reengineering, or organizational effectiveness. This may be understandable when HR professionals lack the competence to add value in these domains; but it is unfortunate that the HR practices so central to creating competitive organizations cannot be integrated, redesigned, and aligned with business thinking.

HR policies and practices should create organizations that are better able to execute strategy (Chapter 3), operate efficiently (Chapter 4), engage employees (Chapter 5), and manage change (Chapter 6), all of which are elements of the competitive organization. This process requires HR champions, whether line managers or HR professionals, who can create value and deliver results. The identity of a firm's HR champion is less important than having one.

What's so? The answer to this question is easy: *HR matters.* HR practices create organizational capabilities that lead to competitiveness. HR champions master, align, and leverage these practices so that employees, customers, and investors receive value.

So What?

If HR matters more to competitiveness than ever before, then both line managers and HR professionals must become HR champions. They must not only appreciate HR issues, but master the techniques for creating value through HR practices.

The Emerging Human-Resource Community

Human resources is no longer the sole responsibility of the HR department, but involves a firm's broader *human-resource community.* The HR community consists of those individuals throughout the organization who are dedicated to leveraging HR practices to devise and integrate organizational capabilities that create value and deliver results.

The membership and balance of the HR community can vary. It may be anchored by HR professionals who understand HR theory and can design world-class HR practices. The HR community may be sponsored by the operating managers primarily responsible for meeting business needs. It may extend to other staff groups who use HR practices both within the group (for example, HR practices applied within the marketing, finance, and information technology groups) and as means for accomplishing group goals. The HR community may be further supported by consultants or other vendors who provide fresh insight and technical expertise. Taken together, these varied roles constitute a viable human-resource community that can create value and deliver results. To create such an HR community, however, HR professionals and line managers must stand forth as HR champions.

Implications for HR Professionals as HR Champions

The HR professional of the future will be dramatically different from the HR employee of the past. Under the rubric of becoming business partners, HR professionals will think more about results than programs. They will focus on and guarantee deliverables from deployment of HR practices that create value for their organizations, developing organizational architectures and using them to translate strategy into action. They will perform organizational diagnoses by applying their organizational architectures to set organizational priorities. HR professionals reengineer HR work through use of technology, process reengineering teams, and quality improvements. They will be the employees' voice in management discussions, ensuring that employees feel their issues have been heard. They will be catalysts, facilitators, and designers of both culture change and capacity for change, establishing a vision for the HR function that excites clients and engages HR professionals.

The HR concept subsumes various roles, and this will continue in the future of the profession. Some HR professionals act as generalists, establishing bonds with clients and creating value by helping to turn strategy into action. Other HR professionals are specialists, mastering HR theory and keeping up with or developing HR innovations. As these individuals become professional within their domains, they are better able to work together to ensure that HR departments deliver value.

Implications for Line Managers as HR Champions

Line managers also must be HR champions. When I taught an MBA course "HR as a Competitive Advantage," I asked the following question on the final exam.

Who is primarily responsible for HR practices within a firm?

a. Line managers.

b. HR professionals.

c. A partnership between line and HR.

d. Consultants.

e. No one, they just emerge.

Most students answered *c*—and I marked them wrong. I hold that the answer is *a;* line managers are *primarily* responsible for the HR practices within a firm. Line managers have ultimate responsibility for both the outcomes and the processes within a firm. They are accountable to shareholders for delivering economic value, to customers for product or service value, and to employees for work place value. To deliver these outcomes, line managers must become HR champions.

As HR champions, line managers need to understand organizational capability as a critical source of competitiveness. They must ensure that every business plan has an organizational action plan for implementation. They ensure that strategic promises to customers, employees, and investors are kept. They must create staff shared-services organizations with multiple delivery mechanisms for staff work. They articulate a new employee contract for all employees that incorporates both stretch goals and the resources to reach those goals. They align the internal culture to achieve the desired market identity by understanding the processes that create shared mindset. Finally, line managers must require that the HR department set high goals (mission, values, strategies), and they should review, monitor, and hold the HR department accountable for reaching those goals.

Implications of the Partnership Between Line Managers and HR Professionals

Ultimately, line managers or HR professionals acting in isolation cannot be HR champions; they must form a partnership. Traditional barriers separate line and staff: Partnerships break down these barriers. Partnerships ensure that, while both parties bring unique competencies to their joint task, their combined skills are more than the sum of their parts. Partnerships imply mutual respect, with partners working together toward common goals in a process enriched by varied perspectives. Partnerships encourage debate and differences, but ultimately find common ground on which conflict is replaced by commitment. A true partnership exists where observers at a staff meeting cannot readily tell the HR executive from the line manager, because both clearly focus on business results.

The emerging HR community is based on multiple partnerships (see Figure 8-1). Line managers bring authority, power, and sponsorship and have overall responsibility for the HR community. HR professionals bring

Figure 8-1 HR Community: A Series of Partnerships

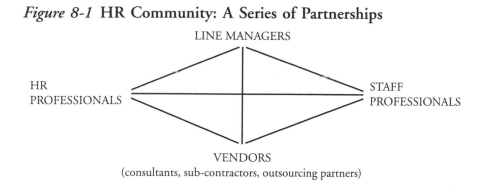

technical expertise. Staff professionals bring technical expertise in their functional areas. Vendors offer technical advice or perform routine standardized work. Collectively, the HR community defines and delivers value.

Now What?

HR communities exist today. Some of these communities are formally defined; others are casual, with vague or shifting relationships. Regardless of the current status of any particular HR community, seven challenges for the future will propel the HR community forward.

Challenge One: HR Theory

Theory fulfills two purposes: First, it explains why things happen, and second, it explains when things happen.[14]

Why HR matters

C.K. Prahalad, a world renowned professor of strategy, meets frequently with groups of HR executives. Among the insights he offers these groups is a challenge. He claims that one reason HR has not become as pivotal to business as it should be is that HR often lacks theory. Theory explains *why* events happen. Theory provides explanations based on logic for how events relate to each other. Theory weaves individual events into predictable and generalizable patterns. Prahalad argues that HR lacks a cohesive theory.

To make HR practices more than isolated acts, managers and HR professionals must master the theory behind HR work; they need to be able to explain conceptually how and why HR practices lead to their outcomes. HR is based on recognizable bodies of knowledge. Familiarity with the theory of learning should be a prerequisite for those in training, development, and education. The theories of motivation should be the foundation for work by those in compensation. The theory of organizational change should be the foundation for HR professionals working toward organizational effectiveness. Reliance on theories creates thoughtful practitioners with solid grounding in the basics of HR practices. Such practitioners are more likely to avoid some of the frou-frou that gives the discipline its negative image.

Explications of HR theory are beginning to emerge,[15] drawing on various streams of academic research.[16] They offer alternative explanations for how HR practices affect business results, including the following:

- **Resource dependence (from political science):** HR practices help the firm acquire a stable supply of scarce resources (intellectual and human capital) that helps the firm to compete.

- **Transaction cost (from institutional economics):** HR practices reduce the costs associated with accomplishing and governing how work is done.

- **Contingency theory (from business strategy):** HR practices align with business strategy to provide a fit that leads to results.

- **Institutional theory (from sociology):** HR practices transfer knowledge and ideas from firm to firm making the best practices of an industry routine.

- **Cognitive psychology (from psychology):** HR practices help create a shared mindset or culture within the firm that reduces governance costs and increases commitment.

Regardless of the preferred theory, managers and HR professionals should abstract from it a higher level of reasoning for their day-to-day work and thus better explain why their work accomplishes its goals.

When HR matters

Theory also leads to contingent thinking. Contingent thinking is based on a series of *if. . . then* equations. It helps HR professionals to avoid playing

HR Jeopardy, in which they begin with the answer, an HR practice, and forget to ask the question.

Too often, for example, HR benchmarking looks for answers about what constitutes world-class or best HR practice. To identify these best practices, HR professionals visit leading companies to review their HR programs, which are then adopted back home. When working with General Electric, I witnessed the pilgrimage to GE by a number of companies seeking to learn more about GE's practices in succession planning, culture change, development, and employee involvement. Many of these visitors, enamored of the GE programs, returned home only to find that they were impossible to implement in their given work settings.

The missing element in these benchmarking visits was contingent thinking. Contingent thinking focuses not only on the practice (the *then* of the *if. . . then* proposition), but on the setting that facilitates the practice (the *if*). General Electric's remarkable success in creating a new culture was the result of a host of contingencies, including strong CEO leadership support, managerial competencies, an organizational history and legacy of innovation, a social architecture through which ideas were readily shared, credibility for HR professionals, and embedded and supportive HR practices (for example, communication, rewards, training, and succession planning).

HR champions need to learn and practice contingent thinking. They need to learn that it is not the HR practice that matters, but the context for the practice. Contingent thinking comes from constantly asking the question "Why": Why did this HR practice work?

Challenge Two: HR Tools

HR history

Originally, hiring and firing people, the traditional core of HR activities, was done by purchasing agents. The logic was that purchasing agents acquired land, equipment, materials, and, by natural extension, people. To an extent because of this dehumanizing attitude, unions emerged to represent employees. To negotiate with the unions, firms needed their own representatives, giving rise to the labor relations specialty within HR.

Other subspecialties followed. The staffing function grew out of the belief that, with testing and assessment, employees could be matched to jobs and their performance increased. Training grew out of the belief that, with proper training programs, employees could develop the skills necessary to do their jobs. Compensation grew out of the belief that, if designed appropriately, compensation systems could motivate employees to higher performance. Appraisal systems grew out of the need to specify the behaviors and outcomes expected of employees so that management goals could become employee goals.

By the late 1970s, most people writing about HR were describing four core HR activities: staffing, development, appraisal, and rewards.[17] As HR professionals mastered these activities at the operational and strategic levels, they could demonstrate value.

The HR standard of the late 1980s coupled these skills with those of organizational design and communications. With the enormous numbers of mergers, consolidations, and acquisitions, learning to create new organizational forms around teams and processes became central to the HR profession. Communication programs became critical vehicles for sharing information with employees and thus became part of the HR agenda.

In developing the HR practices needed for the future, improvement must continue in many of the HR core technologies, including executive development, recruiting and staffing, training and education, rewards and recognition, performance management, employee relations, labor relations, and diversity. New issues, however, represented by the six HR tools discussed below, will present HR professionals with corresponding new questions.

Global HR

Global HR has two implications. First, HR professionals need to articulate the HR ramifications of a global business strategy. A global business strategy focuses on how a company *gets in,* that is, starts doing business in a given country. Many companies see opportunities in China or India, for example, and have prepared strategies for entry into these markets. For these strategies to succeed, however, they must first deal with many basic HR issues. How do we hire people to staff the operation? How do we make sure that the employees working in the country adhere to the firm's culture? How do we create incentives to reinforce appropriate behaviors among employees in the country? How do we build communications programs within and with the country operation? These and other HR questions are critical to an effective global business strategy; HR professionals should understand the choices and consequences of alternative answers to these questions.

Second, HR professionals should be aware of and sensitive to unique country conditions. This focuses attention on how businesses *get work done* within a country once they are in. Laws governing downsizing, for example, may affect how many people are hired and how they are treated. HR professionals should master within-country idiosyncratic policies about hiring (for example, many French firms rely on graphology, or handwriting analysis, as a screening technique), compensation (for example, tax laws in many countries dictate that some compensation take the form of lifestyle perquisites rather than higher salaries), benefits (for example, the employee health and wellness benefits expected may vary by country), or training (for example, apprenticeship programs are common in German companies). Imagine a large matrix. The columns are the countries in which a company operates; the rows are the HR practices. In each cell are some of the unique requirements of that country. HR professionals should be masters of this type of matrix, able to discuss any and all country-specific HR challenges.

Global HR matters and will come to matter more in the future. It matters in terms of business strategy, country practice, and knowledge transfer.

Leadership depth

The leader of the future is not the leader of the present. Defining and creating the leader of the future will be a major challenge for the HR professional. Frances Hesselbein, Marshall Goldsmith, and Richard Beckhard have edited a marvelous book, *The Leader of the Future,*[18] in which a number of prominent theorists on the nature of leadership discuss their views. These essays reveal a number of ways in which the leader of the future will differ from the leader of today.

- Leadership will reside less at the top; it will, rather, be shared throughout an organization.

- Charismatic leaders will be less important than the processes the leaders create.

- Individual leadership will be replaced by team leadership.

- The new leader will be more likely to ask questions than to give answers.

- Leaders will be less likely to look for and accept simple solutions and more likely to identify and live with paradoxes.

- Focus will shift from reliance on purely analytical tools in favor of integration of the analytical and the affective.

- Global thinking and demeanor will replace an exclusively domestic focus.

- Interest in questions and learning will replace focus on solutions and answers.

HR professionals must establish systems that create or discover these future leaders. These systems might include designing and using competence models, tracking the quality of present leadership, finding creative methods for leadership development, and involving senior managers in serious leadership development. HR professionals may come to be judged by the extent to which they develop future leaders.

Knowledge transfer

Two primary factors characterize the learning organization: the ability to generate ideas that have impact and the ability to generalize them.[19] Most large firms generate ideas regularly. Pockets of excellence exist wherever innovative practices exist. Innovations in management, technology, product, distribution, and human resources routinely occur within businesses, plants, countries, or functions.

The greatest learning challenge by far is to generalize these ideas. Generalizing ideas means sharing knowledge across boundaries of time, space, geography, business, or function. Creating systems that transfer knowledge throughout an organization will surely become a critical item in the HR toolkit. Knowledge transfer will help firms reduce cycle time by allowing shared insights to move easily among locations, increasing innovation by building on experience, and making better decisions derived from information from multiple sources. Knowledge transfer confers the same benefits that the learning organization does: It confers the ability to learn faster than competitors do, to respond more quickly to market conditions, to learn more quickly from failures and successes, and to build intellectual and human capital.

Creating the infrastructure for knowledge transfer requires that HR professionals work with information-systems professionals to create computer networks that share information. Basic questions that must be answered to achieve effective systems include the following:

- What do we need to know that we don't know?
- How do we find out?
- How do we share that knowledge with others?

Knowledge transfer, however, involves more than an investment in technology. It means creating a mindset among all employees that values new ideas and innovation and devalues game-playing.

Effective knowledge transfer processes will have implications for who is hired (those able and willing to seek and share ideas), how development is done (by sharing ideas around the world), how incentives are created (to encourage transfer of knowledge), how communications are established (to easily access and share more information), and how organizations are organized (less hierarchy and more information-sharing). HR professionals in some firms are even now being called and considered chief learning officers,[20] an indication of the growing importance of knowledge transfer.

Culture change

In our second round of the State of the Art (SOTA) study for the Human Resource Planning Society, Bob Eichinger and I found a startling result. Asked to identify one out of ten challenges as the single most important facing competitive organizations today, a significant number of leading thinkers picked culture change. Asked to evaluate how well most organizations met each of these 10 challenges, culture change came in last.

A decade ago, *culture change* was viewed as an esoteric, academic buzzword. Today, it has become a maxim for ensuring that the fundamental assumptions, values, mindsets, and thought processes of a firm's employees adapt to changing conditions. Culture change deals less with implementing new initiatives than with changing a firm's fundamental mindset. It deals with information-sharing, treatment of employees, work allocation, and decision-making. Culture change occurs not only inside a firm, among its employees, but outside, among its suppliers and customers.[21]

To accomplish culture change, HR professionals must learn to engage the organization in a series of actions, including the following:

- **Commit to culture change.** HR professionals must learn to build a business case for culture change. Culture change must be a means to enhancing shareholder and customer value.

- **Define a current culture.** HR professionals need a model or framework to describe a firm's culture. The particular framework chosen from the many that have been created matters less than the ability of the HR professional to talk clearly and precisely, using accepted theory and research, about the culture framework chosen.

- **Define the desired culture.** Desired cultures reflect the identity of a firm shared by employees and customers. Identifying the desired culture, using any one of many accepted processes, helps HR professionals to articulate the outcome or direction of culture change.

- **Expose culture gaps.** Gaps between current and desired cultures need to be made explicit so that roadmaps of culture change can be sketched and followed.

- **Prepare and implement culture action-plans.** Culture action-plans may include corporate-wide programs (for example, a quality training initiative or a competence-based hiring practice), reengineered processes (for example, in purchasing, customer interface, or order-to-remittance), or employee engagement activities (for example, running town-hall meetings at which employees act in character with the new culture). HR professionals must creatively turn cultural ideals into real actions.

- **Coordinate culture-change efforts.** In many culture-change efforts, more work is done than is integrated. One solution is to make HR professionals responsible for forming, sponsoring, or chairing a transformation team with the job of integrating parallel activities dedicated to culture change.

- **Measure results.** Often, culture-change efforts begin with big fanfare but end months later with a whimper. HR professionals should be able to measure and document a culture change and its impact on people, processes, and profits.

While these may not be necessary steps for every culture change, they represent some of the basic lessons that will need to be applied by the HR professionals of the future.

Customer-focused HR

As the criteria for HR success shifts from internal factors (for example, reduced costs and increased employee commitment) to external ones (for example, increased revenue and increased customer satisfaction), HR practices need to focus both on employees and on external customers. This double focus leads to new methods of deploying HR practices that involve outside suppliers and customers. Customers will be involved in training sessions, staffing decisions, and employee evaluations. They will join high-performance teams and help create communication plans in which they participate as both receivers and givers of information. These are just a few examples of the new HR tools that will focus on customers as well as employees.

For HR professionals, customer focus has dramatic implications and raises many urgent questions. Where should time be spent *today*? Who in the firm participates in shaping the HR agenda? How many external customers should be involved in designing and delivering HR practices? What relationships across staff groups inside the firm will be required to build these external bridges?

Answers to these questions will change over the next few years as HR professionals increasingly spend time with real external customers, involving them in the design of staffing, training, compensation, organization, communication, and other HR practices. Customers may come to be as involved as employees in the design and delivery of HR practices. HR professionals may find themselves part of a client team, along with marketing, sales, operations, and MIS professionals—all dedicated to serving customer needs.

When employee-focused HR practices shift to customer-focused HR practices, employees and customers both win. Employees win by seeing their work add value to customers, by enhancing their ability to adapt their work quickly to meet customer needs, and by becoming more intimately involved with satisfying customer expectations. Customers win by dealing with supplier firm employees who are true customer resources, by working with suppliers dedicated to their needs, and by reducing the cycle time needed to change how work gets done.

Challenge Three: HR Capabilities

Organizations have capabilities, particular processes they perform well. HR communities must also exhibit capabilities, processes, and practices that serve as criteria for evaluating their success. Traditionally, the effectiveness of HR functions was measured by their accuracy and administrative efficiency. To meet these criteria, HR developed consistency through precision, routines, and reliable procedures.

Today, new HR capabilities must be added to the traditional ones, including the following:

- **Speed:** How quickly can HR work be done without sacrificing quality?

- **Implementation:** How well can new ideas be turned into actions with visible results in terms of employee behavior or benefits to the firm?

- **Innovation:** How able is the HR community to think creatively about solving old problems and about finding solutions to problems it has not previously considered?

- **Integration:** How well does HR work integrate with strategic plans, customer goals, employee needs, and other staff function plans?

Delivering these outcomes will require that HR communities build new capabilities. These capabilities will, in turn, require team building across the HR community, technology leveraging, risk taking, goal sharing about the business impact of HR work, awareness and adaptation of best HR practices, and the personal confidence to take risks and innovate.

Challenge Four: HR Value Proposition

Any business activity should be reducible to a fundamental business proposition based on creating value for customers in economically viable ways. HR professionals must create an HR value proposition, aligning HR practices to simple business realities: serving customers, meeting deadlines, making profits, leveraging technology, and satisfying investors. HR professionals should invest serious time in learning how their work affects these business realities. This is not a new call to arms: This message has been stated and restated in many forms over and over again for the last thirty years. But it is time for HR professionals to stop talking and make it happen. Every HR professional should be able to pass this one-question exam: How does your work add value to this business in economic terms?

The HR investment in the future must focus on *value creation* and on developing a value equation for HR services and products. The HR value proposition raises both simple and complex questions. Simple questions are aimed at making explicit the relationships between HR practices and the three locales of value.

- **Employees:** Morale, commitment, competence, and retention.
- **Customers:** Retention, satisfaction, and commitment.
- **Investors:** Profitability, cost, growth, cash flow, and margin.

Simple logic suggests that HR practices affect each of these practices directly, as illustrated in Figure 8-2.

More complex questions about value creation probe the interrelationships of the four key factors—HR practices, employees, customers, and investors—when action in any one area affects the other three both directly and indirectly. An organizational change to increased use of teamwork (an HR practice), for example, affects employee morale and commitment but also customer satisfaction and profitability, which may, in turn, have further repercussions on employee morale. Sorting out such complex relationships will be among the long-term challenges in creating a complete HR value proposition.

The absence of an HR value proposition leaves the HR profession to justify itself through anecdotes, perceptions, goodwill, and the instincts of senior managers. It is necessary, therefore, to begin the thinking about a more complex HR value proposition. One technique is as follows: On the left side of a piece of paper, list your firm's HR practices. On the right, put your firm's most viable economic indicator of success (for example, return on equity, return on net assets, earnings per share, and so on). The HR value proposition fills the gap, connecting the practices on the left to the performance on the right.[22]

Figure 8-2 **Assessing the Effects of HR Practices on Employees, Customers, and Investors**

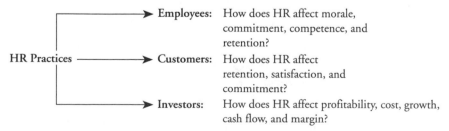

HR Practices ⟶ **Employees:** How does HR affect morale, commitment, competence, and retention?

⟶ **Customers:** How does HR affect retention, satisfaction, and commitment?

⟶ **Investors:** How does HR affect profitability, cost, growth, cash flow, and margin?

Any number of paths can connect HR practices with firm performance.[23] The thought process embedded in this book views HR practices as creating sets of organizational capabilities. Organizational capabilities, the enduring attributes characterizing an organization, create value for the customers served by them. When customer value is created, economic value (however measured) follows. The HR value proposition, therefore, is that HR practices create organizational capabilities that create customer value that in turn creates economic value.

The path I follow to connect HR practices and business performance may not attract everyone, nor should it. But every firm should create and follow a path toward an HR value proposition.

Challenge Five: HR Governance

Governance deals with how work is coordinated. Work has generally been governed within a firm's legal boundaries. In the future, however, governance may take many forms. Organizations today have been defined as networks or clusters and described as virtual and boundaryless. In these organizations, work is governed through relationships and information more than through policy and hierarchy. The largest employer in the 1990s United States, for example, is Manpower, a temporary service agency. Contract employees have become common at many firms, only one example of how outsourcing has redefined how work gets done.

New organizational forms, moving away from pyramids and toward networks, require new thinking about management processes. Careers in a network organization may be more horizontal than vertical. Compensation systems may be tied less to position than to competence. Cultures will cut across internal boundaries rather than be confined within business units. Learning to join together and produce as teams may become as critical to career success as having clear areas of power or control once was.

The boundaries of the firms of the future may be based less on legal and geographic definitions than on knowledge and values. Governance applies within the HR community. It is plausible that the HR community, with internal specialists in staffing, training, measurement, compensation, benefits, communication, organizational design, and so on, will become a virtual organization in which work occurs to set policies and administer HR practices. Rather than create a large internal training staff, for example, a firm might contract for this work with a vendor who would provide everything necessary, from course design to delivery to evaluation. Similar governance arrangements might be developed for staffing, communication, organization design, team-building, policy-setting, and other HR activities. Questions relating to such a transition include the following:

- How does HR organize to deliver value?
- Who does HR work (HR professionals, line managers, or contractors)?
- Where is accountability for HR work?
- How is the structure of the firm's HR community established?

By answering these governance questions, firms create HR functions with a dramatically different look. The function might become very small and serve as a broker of services. It may split into distinct roles, such as centers of expertise, generalists, and service centers, that work with each other to create value. A third possibility would be an HR function housed under one strong central body but with responsibility for ensuring company responsiveness to local needs.

Challenge Six: HR Careers

Even if only a portion of the possible developments discussed in this book come to pass, careers in HR will change dramatically. The traditional career model followed the metaphor of stages, with HR professionals passing through a series of linear stages as they progressed in their careers from apprentice to individual contributor to mentor to strategist. A more apt metaphor in the future may be the career as a mosaic.

In a career mosaic, one's position in the hierarchy becomes less relevant than what one knows. Career paths become less linear as HR professionals increasingly engage in diverse career activities, forgoing a purposeful career plan in favor of career opportunism, responding to the opportunities that arise from any number of sources. A career mosaic may be characterized in terms of three dimensions (see Figure 8-3). First, an HR professional may work in one of four locations: at a site (for example, plant), in a business unit (for example, a product line or a country), at corporate HR, or outside the HR function. Second, in each of these four possible work locations, the HR professional may be a specialist (focusing on a specific

Figure 8-3 HR Career Mosaic

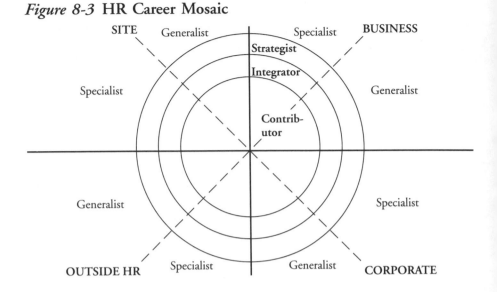

HR practice) or a generalist (integrating HR with other work). Third, particular positions may have one of three career aspects: contributor (working alone), integrator (coordinating the work of others), and strategist (directing policies and procedures).

Figure 8-3 shows the multiple paths that an HR career can take. An employee who has personal commitments to a particular location, for example, may spend an entire career working at that site (top left cell), moving from specialist to generalist and through a series of roles and positions, but all within the single site. Another career path might take an HR professional outside the HR function (bottom left cell) and then back into it. An increasingly common HR career path is to move throughout the mosaic. For example, an HR professional may be hired in as a sales representative selling a particular product; a move into sales management and then into an HR generalist position at a site may be followed by a move into an HR specialist job in a business unit, followed by an HR generalist job at that unit, and, ultimately, a corporate generalist role.

The usefulness of considering the career mosaic is to recognize that multiple career paths exist, many jobs within the HR community are important, and individual competencies are more important than career stages.

Challenge Seven: HR Competencies

HR competence can be conceptualized using a three-domain framework that includes knowledge of business, delivery of HR, and management of change processes (see Figure 8-4).[24] As illustrated in the figure, competencies in each domain contribute in different ways to the overall performance of HR professionals. Knowledge of business explains 18 percent of the performance of HR professionals; knowledge of HR practices explains 23 percent; and change management explains 41 percent. One interpretation of this research is that knowing the business lets an HR professional *join* the management team; knowing HR practices helps the professional *contribute;* and managing change helps the HR professionals *make things happen.*

Knowledge of business

HR professionals add value to their organizations when they understand how the business operates because that understanding helps the HR professional adapt HR and organizational activities to changing business condi-

Figure 8-4 **Relative Competencies for HR Professionals as Business Partners (data from 12,689 associates)**

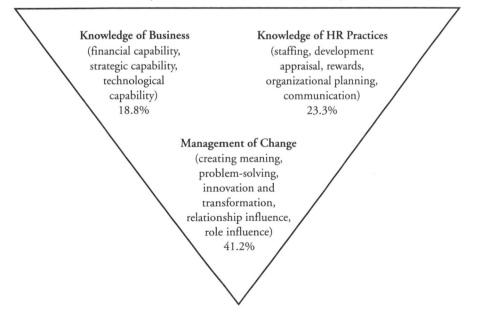

Knowledge of Business
(financial capability,
strategic capability,
technological
capability)
18.8%

Knowledge of HR Practices
(staffing, development
appraisal, rewards,
organizational planning,
communication)
23.3%

Management of Change
(creating meaning,
problem-solving,
innovation and
transformation,
relationship influence,
role influence)
41.2%

tions. Knowing the financial, strategic, technological, and organizational capabilities of an organization are necessary conditions of entry into any strategic discussion. HR professionals who are knowledgeable exclusively in industrial, employee, or human relations may be fully competent in their discipline but still fail to understand the essentials of the business in which their firms compete. Some HR professionals know the technology of human resources but are unable to adapt that technology to business conditions. Business acumen requires knowledge, if not direct operational experience, in functional areas such as marketing, finance, strategy, technology, and sales, in addition to human resources. The HR competence encompassed by the phrase *knowledge of the business* is not the ability *to do* all business functions, but the ability *to understand* them.

Delivery of HR practices

Professionals in the HR function, as those in any other staff function, must be experts in their specialty. The ability to deliver state-of-the-art, innovative HR practices builds the credibility of and respect for HR professionals. HR practices fall into six categories: staffing, development, appraisal, rewards, organizational design, and communication.[25] HR professionals who are perceived as being competent in these categories (depending on experience and position) will be seen as credible designers and implementers of HR systems. Competence in the delivery of HR practice goes beyond knowledge; it requires that the HR professional deliver HR practices to organization members.

Management of change/processes

The rationale for including a change competence domain is that, as the pace of change outside businesses increases (through globalization, information flow, customer expectations, technology, and so on), businesses must change internally to be competitive. Businesses with a greater capacity for change will, over time, be more competitive. Individuals' resistance to change often prevents organizations from adapting as quickly as needed and desired. As HR professionals develop competencies to manage change processes, they can help other organization members to manage change, thus creating an overall organizational capacity for change. HR professionals with competencies to manage change processes demonstrate the attributes of outstanding change agents—they can diagnose problems, build relationships with clients, articulate visions, set leadership agendas, solve problems, and implement goals. The contributing competencies exhibited in change management are knowledge (of change processes), skills (as change agents), and abilities (to deliver change).

Credibility

Beyond the three domains outlined above, however, is a domain of final necessary competency for the successful HR professional: Credibility. Figure 8-5 presents an expanded model of HR competencies. Interviews with HR professionals have yielded insights into what HR professionals can do to acquire personal credibility. The behaviors that enhance credibility include the following:

- **Accuracy:** Being accurate in all HR work.
- **Consistency:** Being predictable.
- **Meeting commitments:** Doing what you say you will do on time and within budget.
- **Chemistry:** Being personally comfortable with peers, subordinates, and supervisors.

Figure 8-5 **Model for Future HR Competencies**

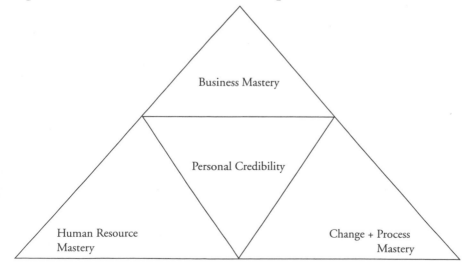

- **Confronting appropriately:** Being willing to disagree and challenge at the appropriate time, in the appropriate setting, and in the appropriate manner.

- **Integrity:** Behaving ethically.

- **Thinking outside the box:** Offering alternative perspectives that might not otherwise be voiced; having a point of view and being willing to express it.

- **Confidentiality:** Maintaining in strict confidence all personal information.

- **Listening to and focusing on executive problems:** Understanding all HR actions in light of the needs of the executive or the business.

These behaviors contributing to credibility are not exclusive to HR professionals; many apply to leadership credibility in general.[26] But a successful career in the HR functions of the future must bring these competencies to bear not on mounting successive career stages, but on building further essential organizational competencies.

CONCLUSION

The information in this book has multiple implications. It should help HR professionals to assess the extent to which their organizations are leveraging their human resource efforts for competitive advantage. It should provide a diagnostic with which to evaluate and improve both HR practices and HR departments. It should help line managers become human resource champions by better understanding and increasing their firm's human and intellectual capital. It should help those who work in human resources to become more professional by focusing more on what they deliver than on what they do.

Ultimately, a firm's human-resource community holds crucial responsibility for adding value and delivering results.

NOTES

Chapter 1

1. *Value* has multiple meanings in management thinking. Economists have argued that value refers to the economic success of a firm, and it is often spoken of in terms of *shareholder value;* see Alfred Rappaport, *Creating Shareholder Value* (New York: The Free Press, 1986). Value has also come to refer to *customer value,* that is, the value that customers perceive in their interactions with a firm; see Richard G. Whiteley, *The Customer-Driven Company* (Reading, Mass.: Addison-Wesley, 1993). *Personal values* and the ideals of individuals can be shaped into *organizational values;* see Robert E. Quinn and J. Rohrbaugh, "A Competing Values Approach to Organizational Effectiveness," *Public Productivity Review* (June 1981): 122–140. Some have worked to connect these various value; see Jac Fitz-enz, *Human Value Management: The Value-Adding Human Resource Management Strategy for the 1990s* (San Francisco: Jossey-Bass, 1990). Traditionally, most writers on this subject maintain that HR practices add value only for employees, by making the company a better place to work. I make linkages among shareholder, customer, and employee values through delivery of HR systems and argue that HR practices create value for all three stakeholders, in that all benefit from effective human resources.

2. The evolution of the concept of organizational capability is summarized in Dave Ulrich and Dale Lake, *Organizational Capability: Competing from the Inside/Out* (New York: Wiley, 1990). Since the appearance of *Organizational Capability,* a number of authors have built on the concept, sometimes using different terms; for example, see G. Stalk, P. Evans, and L.E. Shulman, "Competing on Capabilities: The New Rules of Corporate Strategy," *Harvard Business Review* (March–April 1992): 57–69; Ed Lawler III, *The Ultimate Advantage* (San Francisco: Jossey-Bass, 1992); James Brian Quinn, *The Intelligent Enterprise* (New York: The Free Press, 1992); and Jeffrey Pfeffer, *Competitive Advantage through People: Unleashing the Power of the Work Force* (Boston: Harvard Business School Press, 1994).

3. There is an ongoing debate about what the term *human resources* encompasses. First, HR may refer to the practices of human resources, that is, to how a firm manages its staffing, training, compensation, communication, and other HR systems. These practices, the responsibility of both line managers and HR professionals, over time come to define an organization, giving it a personality (culture), a history (tradition), and a set of values (rules and regulations). Second, HR may refer to the HR function or department, that is, to a generally definable operating unit within a firm. Third, HR may refer to HR professionals, those individuals who work full time in human-resource roles. In this book, I use the term *HR* in all three senses. In some instances, I specify the referent as HR practices, functions, or professionals; in others, the context of the discussion establishes the sense in which *HR* is being used; in still others, I use *HR* to envelop multiple meanings (as, for example, in discussions later in this chapter that encompass issues affecting HR practices, functions, *and* professionals).

4. The Human Resource Planning Society commissioned a study called "State of the Art" (SOTA), in the course of which Bob Eichinger and I collected data from thought leaders in industry who responded to questions about their perceptions of business trends and the HR implications of those trends. The report, presented at the Human Resource Planning Society's 1995 annual meeting, with an update at the 1996 annual meeting, was published as "Are You Future Agile? Are You Going to Be on the Value Chain Train? The First Annual State of the Art (SOTA) Report," *Human Resource Planning* 18, no. 4 (1995): 30–41.

5. This comment by Joe Miraglia was made in personal correspondence with the author, August 1995.

6. Work on customer responsiveness often focuses on maintaining a service orientation, being aware of customer needs, and building relationships with customers. See James Heskett, *Managing in the Service Economy* (Boston: Harvard Business School Press, 1986); K. Albrecht and R.I. Zemke, *Service America* (Homewood, Ill.: Irwin, 1988); Leonard Schlesinger and James Heskett, "The Service-Driven Service Company," *Harvard Business Review* (September–October 1991): 71–82; Leonard Berry, *On Great Service* (New York: The Free Press, 1995); and Benjamin Schneider and David E. Bowen, *Winning the Service Game* (Boston: Harvard Business School Press, 1995).

7. Research on employee and customer attitude can be found in B. Schneider and D.E. Bowen, "Employee and Customer Perceptions of Service in Banks: Replication and Extension," *Journal of Applied Psychology* 17 (1985): 423–433; Dave Ulrich, Richard Halbrook, Dave Meder, and Mark Stuchlik, "Employee and Customer Attachment: Synergies for Competitive Advantage," *Human Resource Planning* 14, no. 2 (1991): 89–102; Bill Fromm and Len Schlesinger, *The Real Heroes of Business and Not a CEO Among Them* (New York: Doubleday, 1993); and Schneider and Bowen, *Winning the Service Game.*

8. See Gary Hamel and C.K. Prahalad, "Strategic Intent," *Harvard Business Review*

(May–June 1989): 63–76; Gary Hamel and C.K. Prahalad, "Competing for the Future," *Harvard Business Review* (July–August 1994): 122–128; and Gary Hamel and C.K. Prahalad, *Competing for the Future* (Boston: Harvard Business School Press, 1994).

9. See Dwight L. Gertz and Joao Baptista, *Grow to Be Great: Breaking the Downsizing Cycle* (New York: The Free Press, 1995).

10. See a summary of the failure rate of change initiatives in Ron Ashkenas, "Beyond the Fads: How Leaders Drive Change with Results," *Human Resource Planning* 17, no. 2 (1994): 25–44.

11. In *The Seven Habits of Highly Effective Leaders* (New York: Simon & Schuster, 1989), Steve Covey distinguishes between production and production capability. *Production capability* is the organizational capability to which I refer; the ability to continually produce products, services, ideas, or results is the essence of organizational capabilities.

12. On the importance of reputation, see Charles Fombrun, *Reputation: Realizing Value from the Corporate Image* (Boston: Harvard Business School Press, 1996).

13. On removing boundaries, see Kenichi Ohmae, *The Borderless World: Managing Lessons in the New Logic of the Global Marketplace* (New York: Harper, 1990); and Ron Ashkenas, Dave Ulrich, Todd Jick, and Steve Kerr, *The Boundaryless Organization* (San Francisco: Jossey-Bass, 1995).

14. On the importance of change, see R. Kanter, B.A. Stein, and T.D. Jick, *The Challenge of Organizational Change* (New York: The Free Press, 1992); Steven Goldman, Roger Nagel, and Kenneth Preiss, *Agile Competitors and Virtual Organizations: Strategies for Enriching the Customer* (New York: Van Nostrand Reinhold, 1994); and Peter Drucker, *Managing in a Time of Change* (New York: Penguin, 1995).

15. On learning, see C. Argyris and D.A. Schon, *Organizational Learning: A Theory of Action Perspective* (Reading, Mass.: Addison-Wesley, 1978); P.M. Senge, *The Fifth Discipline: The Art and Practice of the Learning Organization* (New York: Doubleday/Currency, 1990); and Cal Wick, *The Learning Edge: How Smart Managers and Smart Companies Stay Ahead* (New York: McGraw-Hill, 1993).

16. The Rapid Learning Project, a collaboration between Cal Wick and me, collected surveys from more than 1,300 individuals at thirty firms.

17. Ulrich and Lake, *Organizational Capability.*

18. The argument concerning parity and organizational uniqueness is at the heart of *Organizational Capability,* by Dave Ulrich and Gerry Lake, and has been articulated by Stalk, Evans, and Shulman in "Competing on Capabilities" and by Pfeffer in *Competitive Advantage through People.*

19. The leader of the future is well described in *The Leader of the Future,* edited by Frances Hesselbein, Marshall Goldsmith, and Richard Beckhard (San Francisco: Jossey-Bass, 1995).

20. Excellent work on the process of quantifying HR starts with a number of papers

and books by Jac Fitz-enz demonstrating how HR can and should be quantified; see especially "Quantifying the Human Resources Function, *Personnel* (March–April 1980): 41–52. John Boudreau, at Cornell, in his many papers on the HR measurement issue, includes some descriptions of how firms can take HR measures. See, for example, "Effects of Employee Flows on Utility Analysis of Human Resource Productivity Improvement Programs," *Journal of Applied Psychology* 68 (1983): 396–406; "Decision Theory Contributions to HRM Research and Practice," *Industrial Relations* 23 (1984): 198–217; with C. Berger, "Toward a Model of Employee Movement Utility," in *Research in Personnel and Human Resources Management,* vol. 3, ed. K. Rowland and G. Ferris (New York: JAI Press, 1985); and with Robert Berman, "Using Performance Measurement to Evaluate Strategy Human Resource Management Decisions: Kodak's Experience with Profit Sharing," *Human Resource Management* 30, no. 3 (1991): 393–410.

21. The concept of the *professional* has been bandied about for years. Sociologists have worked to define what it means to be a professional and to determine the impact of professionals on society; see, for example, Terence Johnson, *Professionals and Power* [London: Macmillan Press, 1972), and "The Professions in the Class Structure," in *Industrial Society: Class, Cleavage, and Control,* ed. R. Scase (New York: St. Martin's Press, 1977). Other researchers have examined those who work in specific professions, such as R&D (see Donald Miller, *Managing Professionals in Research and Development* [San Francisco: Jossey-Bass, 1986]), science or engineering (Steven Kerr, Mary Ann Von Glinow, and Janet Schriesheim, "Issues in the Study of Professionals in Organizations: The Case of Scientists and Engineers," *Organizational Behavior and Human Performance* 18 [1977]: 329–345), and high technology (Mary Ann Von Glinow, *The New Professionals: Managing Today's High-Tech Employees* [Cambridge, Mass.: Ballinger, 1988]). All of these authors establish similar criteria for what makes an occupation a profession, and these form the underlying determinants for the definition of *professional* used in this book.

Chapter 2

1. These transitions have been well described in literature on HR roles throughout the 1980s. See M.A. Devanna, C.J. Fombrun, and N.M. Tichy, "Human Resource Management: A Strategic Perspective," *Organizational Dynamics* (Winter 1981): 51–64; M.A. Devanna, C.J. Fombrun, and N.M. Tichy, "A Framework for Strategic Human Resource Management," in *Strategic Human Resource Management,* ed. C.J. Fombrun, N.M. Tichy, and M.A. Devanna (New York: Wiley, 1984), 33–51; L. Dyer, "Studying Human Resource Strategy: An Approach and an Agenda," *Industrial Relations* 23 (1984): 156–169; Dave Ulrich, "Organizational Capability as a Competitive Advantage: Human Resource Professionals as Strategic Partners," *Human Resource Planning* 10, no. 4 (1987): 169–184; Randall S. Schuler, "Repositioning the Human Resource Function: Transformation or De-

mise?" *Academy of Management Executive* 4, no. 3 (1990): 49–60; James W. Walker, *Human Resource Strategy* (New York: McGraw-Hill, 1992); and James W. Walker, "Integrating the Human Resources Function with the Business," *Human Resource Planning* 17, no. 2 (1994): 59–77.

2. The first iteration of this framework was published in Dave Ulrich, "HR Partnerships: From Rhetoric to Reality," *Strategic Partners for High Performance* (New York: Work in America Institute, 1994), 45–61.

3. These two dimensions of organizing thinking about work are consistent with conclusions drawn by Bob Quinn and his colleagues. In the course of extensive literature reviews, they have found that these two dimensions capture much of the variance in management thinking. See R.E. Quinn and J. Rohbraugh, "A Spatial Model of Effectiveness Criteria: Towards a Competing Values Approach to Organizational Analysis," *Management Science* 29 (1983): 363–377, and R.E. Quinn, *Beyond Rational Management* (San Francisco: Jossey-Bass, 1988).

4. Throughout the 1980s, many books and articles appropriately focused on the strategic side of HR. Some of these articles, however, may have fallen into the trap of discounting the operational part of HR in the quest to be strategic.

5. Many individuals have helped clarify the concepts in this cell. In particular, I appreciate the contribution of Pete Peterson, of Hewlett-Packard, who distinguished the role of the line manger, who is responsible and accountable for people, from that of the HR professional, who acts as employee champion. In addition, Debra Engel, at 3-Com, helped coin the term *employee contribution,* which captures the issues in this role.

6. The importance of honoring the past while working for the future is well captured by Alan L. Wilkins in *Developing Corporate Character* (San Francisco: Jossey-Bass, 1989).

7. This study showed that the ability to manage change is central to HR effectiveness. See Dave Ulrich, Wayne Brockbank, Arthur Yeung, and Dale Lake, "Human Resources as a Competitive Advantage: An Empirical Assessment of HR Competencies and Practices in Global Firms," unpublished manuscript, 1993, and Dave Ulrich, Wayne Brockbank, Arthur Yeung, and Dale Lake, "Human Resource Competencies: An Empirical Assessment," *Human Resource Management* 5, no. 4 (1995): 473–496.

8. *Personnel Journal* (December 1993) defined seven criteria for the Optima award. Much of this chapter's information on Hewlett-Packard comes from this article.

9. The original framework for Figure 2-1 was presented in Dave Ulrich, "HR Partnerships: From Rhetoric to Reality." Much of this work was based on experiences with Pfizer and stemmed from Pfizer's efforts to define the roles and responsibilities of its HR professionals.

10. Many insightful HR executives have extended the definition of business partner. In particular, Pete Peterson, vice president of personnel at Hewlett-Packard, has

recognized that *all* HR professionals are business partners, not just those who work directly with line managers. Influencing and supporting this perspective are Sue Cook (Tandem), Debra Engel (3-Com), Ralph Christiansen (Hallmark), Kevin Wheeler (National Semiconductor), and Eileen Wheeley (General Electric).

11. For more on HR professionals as change agents, see Manual London, *Change Agents* (San Francisco: Jossey-Bass, 1988).

Chapter 3

1. These quotes from Ronald Bitner, the CEO, are from a series of internal speeches, presentations, and communications he shared with his employees, customers, and investors between 1993 and 1996.

2. The concept of SPOTS comes from work by Joseph Brockbank and Dave Ulrich, in which they contrast traditional and involving approaches to strategic creation and execution. See Joseph Wayne Brockbank and Dave Ulrich, "Avoiding SPOTS: Creating Strategic Unity," in *Handbook of Business Strategy 1990*, ed. Harold Glass (New York: Gorham, Lambert, 1990).

3. Edward Freedman, in *Strategic Management: A Stakeholder Approach* (Boston: Pitman, 1985), provides the backdrop for the balanced scorecard approach.

4. The balanced scorecard has received increased attention through three articles by Robert S. Kaplan and David P. Norton published in the *Harvard Business Review:* "The Balanced Scorecard—Measures That Drive Performance" (January–February 1992): 71–79; "Putting the Balanced Scorecard to Work" (September–October 1993): 134–147; and "Using the Balanced Scorecard as a Strategic Management System" (January–February 1996): 75–85.

5. In addition to an influential professional body, the HR Planning Society, there has recently emerged an extensive literature on HR planning, including Dave Ulrich, "Human Resource Planning: Linking Customers and Employees," *Human Resource Planning* 15, no. 2 (1992): 47–62; James W. Walker, *Human Resource Strategy* (New York: McGraw-Hill 1992); and Dave Ulrich, "Human Resource Planning and Change: From Antithesis to Synthesis," in *Handbook of Change Management*, eds. Lance Berger and Martin Sikora (New York: BusinessOne/Irwin 1993).

6. See the following works on benchmarking: Kathleen Liefried and C.J. McNair, *Benchmarking: A Tool for Continuous Improvement* (New York: HarperBusiness, 1992); Jac Fitz-enz, "Benchmarking: HR's New Improvement Tool," *HR Horizons* 107 (1992): 7–13; and Ellen Glanz and L. Dailey, "Benchmarking," *Human Resource Management* 31, nos. 1 and 2 (1993): 9–20.

7. Robert Eichinger and Dave Ulrich, "Are You Future Agile? Are You Going to Be on the Value Chain Train? The First Annual State of the Art (SOTA) Report," *Human Resource Planning* 18, no. 4 (1995): 30–41.

8. The debate between core competence and capability is less relevant than the focus

on building internal organizational strengths, regardless of the term used to describe them. Authors who have worked on this dimension include the following: C.K. Prahalad and Gary Hamel, "The Core Competence of the Corporation," *Harvard Business Review* (May–June 1990): 79–91; Dave Ulrich and Dale Lake, *Organizational Capability: Competing from the Inside/Out* (New York: Wiley, 1990); James Brian Quinn, *Intelligent Enterprise* (New York: The Free Press, 1992); and G. Stalk, P. Evans, and L.E. Shulman, "Competing on Capabilities: The New Rules of Corporate Strategy," *Harvard Business Review* (March–April 1992): 57–69.

9. Dave Ulrich, Bob Eichinger, and Mike Lombardo have created a deck or set of cards corresponding to basic organizational capabilities, called the "Organizational Architect," with which managers can sort and identify the critical capabilities they require given a particular business strategy. They can then link these organizational capabilities to managerial competences through the parallel "Career Architect" deck of cards.

10. This is consistent with Treacy and Wiersema's argument that focused strategies are more likely to be successful than dispersed strategies. See Michael Treacy and Fred Wiersema, "Customer Intimacy and Other Value Disciplines," *Harvard Business Review* (January–February 1993): 84–96; Lee Tom Perry, Randall G. Stott, and W. Norman Smallwood, *Real-Time Strategy: Improvised Team-Based Planning for a Fast Changing World* (New York: Wiley, 1993); and Michael Treacy and Fred Wiersema, *The Discipline of Market Leaders* (Reading, Mass.: Addison-Wesley, 1995).

11. See Ikujiro Nonaka's work on the knowledge-creating company, in which capabilities are turned into a stream of ongoing products: "The Knowledge-Creating Company," *Harvard Business Review* (November–December 1991): 96–104; and, with Hiro Takeuchi, *The Knowledge Creating Company* (New York: Oxford University Press, 1995).

12. On organizational architecture, see David Nadler, Marc Gerstein, Robert Shaw, and Associates, *Organizational Architecture: Designs for Changing Organizations* (San Francisco: Jossey-Bass, 1992).

13. Jay Galbraith's star framework has been used for a number of years and can be seen throughout his work. See, for example, Jay Galbraith, *Designing Complex Organizations* (Reading, Mass.: Addison-Wesley, 1973); J.R. Galbraith, *Organization Design* (Reading, Mass.: Addison-Wesley, 1977); J.R. Galbraith, E.E. Lawler III, and Associates, *Organizing for the Future* (San Francisco: Jossey-Bass, 1993); and Jay Galbraith, *Designing Organizations: An Executive Briefing on Strategy, Structure, and Process* (San Francisco: Jossey-Bass, 1995).

14. The 7-S framework was created for McKinsey by Anthony Athos, of Harvard, and Tom Peters, of Stanford, working with Bob Waterman, of McKinsey. It has subsequently been used to describe organizational operations: see Anthony Athos and Richard Pascale, *The Art of Japanese Management* (New York: Warner Books,

1991), and Richard Tanner Pascale, *Managing on the Edge: How the Smartest Companies Use Conflict to Stay Ahead* (New York: Simon & Schuster, 1991).

15. Much of the work on HR measures comes from Jac Fitz-enz, *Human Value Management: The Value-Adding Human Resource Management Strategy for the 1990's* (San Francisco: Jossey-Bass, 1990), and Dave Ulrich, "Profiling Organizational Competitiveness: Cultivating Capabilities," *Human Resource Planning* 16, no. 3 (1993): 1–17.

16. The following are some thorough, currently popular texts that provide overviews of HR practices: Wayne Cascio, Managing *Human Resources: Productivity, Quality of Work Life, Profits,* 4th ed. (New York: McGraw-Hill, 1995); David DeCenzo and Stephen Robbins, *Human Resource Management: Concepts and Practices,* 5th ed. (New York: Wiley, 1995); Gerald Ferris, Sherman Rosen, and Harold Barnum, *Handbook of Human Resources Management* (Cambridge, Mass.: Blackwell, 1995); G. Milkovich and J. Newman, *Compensation* (New York: Irwin, 1995); and Randall Schuler, *Managing Human Resources* (St. Paul: West Publishing, 1995).

17. Chapter 7, for example, shows how organizational diagnosis can be applied to the HR function.

Chapter 4

1. See the discussions of HR reengineering by Arthur Yeung and Wayne Brockbank in "Reengineering HR through Information Technology," *Human Resource Planning* 18, no. 2 (1995): 25–37; and by Dave Ulrich in "Shared Services: From Vogue to Value," *Human Resource Planning* 18, no. 3 (1995): 12–24.

2. The Johnson & Johnson case was presented by Michael Carey, the vice president of human resources at Johnson & Johnson, at a 1994 forum on shared services held in New Jersey and sponsored by the Human Resource Planning Society.

3. Lee Forest, at Amherst Consulting, has done excellent work in creating shared staff service organizations.

4. The Lotus case was presented to a seminar sponsored by the American Electronics Association, October 1994.

5. See a review by Ron Ashkenas of the successes in change in "Beyond the Fads: How Leaders Drive Change with Results," *Human Resource Planning* 17, no. 2 (1994): 25–44.

6. The information from Arthur Yeung comes from materials for his lectures at the university of Michigan and from his articles on reengineering HR. See Arthur Yeung and Dave Ulrich, "Effective Human Resource Practices for Competitive Advantages: An Empirical Assessment of Organizations in Transition," in *Human Resource Strategies for Organizations in Transition,* eds. Richard J. Niehaus and Karl F. Price (New York: Plenum, 1990), 311–326; Arthur Yeung, Wayne Brockbank, and Dave Ulrich, "Lower Cost, Higher Value: Human Resources Function

in Transition," *Human Resource Planning* 17, no. 3 (1994): 1–16; and Arthur Yeung and Wayne Brockbank, "Reengineering HR through Information Technology," *Human Resource Planning* 18, no. 2 (1995): 25–37.

7. In a recent article (*Fortune,* January 15, 1996), Tom Stewart suggested that the HR function "put up or shut up"—either deliver value or be outsourced. In the course of arguing that outsourcing is a viable delivery mechanism, Stewart fails to acknowledge the full range of delivery mechanisms that can be used to deliver HR work. Outsourcing is neither a catchall nor a cure-all; yet, under the right circumstances, it can be a viable means of creating value.

8. The customer-guarantee literature can be traced to a work by Christopher Hart, "The Power of Unconditional Service Guarantees," *Harvard Business Review* (July–August 1988): 54–62. More recent investigations of the concept can be found in Leonard Berry, *On Great Service* (New York: The Free Press, 1995); and Benjamin Schneider and David E. Bowen, *Winning the Service Game* (Boston: Harvard Business School Press, 1995).

9. The concept of boundaries is discussed at length by Ron Ashkenas, Dave Ulrich, Todd Jick, and Steve Kerr in *The Boundaryless Organization: Breaking the Chains of Corporate Structure* (San Francisco: Jossey-Bass, 1995).

10. Kim Cameron, as guest editor of *Human Resource Management,* has identified a series of key factors for successful downsizing: see Kim Cameron, Guest Editor, "Psychological Contracts [special issue]," *Human Resource Management* (Summer 1994); see also Kim S. Cameron, "Strategies for Successful Organizational Down-sizing," *Human Resource Management* 33, no. 3 (1994): 189–211.

Chapter 5

1. The concept of the new psychological contract is well discussed in a special issue of *Human Resource Management* (vol. 33, no. 3, 1994), guest edited by Warren Wilhelm, Martin Gressler, and Denise Rousseau.

2. Challenges of post-reengineered and post-downsized firms are discussed in Robert Johansen and Rob Swigart, *Upsizing the Individual in the Downsized Organization* (Reading, Mass.: Addison-Wesley, 1994); and William Bridges, "Leading the De-Jobbed Organization," in *The Leader of the Future,* ed. Frances Hesselbein, Marshall Goldsmith, and Richard Beckhard (San Francisco: Jossey-Bass, 1995), 11–18.

3. This quote is attributed to Pete Peterson, who strongly advocates that line managers own the responsibility for managing people and that HR professionals support that agenda.

4. There are a number of works on teenage depression. This book draws primarily on Wendy Ulrich, "Multiple Assessments of Affective Context and Referral Practices in Secondary Classrooms" (Ph.D. diss., University of Michigan, 1989).

5. The argument that aspirations should exceed resources is made in Gary Hamel and

C.K. Prahalad, "Competing for the Future," *Harvard Business Review* (July–August 1994): 122–128. Hamel and Prahalad apply the argument to business strategy, but the same logic applies to personal goals and strategies.

6. Yeung provided this analysis during the course of personal conversation with the author.

7. Workout has been described in a number of publications, but the discussion in this book is based on my work with General Electric's leadership team in crafting Workout and on my application of the ideas in several other companies.

8. The concept of reengineering was popularized by Michael Hammer and James Champy in *Reengineering the Corporation: A Manifesto for Business Revolution* (New York: HarperBusiness, 1993).

9. Carl Larson and Frank LaFasto, in *Teamwork* (Newbury, Calif.: Sage Publications, 1989), review dozens of effective teams and explore their underlying processes; Susan A. Mohrman and Thomas G. Cummings, in *Self-designing Organizations* (Reading, Mass.: Addison-Wesley, 1989), review a theory and model of teams; and Jon R. Katzenbach and Douglas Smith, in *The Wisdom of Teams: Creating the High-Performance Organization* (Boston: Harvard Business School Press, 1993), identify processes inherent in high-performing teams.

10. Thurgood Marshall described this military leadership model in a 1992 speech to General Electric employees charged with developing GE's future leaders.

11. For a description of the culture of Southwest Airlines, see Brenda Paik Sunoo, "How Fun Flies at Southwest Airlines," *Personnel Journal* (June 1995): 37–45.

12. This Pepsi story, which earned the Personnel Journal Optima Award in 1995, comes from Dawn Anfuso, "PepsiCo Shared Power and Wealth with Workers," *Personnel Journal* (June 1995): 42–49.

13. The work by National Semiconductor on groupware comes from research and theory developed by the Institute for the Future and is published in Robert Johansen, David Sibbet, Suzyn Benson, Alexia Martin, Robert Mittman, and Paul Saffo, *Leading Business Teams: How Teams Can Use Technology and Group Process Tools to Enhance Performance* (Reading, Mass.: Addison-Wesley, 1991); and Robert Johansen and Rob Swigart, *Upsizing the Individual in the Downsized Organization* (Reading, Mass.: Addison-Wesley, 1994).

14. For a review of trends in development and learning, see Dave Ulrich and Hope Greenfield, "The Transformation of Training and Development to Development and Learning," *American Journal of Management Development* 1, no. 2 (1995): 11–22.

Chapter 6

1. The General Electric change effort is heralded in a number of books, including Richard Tanner Pascale, *Managing on the Edge: How the Smartest Companies Use Conflict to Stay Ahead* (New York: Simon and Schuster, 1991); Robert Slater, *Get*

Better or Get Beaten! 31 Leadership Secrets from GE's Jack Welch (New York: Irwin, 1994); and Ron Ashkenas, Dave Ulrich, Todd Jick, and Steve Kerr, *The Boundaryless Organization* (San Francisco: Jossey-Bass, 1995).

2. Quoted in Jennifer Labbs, "Put Your Job on the Line," *Personnel Journal* (June 1995): 53–57.

3. The story of the culture change at Sears is laid out in the *New York Times,* January 7, 1996. Most of the discussion in this book, however, comes from the author's personal experience of and involvement in the change effort.

4. On change that fails, see Ron Ashkenas, "Beyond the Fads: How Leaders Drive Change with Results," *Human Resource Planning* 17, no. 2 (1994): 25–44; John P. Kotter, "Leading Change: Why Transformation Efforts Fail," *Harvard Business Review* (March–April 1995): 59–67; and John P. Kotter, *The New Rules: How to Succeed in Today's Post-Corporate World* (New York: The Free Press, 1995).

5. Todd Jick, Steve Kerr, and Dave Ulrich created these questions and used them in the Change Acceleration Process (CAP) workshop at General Electric.

6. Summaries of research on change can be found in Noel Tichy, *Managing Strategic Change* (New York: Wiley, 1983); R. Kanter, B.A. Stein, and T.D. Jick, *The Challenge of Organizational Change* (New York: The Free Press, 1992); P.C. Nutt, *Managing Planned Change* (New York: Macmillan, 1992); Ron Ashkenas, "Beyond the Fads: How Leaders Drive Change with Results," *Human Resource Planning* 17, no. 2 (1994): 25–44; Robert W. Jacobs, *Real Time Strategic Change: How to Involve an Entire Organization in Fast and Far-Reaching Change* (San Francisco: Berrett-Koehler, 1994); and Peter Drucker, *Managing in a Time of Change* (New York: Penguin, 1995).

7. Studies of individual change include work on habits such as weight loss, alcohol and drug abuse, cognitive therapy, personal conversion, and exercise habits.

8. Studies of high-performing teams are found in Carl Larson and Frank LaFasto, *Teamwork* (Newbury, Calif.: Sage Publications, 1989); Jon R. Katzenbach and Douglas Smith, *The Wisdom of Teams: Creating the High-Performance Organization* (Boston: Harvard Business School Press, 1993); and Susan Albers Mohrman, Susan Cohen, and Allan M. Mohrman, Jr., *Designing Team-Based Organizations: New Forms for Knowledge Work* (San Francisco: Jossey-Bass, 1995).

9. The team charged with creating a model of change included individuals both inside GE (Jacquie Vierling, Cathy Friarson, and Amy Howard) and outside GE (Steve Kerr, Dave Ulrich, Craig Schneier, John Biel, Ron Gager, and Mary Anne Devanna).

10. Specific results and general conclusions drawn from the use in various change efforts of this profiling tool have been published elsewhere by Steve Kerr and Dave Ulrich. The focus here is on helping HR professionals to identify the critical success factors for change, learn a methodology for translating that knowledge into action, and attain the ability to make change initiatives happen.

11. Regina O'Neill and Robert Quinn, guest editors, *Human Resource Management* 32, no. 1 (1993).

12. Richard W. Beatty and David Ulrich, in "Re-Energizing the Mature Organization," *Organizational Dynamics* 20, no. 1 (1991): 16–30, describe the process of culture change in large, traditional corporations.

13. This group included the following (members of the 1989 Workout team are indicated by an asterisk): Ron Ashkenas of Robert Shaeffer & Associates; Tom Barocci, MIT (now with Barocci & Associates); Jim Baughman,* GE; Dick Beatty, Rutgers University; Jon Biel,* GE (now with Biel and Associates); Wayne Brockbank, University of Michigan; Jim Clawson, University of Virginia; Alan Cohen, Babson College; MaryAnne Devanna, Columbia University; Jack Gabarro, Harvard University; Jeffrey Gandz, University of Western Ontario; Todd Jick,* Harvard University (now at INSEAD); Bill Joyce, Tuck School; Rob Kazanjian, Emory University; Steve Kerr,* University of Michigan (now full-time at General Electric); Bob Miles, Emory University; Len Schlesinger,* Harvard University; Craig Schneier, Sibson (now a private consultant); Deborah Shah,* Shah & Associates; Paul Thompson, Brigham Young University; Noel Tichy, University of Michigan; Kirby Warren, Columbia University; and Alan Wilkins, Brigham Young University.

14. See thoughtful discussions of culture in T.E. Deal and A.A. Kennedy, *Corporate Cultures: The Rites and Rituals of Corporate Life* (Reading, Mass.: Addison-Wesley, 1982); J. Martin, M.S. Feldman, M.J. Hatch, and S.B. Sitkin, "The Uniqueness Paradox in Organizational Culture," *Administrative Science Quarterly* 28 (1983): 438–453; Stanley Davis, *Managing Corporate Culture* (Cambridge, Mass.: Ballinger, 1984); J. Barney, "Organizational Culture: Can It Be a Source of Sustained Competitive Advantage?" *Academy of Management Review* 11, no. 3 (1986): 656–665; and John Kotter and James Heskett, *Culture and Performance* (New York: The Free Press, 1992).

15. See the cover story on culture change in *Fortune,* December 14, 1993.

16. See Linda Smircich, "Concepts of Culture and Organizational Analysis," *Administrative Science Quarterly* 28 (1983): 339–358.

17. See Stanley Davis, *Managing Corporate Culture* (Cambridge, Mass.: Ballinger, 1984).

18. For a summary of the psychological approach to culture, see J.W. Brockbank and D. Ulrich, "Institutional Antecedents of Shared Organizational Cognitions," working paper, University of Michigan, 1988; and Dave Ulrich, "Culture Change: Will We Recognize It When We See It?" in *Managing Strategic and Cultural Change in Organizations,* ed. Craig Schneier (New York: Human Resource Planning Society, 1995).

19. This approach to shared mindset and automatic thoughts was first set out in Dave Ulrich and Dale Lake, *Organizational Capability: Competing from the Inside/Out* (New York: Wiley, 1990).

20. For more on the relationship between culture and performance, see D.R. Denison, "Bringing Corporate Culture to the Bottom Line," *Organizational Dynamics* (Winter 1984): 5–22; and John Kotter and James Heskett, *Culture and Performance* (New York: The Free Press, 1992).

21. The Xerox case is well described in Gary Jacobson and John Hillkirk, *Xerox: American Samurai* (New York: Macmillan, 1986); and Robert Howard, "The CEO as Organizational Architect: An Interview with Xerox's Paul Allaire," *Harvard Business Review* (September–October 1992): 106–123.

22. The literature on reengineering includes Michael Hammer, "Reengineering Work: Don't Automate, Obliterate," *Harvard Business Review* (July–August 1990): 104–112; Michael Hammer and James Champy, *Reengineering the Corporation* (New York: Harper Business, 1993); James Champy, *Reengineering Management* (New York: Harper Business, 1994); and Michael Hammer, *Beyond Reengineering* (New York: Harper Collins, 1995).

23. The concept of *equifinality* comes from systems theory and is discussed extensively in Daniel Katz and Robert Kahn, *The Social Psychology of Organizations* (New York: Wiley, 1978).

24. See Joseph Miraglia, "An Evolutionary Approach to Revolutionary Change," *Human Resource Planning* 17, no. 2 (1994): 1–24; and Joseph Miraglia, "An Evolutionary Approach to Revolutionary Change and the Implications for HR Practice," in *Managing Strategic and Cultural Change in Organizations,* ed. Craig Schneier (New York: Human Resource Planning Society, 1995).

25. Ronald Bitner made these remarks in an untitled presentation to Goldman, Sachs, and Company at the Communacopia II Conference.

Chapter 7

1. Wayne Brockbank, a professor at the University of Michigan, uses the term *HR for HR* to describe the necessity for human resources groups to apply HR principles to their own organizations.

2. Ellig stated this position in personal correspondence with the author.

3. Tony Rucci made these comments at a conference sponsored by the *Human Resource Executive,* Palm Springs, Florida, September 19, 1995.

4. Among the many excellent works on the strategy formulation/implementation process, I recommend, in particular, Jay Galbraith, *Designing Organizations: An Executive Briefing on Strategy, Structure, and Process* (San Francisco: Jossey-Bass, 1995).

5. The concept of organizational capabilities dates back to writings by Igor Ansoff from 1962, and it has more recently been developed, using various terminology, by a number of other authors. Dave Ulrich and Dale Lake, in *Organizational Capability: Competing from the Inside/Out* (New York: Wiley, 1990), use the term *organizational capability,* which was picked up by George Stalk, Philip Evans, and Lawrence E. Shulman in "Competing on Capabilities: The New Rules of Corporate

Strategy," *Harvard Business Review* (March–April 1992): 57–62. Using the term *core competence* in "The Core Competence of the Corporation," *Harvard Business Review* (May–June 1990): 79–91, C.K. Prahalad and Gary Hamel draw on P. Selznick, *Leadership in Administration* (Evanston, Ill.: Row, Peterson and Co., 1957). The following works demonstrate that the core competence argument integrates strategy formulation and implementation: Mahen Tampoe, "Exploiting the Core Competencies of Your Organization," *Long Range Planning* 27, no. 4 (1994): 66–77; and Mark Gallon, Harold Stillman, and David Coates, "Putting Core Competency Thinking into Practice," *Research-Technology Management* (May–June 1995): 20–28.

6. Quoted in an article by Eric Raimy in *Human Resource Executive,* June 1995.

7. The thirteen companies identified in Table 7-6 are not randomly chosen but are companies that have publicly shared their HR strategies through forums such as the University of Michigan's HR Planning, sponsored by the Society for Human Resource Management. Because companies invited to present at these forums are generally seen as leading-edge, they provide good examples of effective HR strategies. In addition, they represent a mix of industry and company size, and have varied histories of HR strategy.

8. See work on HR competencies in Dave Ulrich, Wayne Brockbank, and Arthur Yeung, "Beyond Belief: A Benchmark for Human Resources," *Human Resource Management* 28, no. 3 (1990): 311–335; and Dave Ulrich, Wayne Brockbank, Arthur Yeung, and Dale Lake, "Human Resource Competencies: An Empirical Assessment," *Human Resource Management* 34, no. 4 (1995): 473–496.

9. For Wilhelm's view of the sod-planting metaphor, see Warren Wilhelm, "Revitalizing the Human Resource Management Function in a Mature, Large Corporation," *Human Resource Management* 29, no. 2 (1990): 129–144.

10. A survey reported by *Fortune* in 1995 found that HR jobs paid more than the top jobs in management information systems, manufacturing, sales, and marketing.

Chapter 8

1. See Robert H. Hayes, Steven C. Wheelwright, and Kim B. Clark, *Dynamic Manufacturing: Creating the Learning Organization* (New York: The Free Press, 1988).

2. See M.E. Porter, "Industry Structure and Competitive Strategy: Keys to Profitability," *Financial Analysts Journal* 36, no. 4 (1980): 30–41; Michael Porter, *Competitive Strategy* (New York: The Free Press, 1981); and Michael Porter, *Competitive Advantage* (New York: The Free Press, 1985).

3. See George Day, "Marketing's Contribution to the Strategy Dialogue," *Journal of the Academy of Marketing Science* 20 (Fall 1992): 323–330; Barry Leonard, *On Great Service* (New York: The Free Press, 1995); Benjamin Schneider and David E. Bowen, *Winning the Service Game* (Boston: Harvard Business School Press,

1995); and Frederick Webster, "The Future Role of Marketing in the Organization," working paper, Tuck School, 1996.

4. See Alfred Rappaport, *Creating Shareholder Value* (New York: The Free Press, 1986); and Adrian Slywotzky, *Value Migration: How to Think Several Moves Ahead of the Competition* (Boston: Harvard Business School Press, 1996).

5. See Robert Johansen, David Sibbet, Suzyn Benson, Alexia Martin, Robert Mittman, and Paul Saffo, *Leading Business Teams: How Teams Can Use Technology and Group Process Tools to Enhance Performance* (Reading, Mass.: Addison-Wesley, 1991).

6. See Michael Hammer and James Champy, *Reengineering the Corporation* (New York: Harper Business, 1993); James Champy, *Reengineering Management: The New Mandate for Leadership* (New York: HarperBusiness, 1995); and Michael Hammer, *Beyond Reengineering* (New York: HarperCollins, 1995).

7. See Robert E. Cole, *The Rise and Fall of Total Quality Management* (New York: Oxford University Press, 1995).

8. See Dave Ulrich and Dale Lake, *Organizational Capability: Competing from the Inside/Out* (New York: Wiley, 1990); and E.E. Lawler III, *The Ultimate Advantage* (San Francisco: Jossey-Bass, 1992).

9. See C. K. Prahalad and Gary Hamel, "The Core Competence of the Corporation," *Harvard Business Review* (May–June 1990): 79–91; and Mark Gallon, Harold Stillman, and David Coates, "Putting Core Competency Thinking into Practice," *Research-Technology Management* (May–June 1995): 20–28.

10. See Jeffrey Pfeffer, *Competitive Advantage through People: Unleashing the Power of the Work Force* (Boston: Harvard Business School Press, 1994).

11. See J. Barney, "Organizational Culture: Can It Be a Source of Sustained Competitive Advantage?" *Academy of Management Review* 11, no. 3 (1986): 656–665.

12. See Ikujiro Nonaka, "The Knowledge-Creating Company," *Harvard Business Review* (November–December 1991): 96–104; and Ikujiro Nonaka and Hiro Takeuchi, *The Knowledge Creating Company* (New York: Oxford University Press, 1995).

13. Executive commitment to the softer organizational skills is evident from annual reports in which CEOs' letters increasingly mention organizational issues. In the 1995 General Electric annual report, CEO Jack Welch reviews General Electric's enormous success by highlighting the organizational programs central to that success. The 1995 Coca-Cola annual report focuses on creating a learning culture in the exchange of ideas and knowledge creates future shareholder value.

14. These insights into the power of theory derive from the social sciences; see Kurt Lewin, *Field Theory in Social Science* (New York: Harper, 1951); Thomas Kuhn, *The Structure of Scientific Revolutions,* 2d ed. (Chicago: University of Chicago Press, 1970); and Peter F. Drucker, "The Theory of the Business," *Harvard Business Review* (September–October 1994): 95–107.

15. P. Wright and S. Snell, "Toward an Integrative View of Strategic Human Resource Management," *Human Resource Management Review* 1 (1991): 203–225; and Patrick Wright and Gary McMahan, "Theoretical Perspectives for Strategic Human Resource Management," *Journal of Management* 18, no. 2 (1992): 295–320.

16. See D.O. Ulrich and J.B. Barney, "Perspectives in Organizations: Resource Dependence, Efficiency, and Population," *Academy of Management Review* 9, no. 3 (1984): 471–481.

17. See M.A. Devanna, C.J. Fombrun, and N.M. Tichy, "Human Resource Management: A Strategic Perspective," *Organizational Dynamics* (Winter 1981): 51–64; and M.A. Devanna, C.J. Fombrun, and N.M. Tichy, "A Framework for Strategic Human Resource Management," in *Strategic Human Resource Management,* ed. C.J. Fombrun, N.M. Tichy, and M.A. Devanna (New York: Wiley, 1984), 33–51.

18. See Frances Hesselbein, Marshall Goldsmith, and Richard Beckhard, eds., *The Leader of the Future* (San Francisco: Jossey-Bass, 1995).

19. See Dave Ulrich, Mary Ann Von Glinow, Todd Jick, Arthur Yeung, and Steve Nason, *Learning Organization, Culture Change, and Competitiveness: How Managers Can Build Learning Capability,* monograph prepared for the International Consortium of Executive Development and Research, 1993; and Dave Ulrich, Mary Ann Von Glinow, and Todd Jick, "High Impact Learning: Building and Diffusing Learning Capability," *Organizational Dynamics* (Winter 1993): 52–66.

20. Steve Kerr, at General Electric, and Judy Rosenblum, at Coca-Cola, are the leading exemplars of the chief learning officer. Both have responsibility not only for traditional training and development, but also for learning and knowledge transfer.

21. See Dave Ulrich, "Culture Change: Will We Recognize It When We See It?" in *Managing Strategic and Cultural Change in Organizations,* ed. Craig Schneier (New York: Human Resource Planning Society, 1995).

22. The logic for an HR value proposition is similar to that advanced by Heskett and Schlesinger for the service chain, which shows how and why service leads to business results. See James L. Heskett, Thomas O. Jones, Gary W. Loveman, W. Earl Sasser, Jr., and Leonard A. Schlesinger, "Putting the Service-Profit Chain to Work," *Harvard Business Review* (March–April 1991): 164–174.

23. See Dave Ulrich, "Measuring HR Effectiveness: An Overview of the Territory," *Human Resource Management* (forthcoming).

24. The results of our research on HR competencies, begun in 1988, have appeared in Dave Ulrich and Arthur Yeung, "Human Resources in the 1990s: Trends and Required Competencies," *Personnel Administrator* (March 1989): 38–45; Dave Ulrich, Wayne Brockbank, and Arthur Yeung, "Human Resource Competencies in the 1990s: An Empirical Assessment of What the Future Holds," *Personnel Administrator* (June 1989): 91–93; Dave Ulrich, Wayne Brockbank, and Arthur Yeung, "Beyond Belief: A Benchmark for Human Resources," *Human Resource*

Management 28, no. 3 (1990): 311–335; and Dave Ulrich, Wayne Brockbank, Arthur Yeung, and Dale Lake, "Human Resource Competencies: An Empirical Assessment," *Human Resource Management* 34, no. 4 (1995): 473–496.
25. See Ulrich and Lake, *Organizational Capability.*
26. See J.M. Kouzes and B.Z. Posner, *Credibility* (San Francisco: Jossey-Bass, 1993).

INDEX

ABOUT THE AUTHOR

Dave Ulrich is a professor of business administration at the School of Business, University of Michigan, and the co-director of the university's Human Resource Executive programs, which have been ranked number one by *Business Week, The Wall Street Journal,* and *Fortune* since 1990. Ulrich has consulted and done research with more than half of the Fortune 200. The focus of his teaching and research is on how organizations change, build capabilities, learn, remove boundaries, and leverage human resource activities to add value for customers.

Ulrich is the recipient of many accolades, including listings in *Business Week* as one of the world's top ten educators in management and the top educator in human resources as well as the Pericles Pro Meritus Award for outstanding contribution to the field of human resources. He also generated multiple award-winning national databases on organizations that assess the alignment among their strategies, human resource practices, and human resource competencies.

Professor Ulrich is a Fellow in the National Academy of Human Resources, writes a monthly column for *Human Resource Executive,* and serves on the editorial boards of five other journals. Among his publications are three co-authored books and more than eighty articles and book chapters.